RESEARCHING ACROSS LANGUAGES AND CULTURES

We are working within an increasingly globalised knowledge economy, where researchers collaborate in cross-cultural teams, collect data in a variety of languages and share findings for international audiences who may be unfamiliar with the cultural context. *Researching Across Languages and Cultures* is a guide for doctoral students and other researchers engaged in such multilingual and intercultural research, providing a framework for analysis and development of their experiences.

Demonstrating the link between the theoretical approaches offered by the authors and the practical problems encountered by doctoral researchers, this ground-breaking book draws on research interviews with doctoral students from around the world. Students' written reflections on their experiences are presented as interludes between the chapters. A practical, hands-on guide to planning, conducting and writing up research, the book explores the crucial roles involved in interpreting data across cultures within doctoral research.

Key topics include:

- The role of the interpreter and/or local research assistant in the research process and the ethics of translation
- Constructing knowledge across cultures: addressing questions of audience, power and voice
- Academic literacy practices in multilingual settings
- The doctoral student's role within the geopolitics of academic publishing and forms of research dissemination
- The pragmatics of mediated communication (implicatures, intentions, dialogue).

Researchers who come from and work in monolingual societies often forget that their context is unusual – most of the world live in multilingual contexts, where linguistic shifts and hybridities are the norm. Two authors with extensive experience, together with a number of their existing or former research students, share insights into these issues that surround language and culture in research.

This book will be a useful guide for academic researchers, doctoral students, research supervisors and Masters students who carry out empirical research in multilingual or multicultural contexts and/or are writing about their research for a diverse readership across the world.

Anna Robinson-Pant is a Professor of Education and holds the UNESCO Chair in Adult Literacy and Learning for Social Transformation at the University of East Anglia, UK.

Alain Wolf is a lecturer in Translation Theory at the School of Politics, Philosophy, Language and Communication Studies at the University of East Anglia, UK.

RESEARCHING ACROSS LANGUAGES AND CULTURES

A guide to doing research interculturally

Anna Robinson-Pant and Alain Wolf

with reflective pieces from Achala Gupta, Eleni Konidari, Gina Lontoc, Joanna Nair and Pu Shi

LONDON AND NEW YORK

First published 2017
by Routledge
2 Park Square, Milton Park, Abingdon, Oxon OX14 4RN

and by Routledge
711 Third Avenue, New York, NY 10017

Routledge is an imprint of the Taylor & Francis Group, an informa business

© 2017 A. Robinson-Pant and A. Wolf

The right of Anna Robinson-Pant and Alain Wolf to be identified as authors of this work has been asserted by them in accordance with sections 77 and 78 of the Copyright, Designs and Patents Act 1988.

All rights reserved. No part of this book may be reprinted or reproduced or utilised in any form or by any electronic, mechanical, or other means, now known or hereafter invented, including photocopying and recording, or in any information storage or retrieval system, without permission in writing from the publishers.

Trademark notice: Product or corporate names may be trademarks or registered trademarks, and are used only for identification and explanation without intent to infringe.

British Library Cataloguing in Publication Data
A catalogue record for this book is available from the British Library

Library of Congress Cataloging in Publication Data
A catalog record for this book has been requested

ISBN: 978-1-138-84505-3 (hbk)
ISBN: 978-1-138-84506-0 (pbk)
ISBN: 978-1-315-72836-0 (ebk)

Typeset in Bembo
by Swales & Willis Ltd, Exeter, Devon, UK

CONTENTS

Additional contributors	*vii*
Foreword by Alan Rogers	*ix*
Preface	*xii*
Acknowledgments	*xvi*
Explanation of data sources	*xvii*
Transcription conventions	*xviii*

1 From cross-cultural to intercultural: an alternative
perspective on the research process   1
Anna Robinson-Pant

Reflective piece 1: Language, theory and power –
cross-cultural issues in educational research   19
Pu Shi

2 Multilingual research: accounting for the richness of 'context'   24
Alain Wolf

Reflective piece 2: Dressing with a scarf while undressing
the prejudice   40
Eleni Konidari

3 The pragmatics of doing research across languages: inferences
and intentions   44
Alain Wolf

vi Contents

Reflective piece 3: Cultural connotations in language
   structures – an experiential account of meaning-making in
   the processes of translation   58
Achala Gupta

4 The role of the interpreter/translator in the research process:
   the ethics of mediated communication   63
Alain Wolf

Reflective piece 4: Transcribing language, translating culture?
   Transcription convention and issues on translation in
   educational research   84
Gina Lontoc

5 Writing across cultures: reader expectations and 'crises
   of identity'   88
Anna Robinson-Pant

Reflective piece 5: Writing relationships   112
Joanna Nair

6 Research in a multilingual context: joining an international
   community of researchers   117
Anna Robinson-Pant

Endpiece   136
Anna Robinson-Pant and Alain Wolf

Bibliography   *142*
Index   *152*

CONTRIBUTORS

Achala Gupta, a trained education researcher (MPhil, Cambridge), is currently pursuing her PhD (Sociology, National University of Singapore). Her research attempts to conceptualise education practices in India in the emergence of shadow education frameworks and their intertwined relationship with the system of mainstream education.

Eleni Konidari is a PhD candidate at the University of East Anglia. Her research aims to understand how nationalism shapes people's identities and influences their educational aspirations and opportunities.

Gina Lontoc earned her MA in Language and Literature Teaching from Ateneo de Manila University, Philippines, and completed her PhD at the University of East Anglia. Her research focuses on English as a Second Language (ESL) writing and identity. Aside from her role as a university lecturer in various universities in the Philippines, she has been a consultant and review programme developer for international English examinations.

Joanna Nair is a Visiting Fellow at the University of East Anglia and the Director of Educational Liaison for a non-profit organisation. Her PhD thesis explored understandings of development and of well-being in a rural Nepalese community.

Alan Rogers is Visiting Professor at the Universities of Nottingham and East Anglia. He has published widely in the fields of adult learning and development, adult literacy and informal learning. His recent study, *The Base of the Iceberg Informal Learning and its Impact on Formal and Non-formal Learning*, has been published in the Study Guides for Adult Education, by Barbara Badruch, Opladen 2015.

viii Contributors

Pu Shi is a doctoral student from the University of Cambridge. Her research interests include cross-cultural education, foreign language teaching and teacher development, critical thinking and academic literacy in cross-cultural contexts.

FOREWORD

Alan Rogers

In 1988, working in Bangladesh without the benefit of language, I experienced the following exchange when interviewing a leader of a women's group about literacy.

> *Me to interpreter:* Ask her if she is literate or illiterate.
>
> *Interpreter to the women's leader . . .*
> *Woman back to interpreter . . .*
>
> *Interpreter to me:* She says she has never been to school.
> *Me to interpreter:* I did not ask her that; what did you ask her?
> *Interpreter to me:* I asked her if she can read and write – for, you see, there is no word in Bangla for illiterate!

I realised then some of the jumps that researching through translators involves. The interpreter jumped from 'literate' to 'reading and writing'; the group leader jumped from 'reading and writing' to 'being educated' and from that to 'school', and so she replied accordingly. All the jumps were justified but together they took the discussion away from the key issue. I was seeking to find out how she dealt with the everyday literacy tasks involved in being the leader of a women's group in her context (she got her ten-year-old son and other group members to help).

(And we did manage to go on to have a long and fruitful conversation.)

This kind of situation which occurs frequently in intercultural research is an example of the questions with which this book deals. Of course, there are many deep issues around the spaces in which different cultures encounter each other in development programmes and inter-community research; but in language lies a large territory of potential misunderstandings – especially as 'language' is no longer seen by many as 'a fixed, static and clearly delineable object' bounded with a

x Foreword

locality and a population, but as 'fluid, dynamic and practice-based', constantly on the move (Stroud and Prinsloo, 2015: 56).

Researchers who live and work in monolingual societies often forget that their context is unusual – most of the world live in multilingual contexts, where linguistic shifts and hybridities are the norm and conducting research in such contexts brings to the fore certain facets which are the focus of discussion in these pages. Two authors from different disciplines but with extensive experience, together with a number of research students, share their insights into some of the issues around language in research – not just international, for language can be an issue in intra-national research as well. At the heart of the discussion lie two concepts – context and communication. The variable and changing contexts (plural, for the researcher brings a context as well) determine to a large extent the nature of the research exchanges; and communication involves not just words but meanings, intentions and even assumptions. And as the authors point out, research is not just a twosome, the researcher (and their team) and the researched (whether individual or group or whole community). There is at least one other main party (sometimes overlooked) – those to whom the researcher(s) need to submit their report in thesis, publication or policy statement, such as funders, doctoral supervisors and examiners. Some of these third parties join (often unconsciously) in the construction of meanings of the research – so there are potentially three languages involved. My exchange above was in the context of making a video in English about literacy, to be shown to people in the UK who have never been to Bangladesh or any other so-called 'developing country', and they were in my mind all the time, co-constructing the research.

These are some of the complications the authors unravel in clear stages – the data collection (the authors focus on qualitative research, especially ethnographic, but the same issues face quantitative researchers using large-scale data collection methodologies); the use of field notes; and the writing up. Translation of course is the key element – whether word for word or sense for sense (Alain Wolf's use of historical religious examples is both illuminating and amusing). Deciding which principles to adopt within an ethical framework; finding equivalents which convey not just the meaning but also something of the atmosphere; judging whether 'I have never been to school' is adequately translated as 'I am illiterate' – these are the daily decisions of researchers in interlingual contexts, as is shown by the supplementary pieces providing short accounts of practical experience written by recent or current doctoral students each with his or her own research story. And the book takes the process beyond the research and report-writing-up stages into writing for publication; here Anna Robinson-Pant draws on the recent experience she and her colleagues have acquired through running training workshops for academics in writing for publication.

This book is particularly timely – for international research, especially using teams of researchers from different institutions, is growing exponentially in the search for evidence-based policy-making. But this book is not just for those who research across languages; I would recommend it to all researchers in the social science fields. For there is always a gap between researcher and researched, even in the same community – the researcher is *ipso facto* seen and felt to be a different person from the researched (usually richer, urbanised, more educated and with greater measures of freedom than the researched), speaking a different kind of language. Bridging this gap is not easy. And there is always the issue of interpreting your findings in such a way that someone who was not there will enter into the field as at least an observer, if not a participant observer. Dealing fully with such issues, this book will be a useful item in the toolbox of social and cultural researchers.

PREFACE

Why this guide to researching across languages and cultures?

Collaborating on research in cross-cultural teams, collecting data in a second language, working with translators or writing up findings for an international audience unfamiliar with the cultural context. These are common experiences of today's researchers working within a globalised knowledge economy. Increasingly, doctoral students and other researchers find themselves working in multilingual contexts – possibly acting as or through translators and making choices about which language/s to use in fieldwork and writing up. In these situations, doctoral field research often involves learning informally about intercultural communication and how to translate and interpret both written and spoken texts across cultures.

This book provides a guide for doctoral students and other researchers engaged in such multilingual and intercultural research. Collecting and interpreting data across cultures demands sensitive understanding of different roles and research practices which standard research methodology textbooks rarely touch on. How do local participants, the researcher, an interpreter/translator, and an academic supervisor engage in a process of mediating different meanings? The book identifies a number of themes and concerns that have arisen in discussion with international researchers/supervisees through our own experiences in UK higher education, including: conventions of academic literacies in English as compared to languages in which data was collected, the power differentials related to the choice of academic sources, the semantics and pragmatics of mediated communication (humour, politeness, implied meaning), the role of the interpreter and/or local research assistant in the research process, the ethics of translation and forms of research dissemination.

Recognising that methodological critique and reflection is an essential element of the doctoral process, we aim to do more than simply offering practical advice on how to conduct multilingual fieldwork. By introducing theoretical concepts from the fields of intercultural communication, translation studies, academic literacies and postcolonial theory, we set out to provide a framework for researchers to analyse and develop their own experiences of researching across languages and cultures. It will soon be apparent to the reader that both authors come from a qualitative research background. Whilst this has inevitably influenced the approaches we introduce and the examples of field research and writing drawn on, we believe that the book will have much relevance for those using quantitative approaches in intercultural research too. In particular, we hope that the book will encourage doctoral students to write about and share their insights into multilingual and intercultural research – having noticed that this is a dimension frequently hidden or missing in accounts of methodology within the final thesis. Recognising that the doctoral degree is usually one step on a longer research journey, we invite the reader to take up the challenge to explore innovative ways of constructing and disseminating knowledge beyond the PhD.

Origins and form of the book

The idea for this book emerged from developing advanced doctoral training workshops together at our university on 'Researching across languages and cultures'. As will become apparent in the book, we have quite different disciplinary backgrounds and this has been a rich source of learning from each other: Alain in linguistics and theology; Anna in education and development studies. This has influenced the material we have drawn on as illustration - whereas Anna has discussed situations that arose when conducting empirical fieldwork in the South, Alain has taken excerpts from religious texts to develop his analysis of approaches to translation or discourse analysis. Our interaction through the planning of the workshops enabled us to share and bring together different methods and concepts that have shaped our understanding and research approach.

After each workshop, student participants were invited to write about their research experiences. Those responses were of particular interest because they demonstrated the link between the theoretical approaches offered by us as workshop convenors and the practical problems encountered by the doctoral researchers. These reflective pieces form interludes between the various chapters in this book, offering a different perspective from that provided by us as authors and doctoral supervisors[1].

We also draw extensively on interviews, email correspondence and focus group discussions conducted with doctoral students over the past year. Semi-structured interviews were held with current doctoral and some Masters/MPhil students in anthropology, education, sociology, linguistics and development studies in two universities in the UK, as well as in universities in Iceland, Nepal and Korea. This research was approved by the research ethics committee in our respective university departments. As well as following the standard ethics protocols, we tried to maximise opportunities for research participants to 'speak back' to us as researchers.

xiv Preface

Immediately after each interview, students were invited to read and comment on a summary or transcription of the discussion and to give any further reflections. We also sent drafts of the chapters to those being quoted there and had many interesting conversations about our differing interpretations or readings of the data. The participants were then able to make a more considered decision about whether they would prefer to be anonymised (and to suggest a suitable pseudonym if they wished) or for us to use their real names. All of these interactions have influenced this final version of the book and we are grateful to the doctoral students who engaged in this process at a very busy time of their lives.

Having conducted research with doctoral students since becoming a university lecturer in 2000, Anna also returned to interviews and writing conducted previously. This was especially useful for gaining a longitudinal perspective on doctoral research experiences and what students did next, as in the examples in Chapter 6 which build on her book, *Cross-Cultural Perspectives on Educational Research* (2005). Some of the examples were taken from interviews conducted for a joint paper with Dr Tesfay Tsegay at the British Association for International and Comparative Education conference in 2012 (updated through email discussion with participants in 2016). Data cited from 2010 was collected and analysed collaboratively with Dr Anna Magyar as part of a university teaching fellowship, benefiting greatly from her insights from a long experience in academic literacies research. This project led to us making a DVD with international doctoral students – several of whom are quoted in this book.

Writing this book has meant engaging directly with many of the issues that we discuss around researching across languages and cultures. Coming from quite different academic disciplines with differing expectations regarding academic voice, literacy conventions and audience, we first had to decide whether to present a unified authorial voice and presence throughout the book. Finding it impossible to develop a single voice throughout, we opted to retain our individual voices and identities in most of the chapters but have written this introduction and endpiece together as 'we'. So Chapters 1, 5 and 6 are written by Anna, and Chapters 2, 3 and 4 are written by Alain. We hope that retaining our two voices in this way will also give the reader a sense of the initial dialogue we engaged in. The central theme of moving from a cross-cultural to an intercultural perspective on research is re-visited throughout the book through our differing theoretical resources and experiences as researchers and doctoral supervisors. The structure of the book is informed by the conventional chronology of a research process, with the aim of integrating an intercultural and multilingual perspective. So we start from theoretical conceptualisation of the research problem in Chapter 1, moving to data collection and analysis in Chapters 2, 3 and 4 (in relation to translation in data collection and interpretation) and writing/disseminating research (Chapter 5 and 6).

Finally, there is the question about who will read this book? Whilst we started off primarily with doctoral students in mind, as we moved into the context of the geopolitics of academic publishing and dominance of English language research literature, it became clear that the book has a wider potential audience. A central argument of the book is that supervisors and other faculty can learn much from engaging in critical discussion with students researching across languages and cultures - particularly international students with their experience of mediating different academic literacy practices and languages in the UK academy too. As the voices of students engaged in intercultural research are such a rich resource within the book, we hope that established academics will find much to reflect on here too.

Anna Robinson-Pant and Alain Wolf
April 2016

Note

1 The full set of unabridged reflective pieces was published as a Centre for Applied Research in Education (CARE) Working Paper 1, available to download at: https://www. uea.ac.uk/documents/595200/0/CARE+Working+Paper+1.pdf/e2b7032b-c7e8-4fff-9b0e-f6fb8e10c486

ACKNOWLEDGMENTS

During the early stages of our research we benefited greatly from exchanges with students and colleagues – particularly Dr Anna Magyar (who co-directed with Anna some of the research projects discussed here) and Prof. Fred Dervin. The book also grew out of an institutional collaboration between the School of Education and Lifelong Learning and the School of Politics, Philosophy and Language and Communication Studies at the University of East Anglia. Much of the theoretical and practical material presented in this study came up in the course of joint workshops we led in the context of advanced doctoral training. The debt we owe to our workshop students and participants is considerable: many thanks are due, in particular, to Pu Shi, Eleni Konidari, Achala Gupta, Gina Lontoc and Joanna Nair, for writing up their methodological reflections for this book.

Above all, we would like to acknowledge all the doctoral students and other researchers in universities around the world who were so generous in sharing their ideas and time with us through interviews and informal discussion during the later stages of finalising this text. We have learned so much from interacting within this global community which formed around the book. We were delighted that Prof. Alan Rogers agreed to be our 'critical friend' at the last stage. His insightful comments helped us identify gaps and ways in which we could develop stronger connections across the book.

Finally, the dedication of this work goes to our respective partners and family, without whose forbearance and inspiration this study would never have seen the light of day.

EXPLANATION OF DATA SOURCES

As indicated in the Preface, we have drawn examples and analysed data from a variety of sources. In order to simplify the text, we have cited only the year after quotations from interview data. However, as the reader may like to return to the original sources and more detailed accounts of the various studies/projects, we include full details below.

2014, 2015, 2016: this data was collected specifically for this book. Semi-structured interviews were conducted by Alain Wolf with doctoral students in Linguistics and Education from two universities in the UK. The data collected refer to a variety of research contexts in international and European countries – Brazil, Saudi Arabia and Italy to name a few – and in such varied fields as linguistics, education and translation studies. Anna Robinson-Pant conducted interviews with doctoral and some MPhil students in universities in Korea, Nepal and Iceland in 2015 and early 2016. The choice of countries was based only on practicalities – in that she could combine the interviews there with other university business.

2012: data was collected for a collaborative research project with Tesfay Tsegay, presented at the BAICE conference 2012 in Cambridge. Follow-up email discussion was conducted in 2016. The students cited here also wrote and were interviewed about their doctoral experiences in Robinson-Pant (2005) and Robinson-Pant (2009).

2010: this data is drawn from a University of East Anglia Teaching Fellowship project, 'International Research Students: reflections on PhD supervision' (and the DVD produced), conducted by Anna Magyar and Anna Robinson-Pant. A fuller account of the findings and methodology can be found in: Magyar and Robinson-Pant (2011). Where quotations are taken directly from the DVD, this is indicated.

TRANSCRIPTION CONVENTIONS

The transcription conventions adopted in this book reflect the international and mediated nature of the topics under investigation. It is important to note that the book does not go below syntactic and pragmatic levels of description so that a phonetic description is not deemed necessary.

The transcription/translation conventions adopted in this book are as follows:

- Transcriptions aim to combine legibility with faithfulness to oral output.
- Words and concepts are frequently presented in the source language wherever it is felt that readers need to be given access to a culture-specific concept which requires disambiguation and explicitation.
- A literal translation into English is provided wherever possible in order to give the reader as much understanding of the original text as possible. This happens especially in cases where the analysis of the material depends on a close reading of the original text/utterance (see Chapter 4 for example).
- Where the person interviewed/referred to spoke in a language other than English, the translation process is discussed in detail to ensure that the source utterance has been understood in the appropriate context and that the translator's/interpreter's stance is fully considered.
- Where script other than the Roman script is involved – the Devanagari script, the Arabic script or Chinese characters, for example – words and utterances are presented, wherever possible, in the original script. A transliteration is also provided to enhance reader's access.

1

FROM CROSS-CULTURAL TO INTERCULTURAL

An alternative perspective on the research process

Anna Robinson-Pant

Introduction

Research methodology textbooks often mention language and culture as additional factors that should be taken into account when planning research, particularly if the researcher is collecting data in multilingual or unfamiliar cultural contexts. By contrast, our starting point in this book is to consider language and culture as central to research methodology. This chapter sets out to introduce alternative theoretical lenses that can help to challenge the notion that any research study is 'culture-free' and point to ways of moving beyond a 'technicist' approach. Instead, I take an ideological perspective on power, language and culture, raising questions which the rest of the book will explore in more detail. What part does language play in shaping the relationship between researcher, and research participants and the audience of a research text? How have cultural values influenced the research design and research questions? Taking the concepts of culture and language at face value often leads to an emphasis on identifying contrasts and how to bridge these differences. Rather than focusing on the 'cross-cultural' in this way, we introduce a more dynamic concept of culture and language in this book as processes that influence research design, data collection, analysis and writing.

This chapter is written by Anna, an ethnographer in the field of education and development. I am still making this journey from 'cross-cultural' to 'intercultural' perspectives in research, and consider myself a relative newcomer to applied linguistics debates. By contrast, Alain describes himself as 'very much steeped in theoretical discussions such as how sentences are not by themselves able to generate meaning without an appeal to the communicative context in which they are uttered' (see Chapter 2). This leads him to ask questions about how context may be defined as fundamentally related to speakers' intentions (see Chapter 3).

2 Anna Robinson-Pant

These intentions are further problematised in the multilingual research context when researchers find themselves acting as or through translators (see Chapter 4).

For my part, like many other researchers in the field of education and international development, I have tended to view translation and communication with respondents in a multilingual situation primarily as a practical problem to be overcome. As a PhD student in Nepal in the 1990s, I conducted research with adult literacy programmes where spoken and written interactions took place in several languages, including Nepali, English and Newari (a language spoken mainly in the Kathmandu Valley). Though I had learned to speak Nepali, when observing adult literacy classes I was often dependent on literacy teachers to explain to me in Nepali or English what was happening in Newari. My fieldnotes were taken mainly in English, but also contained Nepali and Newari extracts from conversations and participant observation, transcribed by me in Romanised rather than Devanagari[1] script. The decision to transcribe Nepali direct speech into Romanised script or to translate the meaning directly into English in my fieldnotes was taken for purely pragmatic reasons – that I wanted to capture as much as possible, and it was easier and quicker to do this in my first language and using a familiar script.

With regard to oral interaction, I soon discovered that whether I chose to speak English or Nepali very much influenced the kinds of conversations and interviews I had with people – the same person would tell me a different story in Nepali, as compared to the response they gave in English. I was aware that my language decisions as a researcher were not simply influencing who could communicate with me, but were also connected with my and their differing identities, cultural values and the perceived purposes of my research. English was associated with foreign aid agencies, particularly the US organisation whose literacy programmes I was researching in a rural community. Several concepts being introduced through their development programmes could not be or were not translated into Nepali but remained in English (notably, the word 'gender'). An important dimension of my research focused on finding out how people felt about international development, analysing how different languages already used and being introduced through the literacy programme were influencing new power hierarchies within communities (see Robinson-Pant, 2001).

Despite this focus on language issues within the literacy programmes and communities where I researched, I overlooked an opportunity to analyse my own research practices with regard to decisions around language and literacy. This is perhaps not surprising. Looking through textbooks on qualitative research for social scientists, I found that many authors addressed 'language' as a technical hurdle – rather than an opportunity to interrogate research relationships, the multiple identities of researcher and researched, and the complex process of translating fieldwork data into final research text. Since my PhD study, I have drawn on theoretical resources from the fields of intercultural communication, translation studies, academic literacies and postcolonial theory in order to work out strategies for engaging with and analysing hidden voices, identities, relationships and texts within the research process.

In this chapter, I aim to share some of the theoretical lenses that have helped me to investigate more critically multilingual communicative practices within social science research processes – and to which we will be returning throughout this book. Although I draw here primarily on my own experiences as a researcher in education and international development, the analysis also includes insights from doctoral students with whom I have worked as supervisor and researcher here in the UK.[2] I begin by looking at the ways in which doctoral students – who like me do not have a linguistics background – have approached the task of translation.

The researcher as amateur linguist

> I did my research in Swahili so I had to transcribe all my data then translate it in English and sometimes when you think in another language, even when I put down my sentences when sometimes in the supervision, my supervisor will ask me, what do you mean here? I will change things from backwards forwards because of how we speak in Swahili and I had to transcribe it and give to someone to proofread to be sure of the tenses and everything.
>
> *(Scholastica Kazidi (formerly Mokake), in DVD interview, 2010)*

This account from Scholastica Kazidi, a PhD student in a UK university who conducted her field research in Tanzania, gives an insight into the practical difficulties involved in translating the data from Swahili (her mother tongue) into her final thesis text in English. Her concern was primarily with the labour involved because of this extra layer of textual production – transcribing and then translating the data – and then expanding on the meaning orally to her immediate audience, her supervisor. The process was time-consuming but also, for this student who was a social worker not a linguist by profession, involved venturing into an area where she lacked confidence and experience. Her description of changing the text 'from backwards forwards' and not being able to convey the exact meaning in English vividly conveys the frustrations of someone who has unexpectedly found herself thrust into the role of translator.

Comparing Scholastica's experiences with advice from 'outsider' educational researchers – like myself – who conducted research in multilingual contexts, I found a similar emphasis on 'learning by doing' or informal learning as the researcher turned translator. From his experience of researching science education in Malaysia, Lewin (1990: 138) warned: 'there are no wholly literal translations for complex constructs between languages. There are no right translations, only better or worse ones which need careful consideration in terms of the nuances they reflect' (see Chapter 4 for an overview of translation strategies which have been used in multilingual data collection).

4 Anna Robinson-Pant

Discussion in fieldwork guides also focuses on the time-consuming and technical business of translation and learning a second language. Devereux advised – based on his experiences of doctoral research in Ghana – on whether or not an outsider researcher should employ a translator or choose to learn the local language themselves:

> I challenge the golden rule which insists that learning the local language is essential for successful fieldwork . . . Learning the language is a 'data collection exercise' in its own right, and the investment of valuable time and intellectual energy in acquiring this knowledge should be assessed alongside the imperative to collect other kinds of data.
>
> *(Devereux, 1992: 43)*

By describing language learning as another form of 'data collection', Devereux implied that this additional task may actually undermine the 'real' data collection by diverting the researcher's time and energy onto a secondary activity. He went on to set out three possible scenarios for the researcher who is deciding whether or not to learn the local language (ibid.: 46). These range from the researcher who is fluent and can conduct the interview alone, to the researcher who partly understands the local language but works with a translator to interview respondents so that s/he can interject and ask additional questions through the translator. The third scenario involves the researcher delegating the interviewing completely to research assistants and not necessarily attending personally, but discussing the data afterwards with the research assistants/translators. The possible roles that Devereux described – from the researcher who attempts to communicate directly with respondents, to the researcher who is not physically present in interviews – were discussed largely from the perspective of efficiency of communication.

Discussion on language and translation issues within research in my field (comparative education and international development) has been dominated by these concerns about the cost of translation (in terms of time and resources spent on assistants) and effectiveness (whether the translation is accurate). Looking at Devereux' three scenarios from a methodological perspective, what emerges as more significant is the different relationship established between the researcher and participants in these situations, depending on whether communication is being mediated by a third party (the research assistant-cum-translator). There is also the question of whose voices are dominant within each scenario and how the researcher decides to represent in written text the different identities (researcher, respondent, translator) shaping the data. The researcher's decisions about when and what to translate and whether to use a translator can thus be analysed as an important but often hidden aspect of the research process.

Recognising the need to consider the ideological dimension of decision making around language, I turned to three research fields where the starting point seemed to be a recognition of inequality in relation to knowledge construction and communication: intercultural communication, decolonising research methodology, and academic literacies. The next section will introduce some of the conceptual tools that I have used in interrogating my own research practice. Adopting the perspective of research as an intercultural encounter, I look at the implications of this approach for analysing the research relationship, research interviews and writing up. Taking the stance that most social interactions are textually mediated (Barton and Hamilton, 2005), I use the term 'communicative practices' as my entry point to an analysis of multilingual research practice. This can help to avoid focusing only on oral interaction when analysing processes of collecting empirical data, and only on literacy practices and written texts when discussing language issues in relation to writing up. Chapter 5 will explore how all stages of the research process are shaped by written as well as oral texts. I begin this analysis by taking concepts from postcolonial theory and intercultural communication to investigate empirical data collection practices, before moving on to look at writing up through the lens of academic literacies.

Developing an alternative lens on fieldwork practice in multilingual situations

Insider or outsider? Deconstructing the research relationship

> Having been immersed in the Western academy which claims theory as thoroughly Western, which has constructed all the rules by which the indigenous world has been theorised, indigenous voices have been overwhelmingly silenced.
>
> *(Smith, 1999: 29)*

> Decolonizing research provides a site of agency for decentering colonial knowledge.
>
> *(Jankie, 2004: 101)*

> I have always been disturbed by the way in which the Euro-Western research process disconnects me from the multiple relations that I have with my community, the living and the non-living.
>
> *(Chilisa, 2012: 3)*

Analysing the research process through the 'decolonising methodology' lens provided by writers like Smith, Jankie and Chilisa shifts the emphasis from concerns about micro level communication between individuals in the research setting, onto consideration of how global inequalities and historical processes, particularly colonisation, have shaped and continue to influence the construction of knowledge. Smith (1999: 5) argued that 'research is not an innocent distant academic exercise but an activity that has something at stake and occurs in a set of political and social conditions'. Her account of the ways in which Western research practices have distorted and silenced Maori communities' knowledge in New Zealand illustrates

6 Anna Robinson-Pant

how the research relationship can be analysed in terms of cultural and political values. Suggesting that decolonising research did not imply 'totally rejecting Western theories', Jankie (2004: 101) focused on the relationship between 'native and non-native' researchers:

> Collaboration pushes researchers like myself to acknowledge and consider the relevance of our academic knowledge and hybridised identities and experiences in the construction of research knowledge.

Key to decolonising methodology analysis is the recognition of hierarchies of knowledge, influencing not only whose voice is heard but also how that knowledge is being produced. Mutua and Swadener (2004: 2) ask the question 'Who defines and legitimizes what counts as "scholarship"?' Writers have examined the assumptions behind what might be regarded as the hidden texts and practices that shape research outputs, particularly research ethics procedures. Explaining that Maori communities did not promote the same Western notion of individual autonomy, Smith suggested that there was more collective responsibility for maintaining social order and for ownership of property and assets. Consequently, the practice of requesting a respondent to sign individual consent for their photograph and interview to be used in a research text challenged such beliefs and also privileged written contracts over oral agreements. Smith's work marked the starting point of a growing critique of research ethics procedures and assumptions which had often been taken for granted in many UK, US and Australian universities (see Robinson-Pant and Singal, 2013, for a review of this literature).

Writing from her position as a university professor in Botswana, Chilisa (2012: 113) built on Smith's ideas about indigenous practices and beliefs to articulate what she terms a 'relational ontology' and address her uneasy feeling of detachment through Western research processes. Chilisa argued that within a postcolonial indigenous research paradigm, the researcher recognises the centrality of relationships to the research process – relations with people, with the environment, with the 'cosmos' and with ideas: 'The researcher becomes part of circles of relations that are connected to one another and to which the researcher is also accountable' (ibid.). This is in sharp contrast to the situation that Smith described where the researcher was accountable primarily to their institution or funding agency, and where their practice was shaped by institutional values and priorities, such as the need for legal protection through written consent forms. It is not just that such Western communicative practices were seen as inappropriate in indigenous communities, but also that the resulting research would lose value. As Wilson (2008: 130) discovered in relation to research with indigenous people in Canada, 'participants did not want anonymity because they understood that the information imparted or the story offered would lose its power without knowledge of the teller'. Chilisa also saw the dominance of Euro-Western languages as integral to 'the role of imperialism, colonisation and globalisation in the construction of knowledge' (ibid.: 117), as I will discuss later in relation to the writing up of research.

This analysis of the research process from a postcolonial perspective shows how language choices can be seen in relation to wider debates about the role of the researcher in the construction of knowledge. Though a researcher may make decisions about which language to use for interactions with participants on practical grounds (as I did in Nepal), they also need to take account of the hierarchical relationships between languages within their research setting. For instance, the gendered dimension – that women might not be familiar with a language of power (English) due to lack of access to schooling – influenced which languages I chose to use in communicating with research participants in Nepal. All these decisions taken at an individual level have implications not only for the researcher's relationship with participants in the field research, but also for how they appear to privilege certain knowledges and practices.

Questions about how to negotiate access and conduct research activities with regard to language are thus as pressing for the insider researcher who speaks local languages as for an outsider researcher – since both insider and outsider researcher[3] may be introducing new communicative practices such as focus group discussions or consent forms. Similarly, questions about whether to employ a translator or research assistant or try to communicate directly with participants could be considered in relation to North-South[4] relationships of power. For instance, the Northern researcher who is constructing their identity within a new community may need to be aware of ascribed identities (the most obvious being 'Western' or 'rich') and that by delegating language work to assistants, they could be seen as continuing colonial relationships of power between 'Western' researcher and local informant. In some ways, the literature on decolonising methodology is problematic in this sense – the polarisation of 'Western' and 'other' can tend to downplay the individual's agency in constructing and challenging identities and relationships that go beyond these often essentialised and stereotyped identities. Hrefna, an Icelandic doctoral student researching in Greece and interviewed for this book, reflected on this notion of 'culture' in relation to her fieldwork: 'I had expected to research the exotic but I ended up being the exotic myself, mostly to other Greeks and some international scholars!' (Interview 2016)

To counter such processes of 'otherisation', I found that theoretical approaches from intercultural communication encouraged me to look more closely at the intercultural encounter between researcher and research participants. This theoretical lens can provide a way for analysing communicative practices (such as interviews and focus group discussions) facilitated by the researcher with respondents.

Intercultural communication and research interviews

> Terms of cultural engagement, whether antagonistic or affiliative, are produced performatively . . . the representation of difference must not be hastily read as the reflection of *pre-given* ethnic or cultural traits set in the fixed tablet of tradition.
>
> *(Bhabha, 1994: 2)*

8 Anna Robinson-Pant

Taking this concept of culture as performed (rather than 'pre-given') into discussions about the multilingual research encounter can help to illuminate the process rather than focusing only on the end product of research. Alain uses this notion of performativity in Chapter 3 to show how meaning is not only recovered by researchers and the researched, but also acted upon through forms of interaction which involve the use of diverse and sometimes unexpected strategies. This contrasts with the tendency to adopt an essentialised view of culture, generalising for instance about how Thai people behave as compared to Germans – a view encapsulated in Hofstede's (1991) influential work which has informed many cross-cultural training programmes. Chapter 3 provides an overview of the early days of what is now known and often criticised as 'cross-cultural pragmatics' (theoretical work which aimed to offer comparisons across seemingly stable and identifiable national cultures).

Rather than assuming that indigenous or Western values are static, Turner (2011: 14) challenges the notion of 'solidified, naturalised intellectual cultural values and stability of conventions' to suggest that there are points of 'transformation': 'intercultural communication has itself a performative dimension, whereby in being enacted, it inevitably changes types of exchanges' (ibid.). Though analysing 'languaging' practices in the specific context of higher education, Turner's account could be extended to give insights into the ways in which doctoral research practices (like consent forms and ethics protocols) in informal settings and communities could be transformed through the intercultural encounter. An intercultural approach to research thus shifts attention away from identifying national characteristics and norms to a focus on the individual encounter, enabling us 'to understand how and when culture plays an active role in shaping and influencing our meaning-making endeavours' (Sarangi, 1995: 26). Writers on intercultural communication have emphasised the potential for new meanings to be generated and, by implication, for the construction of new knowledge through individuals communicating with each other across cultures (Holliday, Hyde and Kullman, 2004; Holliday 2011). In contrast to the macro perspective on construction of knowledge taken by the decolonising methodology theorists discussed earlier in this chapter, Byram advised, for instance, that we need to focus on 'encounters between individuals with their own meanings' (1997: 31).

Within all these texts, there is a strong sense of the informal learning that takes place through an intercultural encounter, whether in the classroom or outside, intended or spontaneous (see Rogers' (2013) account of informal learning characteristics). This could be compared to the learning involved in the intercultural communication between a researcher and her/his respondents. Risager (2007: 85) suggests that 'to learn a foreign culture is to develop from an ethnocentric to a relativist standpoint and thereby become conscious of one's own identity'. In the context of a multilingual and multicultural research encounter, both researcher and the informants are learning a 'foreign culture' (in terms of the research practices as well as differing cultural values) which can be a source of dynamic transformation. From this perspective, questions about which language/s to use in research interviews could take into account opportunities for intercultural learning, rather than considering only efficiency of communication. An example comes from my interviews for this book with students in Iceland, where Monika (originally from Poland) tried out a new method for data collection, story crafting, to encourage newly arrived children to tell their stories in Polish and Icelandic. She saw this as more empowering than using a translator to 'speak for them' (Interview 2016).

Such opportunities relate partly to questions around power, control and ownership of the research space. Hrefna, the Icelandic student conducting research with refugees in Greece, explained how her relationship with a respondent was shaped by their differing cultural expectations and identities:

> I interviewed a Pakistani man at my house with a young Greek male interpreter. But I could see that the Pakistani was not comfortable at all and would not eat anything I offered. Later he was adamant that I should meet him for a coffee . . . We had coffee in a public place where he paid for the coffee. We are taught in methodology courses that we should be the one that offer refreshments to our interviewees as we are indebted to them for sharing with us their time and stories, but I saw it was important for him that he could do something for me and we then had a more relaxed and intimate atmosphere for the interview. It shows that location and gender roles are important too. I had to be in his culture so that he could be the provider, particularly as in Greece his masculine status was under much scrutiny.
>
> *(Interview, 2016)*

This example offers a different perspective on debates about how far North/South hierarchies dictate or influence research relationships – giving an insight into how both researchers and participants can mediate such expectations. Kamler and Threadgold (2003) give a similar example from their research with older Vietnamese women in the UK, noting that 'food functioned as a language in this context' (ibid.: 149). They describe how once participants started to converse with each other in their mother tongue, the researchers felt they were losing control over the planned research activities.

The researcher's decision about whether or not to use a third party as translator takes on a different significance when viewed through the lens of intercultural communication. The concept of 'face' as 'the negotiated public image, mutually granted each other by participants in a communicative event' (Scollon, Scollon and Jones, 2012: 48) provides a way of analysing how the intercultural encounter might change with the introduction of an additional person. As Scollon et al. (ibid.: 51) emphasise, the 'choice of language is also a matter of negotiation of the face of the participants', since which language they use relates to their relative statuses and assumptions about such differences.

Taking this perspective on Devereux' three scenarios for the outsider field-worker discussed earlier, we can analyse how the relationship might change if

10 Anna Robinson-Pant

the researcher worked with a translator or if they communicated instead directly with participants. Introducing the concept of 'face' illuminates the limitations of analysing the communication only in terms of explaining what responses mean in a different language, rather than looking also at how meaning is being constructed. In a situation where a translator is being used, researcher and respondents are negotiating face not only with each other, but also with the translator, thereby introducing greater complexity into the research relationship. The discussion of face also brings up new questions about who should be selected as a translator: whereas someone from the local community may know the local language (including familiarity with communicative practices, such as interpreting the meaning of silences) and facilitate access, the relative status of translator and respondent may influence their interaction and the translator's interpretation in ways unperceived by an outsider researcher. As Andrews (2012) discusses, the interpreter is not only translating data but is also an active player (almost a co-researcher) in generating meaning with respondents through interviews and discussion. These questions around how to take account of the richness of context – in terms of the 'static' external and the 'dynamic' social/psychological context – will be explored in the next chapter.

Fieldwork in a multilingual situation thus involves questions about identity, power and control over research processes that go beyond language as a technical concern. This is not just an issue faced by outsider researchers unfamiliar with the languages spoken, but also of central concern to all those researching in multilingual and multi-ethnic communities. The facilitation of research activities and the relationship between researcher and researched can be affected not only by the language/s of communication, but also by assumptions about status, values and intentions held by both. Such assumptions can also be influenced by historical relationships around power and inequality, played out through prescribed communicative practices (such as a university's ethics protocols) which often shape interaction within the research process. The picture is complicated further when a translator is involved too, both in terms of negotiating face and identities, and interpreting meaning.

I have so far focused on how meaning is constructed within fieldwork situations through oral interaction, but it is also mediated through written texts – particularly the researcher's fieldnotes and interview transcriptions. I will move now to look at the process of transforming fieldwork material into the final research text. Here I draw on theoretical concepts from research on academic literacies as a lens to analyse the specific writing and reading practices that doctoral students engage in.

'Textualising research into knowledge' (Sengupta, 2005): a multilingual perspective on writing

The view of writing as simply translating oral data has fed into the assumption of a linear progression from oral to written text and the phrase 'writing *up*'. Those working within an indigenous research paradigm have challenged the hierarchical notion of written knowledge being superior to visual and spoken representations of knowledge. However, I would take this further to suggest that it is as problematic to separate oral and written knowledge in this way as it is to polarise 'Western' and indigenous values and practices. Taking Street's (1984, 1993) concept of a continuum of oral and literacy practices in all societies (as opposed to Goody's (1968) 'Great Divide' between literate and oral societies), I start from the understanding that writing is integral to the whole research process – not just the end point.

Research on 'academic literacies' (Lea and Street, 1998; Lillis and Scott, 2007) can provide a way of exploring how institutional practices and values have influenced the kinds of texts that count as research within multilingual contexts and how researchers – including doctoral students – make decisions about which language/s to use in their final thesis. In their book on writing in UK universities, Jones, Street and Turner (1999) defined a shift from conceptualising academic literacy as around skills and effectiveness, to considering epistemological issues, particularly what counts as knowledge and who has control over it. Rather than the assumption of one homogeneous academy, they viewed writing as constructed according to particular conventions in different academic contexts (hence the term 'academic literacies' in the plural). Lea and Street (2010: 370) explained that the concept of identity is central, giving 'particular attention to the relationships of power, authority, meaning making and identity that are implicit in the use of literacy practices within specific institutional settings'.

Within the university context and the doctoral degree, the hierarchical positioning of teacher/supervisor and student can influence whose meaning dominates and how meanings are contested and mediated. Taking the conventional relationship between the researcher and researched as similar in some respects (particularly the researcher, like a teacher, having greater familiarity with and control over the dominant discourse), academic literacies research offers insights into how research writing even outside academia can be similarly shaped by institutional values and practices.

Questions of voice and writer identity become more complex in writing that emerges from multilingual research processes. As well as viewing the identities of researcher and researched in relation to the cultural, linguistic and political fieldwork practices that I discussed earlier, writing a text opens up new relationships and identities beyond the immediate context. Ivanic (2005: 398) developed the model of a four-leaf clover to illustrate four aspects of writer identity: the autobiographical self (sense of their roots), discoursal self (representation of himself/herself in the text), relational dimension (assumptions about the reader's expectations) and the authorial self (sense of authority in the text). The writer may need to construct each of these identities in relation to language and cultural factors beyond the society where they have conducted the fieldwork. Moving from fieldnotes to the final research text involves decisions about who the audience will be (including what languages they are familiar with) and also how the writer/researcher wants to or is expected to represent their identity in the text. For instance, the doctoral student

12   Anna Robinson-Pant

Hrefna explained that this was not just about language or genre but around her ideological stance and topic too: 'I left my Icelandic identity behind in terms of my language decisions [to write in English]. But the emphasis on gender is for me very Scandinavian.' (Interview, 2016)

The discoursal self and the authorial self may be shaped by institutional values and practices, particularly for the doctoral researcher who is writing within a higher educational institution with particular expectations about genre and style. George, a lecturer from Nigeria, when writing up his PhD research findings in a UK university explained that in his fieldwork context, these dilemmas about how identity and voice were represented in text went beyond questions about which language or language competency. He found that he was debating whether to write in a different English from that spoken and written in his fieldwork context, in order to meet the criteria of 'good' academic English in his UK university department:

> So what I'm trying to say is that sometimes . . . writing is also a culture – your piece of writing can explain the kind of culture you portray . . . That if your culture is not purely English culture, you're not likely going to write very strong acceptable English, that would be within the English culture. So you have to struggle, to move from your culture to the English culture.
>
> *(Interview, 2010)*

Another example comes from Canagarajah's (2002) ethnographic study in Sri Lanka. Returning to the University of Jaffna after studying for a PhD in the US, Canagarajah compared his and his colleagues' assumptions about what made a 'good' academic text in English. Responding to an article he had published in the US, they identified his dominant authorial voice and critical stance as 'unnecessarily and unproductively contentious', displaying the self-centred values ('aggressive individualism') that they associated with US universities (ibid.: 141). This contrasted with the values within the Jaffna academic community, which promoted cohesion and traditional rhetoric. These differences illustrate the ways in which the four 'selves' of writer identity outlined in Ivanic's model of the four-leaf clover can each be contested in relation to language and culture: for instance, the 'discoursal self' in this case could draw on academic discourses from both the US and Sri Lankan contexts.

These questions about how to write up research conducted in another language or cultural context are closely linked to our reading practices. Although we sometimes make conscious decisions about whether to cite literature that was written in another language, we may not even realise the ways in which 'we are authored by texts' (Pennycook, 1996: 209). Turner (2011) traces the genealogies that may have influenced an academic text, pointing to the ways in which the indicators of quality in English academic writing – brevity, concision and clarity – come directly from assumptions within Western philosophy. An example given by Janina, a doctoral researcher interviewed in Iceland, suggested that her supervisor (originally from Canada) was reading her draft proposal with what she called 'Anglo Saxon eyes':

> He said he was expecting relevant information first and then the background . . . They read the first sentence and if they like it, jump onto the next. Just knowing this is useful to me – that I should sum up in the beginning.
>
> *(Interview, 2016)*

Janina pointed out that the supervision meeting provided an important opportunity to discuss their differing ways of both reading and writing a research text.

Disseminating research and the geopolitics of academic publishing

The sources that academic researchers draw on to analyse and present their work are frequently taken from 'centre-based' (published in the US, UK and Australia) journal publications in English. This hierarchical notion of what is an acceptable or good academic reference is thus perpetuated through the geopolitics of academic publishing. As Canagarajah (ibid.) points out, scholars in the South lacking familiarity with centre[5] journal rhetorical conventions are less likely to be able to publish their work for a wider audience. From a multilingual perspective, this means that decisions about which language to publish in or which English to write in may be determined by considerations about career progression or social status, rather than who would benefit from the research findings. The dominance of English in academic publishing is not only a challenge faced by researchers in postcolonial societies, as Lillis and Curry (2010) illustrated from their research with European academics. A German student studying in a UK university explained to me how she would continue to publish in English after her degree in order to engage with academic audiences in Germany as well as further afield:

> I wrote my masters in English in Germany because it was political science and as the literature is in English, there is none in German. What's the use of publishing in German? If there is an international focus, the course is usually in English.
>
> *(From interview, Robinson-Pant and Street, 2012)*

Many researchers – particularly those enrolled in doctoral programmes at UK and US universities – do not face a choice about which language to write up in, as this is prescribed by their institution. This was the case for me when writing up doctoral research conducted in Nepal. The knowledge that I would be writing the final text in English influenced my decisions about which language to use for producing intermediate texts, such as fieldnotes and policy analysis. Although Chilisa (2012) recommends publishing research in bilingual texts where there is a choice (for instance, in a local language and a global language), many researchers would not have the financial and linguistic resources to do this. Also, as I discovered in my own case, when I published a Nepali summary of my full English version thesis, those Nepali-speaking readers who were interested in this kind of research text had been educated in and spoke fluent English.

Analysing how writers draw on theoretical texts, Nelson and Castello (2012: 45) reflect on what happens to the authorial voice when voices of other writers are appropriated from a different language – including the possibility of 'revoicing' translated texts. They see this as a tension between 'domesticating' and 'foreignising' a voice, relating to the decision as to whether to 'reproduce the voice or replace it with another voice' (ibid.). In the context of higher education, they question whether a student would be able to incorporate non-conventional features to emphasise their own identity in a text in English without it being considered lesser quality writing. Michael-Luna and Canagarajah (2007) introduce the possibility through their notion of 'code meshing' (as opposed to the ideal of 'pure' language or code-switching) to create a space for multilingual writing in research. They suggest that in this way the multilingual speaker can 'deliberately integrate local and academic discourse as a form of resistance' (ibid.: 56), thereby transforming the dominant academic literacy. Researchers attempting to recreate their respondents' identities in English could draw on such strategies, as I discuss in Chapter 5.

This section has explored the dilemmas facing researchers writing in multilingual contexts, drawing on an academic literacies lens to investigate issues of power and inequality in knowledge construction. In contrast to the previous section about fieldwork, I am seeing the 'multilingual context' here not in bounded geographical terms, but taking into account the author and reader identity too. The researcher may be collecting data in a monolingual context, but in a language that is not their mother tongue, or they may intend to write for an audience who speak different languages. The concept of hierarchies of literacies and languages being shaped by institutional practices and values provides a way of analysing how the researcher makes the decision about which language/s to write and publish in. The researcher is often constrained in how far s/he can make these decisions alone – sometimes directly by the required language medium of their institution, but also indirectly by the theoretical resources available. The geopolitics of academic publishing has led to a situation where researchers are less likely to be able to access literature in non-standard forms or minority languages, since centre-based journals in English dominate in a hierarchical model of global knowledge production. These factors may prevent indigenous researchers and others working in multilingual contexts from citing references from research in their local area or reflecting indigenous knowledges. Engaging with theoretical concepts from academic literacies and the geopolitics of academic writing can point to one way for such researchers – including during a doctoral degree – to challenge and transform unequal relationships around knowledge construction through their writing. Chapter 6 will look in more detail at the roles that doctoral students and supervisors can play in this process.

Conclusion: exploring hidden voices, identities and texts

I began this chapter with some of the common questions and dilemmas raised by educational researchers in the South – around how to collect data effectively in multilingual settings, and above all about how to communicate and translate that data without losing too much time during a doctoral degree. As my own research journey so far has illustrated, shifting attention from those practical concerns to the power relationships between researcher and research participant in terms of both macro and micro levels of knowledge production raises very different issues about how to work across cultures and languages. This chapter concludes by looking at such questions in order to explore the implications for how researchers can work and publish for and/or with diverse groups.

Accounts of doctoral students conducting fieldwork in multilingual settings and writing research texts in their second language or for multiple audiences give an insight into the shifting identities of the researcher as s/he facilitates and mediates communication across cultures and languages. This perspective draws not only on a different conceptualisation of academic literacy but also of mobility. Writing from the discipline of geography, Brooks and Waters (2011: 129) identify a 'new mobilities' paradigm, which 'interrogates the social, cultural and political meanings of "mobility"'. Rather than examining migrants' experiences at home and/or overseas, they suggest that we should focus on 'the actual process of and meanings attached to mobility itself' (ibid.). Rizvi's (2010) discussion of international doctoral students operating within 'transnational spaces' also connects with this idea and explores the ways in which such researchers negotiate between the demands and expectations of their home and host (overseas) institutions. As the quotations from doctoral students in this chapter illustrate, their experiences of research and writing across cultures and languages are intertwined with the process and meanings of migration, even if this was seen as only a temporary move for the doctoral degree.

This emphasis on learning through mobility and migration relates to my earlier discussion about the intercultural encounter in field research. Knowledge in such settings is being produced through the dynamic relationship between researcher, researched and possibly translator, and their institutional, cultural and political values. For the doctoral student, this process is also shaped in the short term by the supervisor-supervisee relationship, mediating differing expectations and understandings. The challenge for the researcher has often been discussed only in terms of dilemmas about which language to use for interviewing or taking notes, how or when to use translators or comparing different translations of data. However, the methodological implications of multilingual research stretch beyond contestation over interpretation of data collected in multiple languages and literacies. The focus on how meaning is constructed within the new mobilities literature and the indigenous research paradigm suggests that the more important question for the researcher might be: *how can I share with the reader (and in the case of PhD students, my supervisors) the experience of writing across cultures and languages, in terms of multiple and shifting identities?* Such an approach would perhaps require a multi-vocal, multi-genre, layered research text, whereas the tendency is to produce a text with a unifying narrator's voice that denies any of these tensions and movement between identities.

Literature on the geopolitics of academic writing and decolonisation of research literature points to the ways in which the research process and research texts may be shaped by hidden texts and literacy practices. With the growing influence of research ethics procedures in UK and US universities (Sikes and Piper, 2010), such texts might include published codes of practice governing researcher conduct. These in turn may require researchers to use literacy practices, such as gaining informed consent in written form, which are unfamiliar in the field research site (see Hamid, 2010; Shamim and Qureshi, 2010). Such hidden texts can construct the research relationship and dynamic in ways that influence the whole process of data collection, analysis and writing up. As discussed earlier, the researcher may not even be aware of the texts that are influencing their own writing conventions and style, such as assumptions influenced by the European enlightenment which associate clarity and transparent writing with rational, objective thinking (Turner, 2011). Alternatively, the researcher may have read and been influenced by researchers who draw on other genealogies of knowledge, but choose not to cite this literature directly, particularly if it has not been published in high status English-language journals.

The underlying question that the researcher needs to address in relation to these concerns might be: *will the reader be aware of all the texts (published and unpublished) shaping the ideas in the final research report/thesis/article, and influencing practices in the fieldwork?* By reflecting on all the texts (oral and written) that have influenced their research process, the researcher is then encouraged to problematise their own position in constructing knowledge. This relates directly to postcolonial debates about hierarchies of knowledges and languages, and the irony that in order to find out more local knowledge, the indigenous researcher may have to read about it in a journal published in a foreign language for an international audience.

Researchers writing within a participatory action research paradigm have long struggled with dilemmas around ownership of text and representation of voice. *How can research conducted collaboratively with a community be represented in ways that take account of the participants' expectations and experiences, yet also meet the academic researcher's agenda?* Within a multilingual context, the issues are similar: *how can a research text (particularly if published only in one language) based on bilingual or multilingual fieldwork incorporate or even simply acknowledge such voices?* The voices in this situation are not only those of researcher and research participants but in the case of research conducted through an interpreter, a third party who is not necessarily involved in writing the final text. From my experience in participatory research, I would approach this question from a wider perspective than simply considering 'whose language' or 'whose voices' are within the final text. Writing on research directions on teacher education in the South, Khamis (2011) argues that the reliance on Human Capital Theory has determined the research questions to be asked and researched.[6] The whole research process thus needs to be interrogated in terms of *who has control over the aims, methods and outputs at various stages?* – rather than just considering who owns and whose voice is acknowledged in the final text. This is partly about issues of language – and whether respondents can relate directly with the researcher or how the research space is being created in a second language. But it is also about the flexibility of the research approach and aims. The ideal outcome of the research process for some communities may not be a written text – whether in an indigenous language or English – but a more tangible contribution to improving their lives.

I have highlighted some questions around researching across languages and cultures that emerged from conceptual debate in the fields of decolonising research methodology, academic literacies and intercultural communication. The aim of this book is for the reader to develop an alternative framework for analysing the relationships, identities and voices of researcher and researched within their specific research context. The questions in the box below provide a starting point for reflecting on a research study through the lenses introduced in this chapter.

Box 1

Questions for further reflection

- How did I decide on my research questions and choice of research area?
- Whose values and priorities have influenced the design of my study, including the ethics procedures? How can I engage with and take account of alternative knowledges?
- How could certain key theoretical concepts and debates (such as 'learner-centred approach') informing my research be problematised within other cultural contexts and research traditions?
- Which literature (and in which languages) have I chosen to read and cite from and why?
- Which languages am I using to record and analyse data? Who is involved in the decisions about which language/s to use?
- How am I using translators or acting as a translator myself? How will this influence the data collected and analysis of findings?
- Whose voices can be heard in my final written text and how do I go about this?
- How do I represent myself (and my differing identities) in the text?
- What forms of research dissemination (oral, visual and written) will I conduct and how do these take into account issues around culture, language and audience?

18 Anna Robinson-Pant

As we have seen in this chapter, the researcher's role and interaction with people and texts can be viewed in relationship to global hierarchies around knowledge construction beyond their immediate context, whilst acknowledging the potential for transformation through the intercultural research encounter. In the following reflective piece, Pu Shi addresses this dilemma that she faced as a doctoral student in the UK. She wanted to draw on the work of Chinese scholars but recognised that 'if I abandon all the "Western" terms and start all over again from Chinese concepts, I would disconnect myself from the language of the "international" community'. Such tensions are not unique to international students, but as Pu Shi points out, non-Western researchers could be seen to have an advantage in this respect: 'Everyone has assumptions, but for those non-Western researchers, they are more often put into the position of having to justify themselves as they enter the "international" community, simply because some of their assumptions are different from the prevailing ideology'. This chapter is a first step towards encouraging all doctoral students (and their supervisors) to take a similar critical perspective on their research process.

Notes

1 Devanagari script is used for writing Nepali, Hindi and several other South Asian languages.

2 Detailed accounts of the research studies with UK doctoral students from which I cite here can be found in: Robinson-Pant 2005, 2009; Magyar and Robinson-Pant 2010, 2011 and Robinson-Pant and Street 2012. As I am reflecting on insights from a range of studies conducted over a period of twelve years, it would be difficult to explain the methodology of each within this chapter. However, as I am all too aware of the limitations of using extracted data that is not fully contextualised (particularly as the above studies adopted an ethnographic and/or participatory approach), I have cited the original studies where readers can find the full account.

3 The concept of 'insider-outsider' has limitations and can lead to a polarised and dichotomised view of culture (see Robinson-Pant, 2016) as will be explored further in Chapter 5 in relation to the related terms 'emic-etic'.

4 I have chosen to use the term North-South to discuss unequal global relationships, in preference to centre/periphery, West/East, developing/developed countries or first/third world (all of which carry similar meanings). However, much of the literature cited here (particularly postcolonial theory) tends to refer to the West and Westerners – in which case, I have used that terminology. In Chapter 6, I switch to centre/periphery, reflecting the research literature on academic publishing.

5 Research in this area tends to use the terms 'centre' and 'periphery' rather than North/South. As Canagarajah (2002: 7) notes, these concepts from dependency theory focus attention on 'the intellectual and material inequalities between the *center* (referred to . . . as the West) and *periphery* (typically communities colonised by European intervention)'.

6 This is similar to the point that Pu Shi makes in Reflective Piece 1 about a task she was given in class to decide which of a list of ten human rights was more fundamental. She was uneasy with the underlying assumption – that rights are fundamental – and felt along with some Chinese classmates that 'responsibility was more fundamental because rights cannot be guaranteed'.

Reflective piece 1: Language, theory and power – cross-cultural issues in educational research
Pu Shi

My interest in cross-cultural education comes from my personal experience of studying in China and the UK. In my doctoral project I compare how Chinese postgraduate students learn to write literature reviews in different settings in China and the UK, hoping to understand how different epistemological cultures and academic conventions influence students' learning. As I think of my learning experience in these two countries, I can see how different cultures shape people's understanding of academic research, of how research should be conducted and what knowledge could be seen as valid. I have also realised that learning to do research is much more than a simple process of producing a paper. It is essentially about acquiring the language used by an academic community, learning to

FIGURE 1.1 The Great Wall in the photograph symbolises a boundary between different cultures. The two people who are walking down the wall are actually standing at the boundary of cultures and are thinking of how to deal with cross-cultural issues – and as can be seen, there's still a long way to go.

participate in the dialogues within that community and eventually being able to use that language to achieve certain 'personal and social goals' (Fairclough, 1989: ix). In cross-cultural settings, educational research is not only about communicating and negotiating differences but also about dealing with power relations and cultural politics. It is from this perspective that I reflect on my research experience.

Before coming to studying in the UK, I obtained a Masters' degree in China in second language education. Most of our courses in that programme were conducted in the English language: most reference books were in English; most theories we learned were produced by Westerners (mainly Anglophone authors); most essays and the final dissertation were written in English. That was partly because we were trained to be English teachers and were keen to maximise the opportunity to read and write in English. Although we were all conducting research within the Chinese context, the use of the English language inevitably led us to use information stored in the English language. It also led to a tacit preference for citing English sources written by English native speakers. It was thus not a mere coincidence that most of the concepts and theories that we used in our research were constructed by Western authors. Although those concepts and theories did provide powerful tools for analysing issues in China, what I sometimes found difficult was that, once the reality was defined in Western terms, some indigenous Chinese concepts would be assigned different meanings because they did not have equivalents in English. For example, the term *da hao ji chu* '打好基础' (to build a solid foundation) is frequently used in the English language curricula in China, meaning that one cannot use a foreign language well without mastering its basic grammar and vocabulary. However, in the current field of second language education, the discourse is very much dominated by terms such as 'communicative approach' or 'task-based approach'. Under such circumstances, to design a research study based on the principle of '打好基础' (*da hao ji chu*) is very likely to be regarded as outdated or biased towards a certain ideology. What is worse is that some positive concepts in Chinese would carry negative connotations when they were translated into English. In my previous research, I found it quite awkward that a mere intention to describe the situation in China looked like a critique just because terms such as 'hard work' and 'unity' (as opposed to diversity) sounded negative in English.

My awareness of this issue was raised by my experience in an MPhil course in the UK on Politics, Development, and Democratic Education. In Western educational institutions, there is a general impression that most Asian students are often silent in class. Research has already shown that there are complex reasons behind their silence. Some people think it relates to their language proficiency or the psychological needs to maintain their self-image (Siegal, 1995). Others think that it relates more to their cultural background, such as the preference for 'discretion over conjecture for novices' (Yates and Trang, 2012: 22). While those explanations were all true to some extent, what I experienced as a Chinese student was that we were sometimes silenced because we couldn't find a language to express our understanding. In other words, what we knew did not connect to the concepts used in the classroom. For example, once we were given a list of ten human rights in a seminar and we were asked to talk about which of them were more fundamental. I saw an assumption behind that question: rights were fundamental. However, I (and some other Chinese classmates) personally thought that responsibility was more fundamental because rights could not be guaranteed unless someone was willing to shoulder certain responsibility. Communication was very difficult under such circumstances when the two parties did not agree with what each other seemed to take for granted. It was at such moments that I felt the immense barrier in cross-cultural communication.

Such incidents did not appear in my previous learning in second language education, probably because most research on language teaching adopted a psychological approach and discussed cognitive and pedagogical concepts which seemed to be 'scientific' and universal. However, as I revisit the literature in second language education, many pedagogical terms are no longer 'scientific'; they look more like representations of a certain culture and ideology. Take 'learner-centred approach', for example. Due to the promotion of the learner-centred approach in the prevailing academic discourse, teacher-lecturing has been dismissed as ineffective and 'boring'. However, in my personal experience, many good lectures are inspiring and motivating while many activities involving student participation could be boring due to their poor design. As I believe, allowing students to talk in class is only one of the many ways that can promote learning and the effect of a pedagogical method eventually depends on whether it fits into a specific context and how well it caters for students' needs.

The dominance of Western educational discourse sometimes leads people to underestimate the importance of understanding local contexts. During the 1990s, some policy makers in China saw the success of the communicative language teaching approach in the West and hence required English language teachers in China to follow suit. Such requirements deprived the teachers of the freedom to choose the best methods for their own students. When it later turned out that the communicative approach was not effective in China, this was attributed to teachers' incapability and the negative social environment in China. However, the 'communicative approach' is only one of the many alternatives that can help students to learn foreign languages – who says that we *have to* use it? Although traditional pedagogies do have problems, they also have their strengths. However, the prevailing Western discourse does not seem to provide the language to defend the valuable parts of traditional pedagogies because those pedagogies are conceptualised in negative terms in the first place, in terms such as 'teacher-domination'. In today's globalising world, it is necessary to learn from the successful experience in education in other countries. However, things become more complex when there is a power relationship involved in the learning process. As a researcher from a non-Western society, I witnessed how 'Western learning' could both benefit and hamper the development of education in China. I am worried that as these Western concepts become dominant in the academic discourse in China, the indigenous Chinese concepts might disappear

22 Pu Shi

from our view and I would have no choice but to examine the reality from a Western lens.

This issue became clearer to me as I read into the literature on the history of education in China. According to Ye Lan's (2005) account, most of the major concepts used to develop the Chinese educational system are borrowed from abroad, from the Soviet Union during the 1950s–1970s and from the UK and US since the 1980s. It is not exaggerating to say that our view of education in China has been largely presented to us as feedback from the Western discourse. For non-Western researchers, this raises a question: whose voice do/should/can we represent? This question is concerned with the positioning of the researcher. Canagarajah identifies himself as 'a periphery scholar now working in (and writing from) the centre' (2002: 7). Right now as I am working on my PhD in the UK, I also find myself in this position. While I have the intention to promote the voice of Chinese scholars in the international academic world, my current work is inevitably adopting 'Western' concepts and theoretical frameworks. This is a peculiar position, i.e. speaking on behalf of the marginalised groups 'through the very channel of their intellectual domination' (ibid.: 7). It is a controversial issue for scholars from marginalised cultures. Practically, I have not found a better alternative because if I abandon all the 'Western' terms and start all over again from Chinese concepts, I would disconnect myself from the common language of the 'international' community. I believe that communication is important and that there must be a common ground for people from different cultures to communicate on. Apparently, the common ground is now largely defined by the Western discourse.

Despite the frustration about our disadvantaged position in the cultural politics in the academic field, I must also say that I have gained a lot as I negotiate the conflicting positions of myself as a researcher standing between different cultures. By observing the writing of 'periphery' authors such as Canagarajah, I have realised that those authors do have an advantage: they tend to be good at clarifying the hidden assumptions underlying their own arguments. Everyone has assumptions, but for those non-Western researchers, they are more often put into the position of having to justify themselves as they enter the 'international' community, simply because some of their assumptions are different from the prevailing ideology. The constant need for justifications has the potential to bring out robust research with a high level of criticality and would, I hope, help with the promotion of marginalised voices in the long term.

In a broader sense, cultural politics is not only about being Western or non-Western; it exists in many aspects of social life and anyone can be put in a marginalised position on certain occasions. As educational researchers, every decision that we make in our research could be a political decision regarding what rules we choose to abide by, whom we choose to stand with and whom we choose to forget. As I believe, being a researcher requires a deep critical awareness of how power relations can be reproduced through the concepts and language that we use in our research. Such awareness may bring pain to our research process.

However, it also makes our work meaningful, exciting and rewarding. Dealing with cross-cultural issues makes research a tortuous journey. Sometimes I find myself feeling so powerless that I cannot help polarising between 'our' group and the 'others'; at other times I feel empowered enough to look beyond conceptual distinctions and to live with multiple identities that transcend cultural boundaries. The process of conducting cross-cultural research has revealed to me the delicacy of how language mediates human activities. It has opened up more ways of looking at the society and has also enabled me to look deeper into myself. That is how research could be liberating despite all its difficulties. It is essentially an attempt at understanding what human life is about and what it means to live as an individual in this big, complicated world. It is based on this reason that I believe cross-cultural research to be a valuable experience.

2

MULTILINGUAL RESEARCH

Accounting for the richness of 'context'

Alain Wolf

The context: a need for definitions

> The context for what follows is that so much research [. . .] is either conducted by researchers from a very different culture or dominated by research traditions within a different culture. How can people from one culture really understand the problems and contexts of a very different society? [. . .] How can researchers from one tradition get inside the minds of people and societies from very different traditions? And furthermore, if they do, how can they communicate that understanding to people who have not attained the insights that the researchers' reports depend upon?
>
> *(Pring, 2011: 77)*

The interactions between the researcher and the researched are often assumed to be determined by the context in which they take place. As the above quotation from a collected volume on research methodologies across cultures suggests, the key questions are to do with what constitutes real understanding as opposed, presumably, to understanding that is superficial. There is, too, an obvious sense that real understanding means faithfully representing the intentions behind people's utterances, metaphorically expressed by Pring (2011: 77) as a way of getting inside their minds. Then finally, there is the question for researchers of further representation in the act of dissemination (as introduced in Chapter 1), whether it is in a PhD thesis or a research report in a published article: how do researchers communicate the understanding they have gained in a language and in a culture that is different from the one they have engaged with?

It is important to ask these questions in the context of research since the support given to economically less advantaged countries often depends on the findings of research projects funded by international agencies. And as Pring (2011: 77) points out, such support is often given 'on certain terms'. The consequence of this is that an increasing amount of attention is now being paid to the cross-cultural 'context' of research, with writers devoting much space to reflecting on the various aspects of the situation in which their study took place (see Halai and Wiliam, 2011). These writers, however, tend to assume that the notion of 'context' is largely unproblematic, and needs no further definition. Linguists have taken a different view. They have raised a number of questions about this concept and have generated a great deal of debate. Some (see the ethnographer Hymes, 1974, the sociolinguist Fishman, 1972, and the functionalists Halliday and Hasan, 1976), take a view of context as stable, i.e. as a given that exists before an inter-action is processed. More recently, other linguists (Sperber and Wilson, 1986; Clark, 1996; Žegarac, 2009) have perceived context as dynamic, i.e. as being continually constructed while the interaction is going on, thereby focusing on its internalist and psychological dimension. It must be said that this understanding of context as dynamic is often overlooked by writers conducting research across cultures. Indeed, their descriptions of the background to the research tend to have, as Žegarac (2009: 30) observes, a 'distinctly externalist-descriptive flavour'. Cognitive-psychological explanations of the context are very few and far between in the literature and I shall want to redress the balance here. Finally, other lin-guists take both views (see Brown, 1995; Wolf, 1999), namely that the external social/geopolitical context is a static construct, whilst the cognitive/psychological context, i.e. participants' beliefs/roles during an interaction, is dynamic. This will be my own position here. I will attempt to give a brief outline of how linguists in the field of Pragmatics[1] have come to approach the notion of context, and the implications this has for the methodological strategies of doing research across cultures. First, I will want to discuss the stable features of context based on an overview of Hymes' (1974) SPEAKING categories to show how the utterances[2] of the researcher and the researched can often be interpreted in terms of relatively unchanging and enduring ethnographic and sociopolitical categories. Second, I will explore the more dynamic aspects of the cognitive/psychological context to show what mechanisms are required in the course of interactions in order to achieve understanding between cultures.

The main aim of this chapter, then, is to explore the notion of context in a way that emphasises the logical possibility of 'a unity of understanding' between cultures (see Pring, 2011: 79). In other words, it argues that the apparent difficul-ties of accessing context across cultures are not logically different in kind from the difficulties researchers experience in carrying out research with individuals from widely different backgrounds within the same language. Pring (2011: 79) illus-trates this by giving the example of a middle-class, middle-aged male researcher from the South of England researching working-class, female adolescents from the North of England. What is important for our discussion here is that understand-ing the context is not different in kind when it comes to doing research across cultures from what it would be in intra-linguistic exchanges. The difference is in the degree of negotiation needed for understanding to occur. This is not to say that one is seeking, in Pring's (2011: 80) words, 'grounds for certainty', for that is

26 Alain Wolf

not attainable. But it is to say that we must not exaggerate, as has been fashionable of late, misunderstandings between cultures, thus over-emphasising their different perspectives on political, social and religious world views. Exploring ways in which successful communication is attained cross-culturally seems to me by far the more philosophically sound and generous enterprise.

As in all chapters, I will base much of my analysis on examples drawn from the literature, and on interviews with doctoral students engaged in recent research across cultures.

Stable features of the context

In an ethnographic approach to sociolinguistics, Hymes (1974) identified eight components of the situational context. Although, as will become apparent in this chapter, he was aware of the psychological nature of the non-linguistic context of situation[3], he tended to focus on its external and stable features from the viewpoint of an omniscient observer, so to speak. This 'externalist-descriptive' approach has been criticised in contemporary writings (see Žegarac, 2009: 31), especially when it comes to giving an account of interactions across cultures. This being said, I believe Hymes's components are a useful template from which to start analysing the stable, unchanging features of the context of situation in my analysis of intercultural research contexts. In order to make the set of components mnemonically memorable, Hymes used the letters of the term SPEAKING for each of the components:

'S' for Setting

Setting refers to 'the time and place of a speech act' (Hymes, 1974: 55). The setting as physical environment can change, of course, but the expectation is that the physical setting of an event endures over a certain period of time. The physical circumstances of an interaction can greatly influence how it is interpreted by participants. An interview, for example, carried out in your own home on a one-to-one basis is likely to be perceived as less formal than one taking place in a huge civic hall in front of six interviewers sitting around a table on a raised platform. 'Setting' has an influence on what Hymes refers to as 'scene', i.e. the 'psychological setting' of the event. Scene can be set preceding the interaction, but in cases where this has been left vague, participants may redefine the event during the course of an event from 'formal to informal' or from 'serious to festive' (Hymes, 1974: 55). To be sure, Hymes, without explicitly saying so, does imply a certain amount of instability in the features of time and place. Although I will return to these categories later when I outline the dynamic features of context, now seems an appropriate time to devote some space to what I would consider to be a typical description of the physical context in a recent study of women's education in Pakistan (Pardhan, 2011).

When she recalls her MA study of the underlying processes of gendered educational experiences in Pakistan, Pardhan (2011: 117) describes the setting and scene of her interaction with the researched vividly, systematically considering the implications and expectations created by the physical environment. She introduces the *setting* as the 'remote, mountainous, rural village of Booni Valley, Chitral Dictrict' and refers to the harsh geographic conditions which have an influence on the *scene* of women's lives as they are involved in agricultural activities. Imperceptibly and very gradually it is the focus on *scene* which adds richness to her description of context. We are warned in the introductory pages by way of metaphors, that 'she found herself on a lonely journey, uncertainly navigating predicaments in diverse aspects of the research design'. As she started on research, she recalls being 'excited to take the opportunity to carry out fieldwork in such a rugged, rustic context' (Pardhan, 2011: 136). But the festive aspects of *scene* soon give way to the realisation that her gender would have a serious impact on the research. Within the prevailing norms of the patriarchal context, she would require a male escort to accompany her to the villages and her female research collaborator's male colleagues would have to explain the study to the men of the household in order to seek their permission for Pardhan to interview the women. In the psychological context of scene, certain elements have an enduring quality whilst others change abruptly without warning. In this respect, Pardhan (2011: 134) describes her interviews with participants in her study mediated by her research collaborator/translator:

> Often during the interviews, a question or a probe that I asked would be translated – resulting in the research collaborator and research participants engaging in a lengthy conversation about common experiences and relationships. When I inquired what they were talking about, the research collaborator would explain that it was not related to the study.
>
> *(Pardhan, 2011: 135)*

Pardhan's description of scene is remarkable. Of note in particular is the interplay between the stable features of context, i.e. the *setting* of a Muslim village in Chirtal District, and the dynamism of *scene*: Pardhan describes her assumption that she would be invited to engage in the conversation between her collaborator and participant based on her own background experience of how research is carried out. When the assumption is cancelled, she is compelled to redefine the event from one of anticipation to uneasy surprise. In another dynamic change to the interaction, surprise gives way to resolve:

> I had to be sensitive, patient and trusting of the situation. Nevertheless I felt I had to cede power in how I directed the research and built relationships with research participants.
>
> *(Pardhan, 2011: 135)*

28 Alain Wolf

But the dynamism inscribed at the heart of any interaction suggests that this is not the end of it. And as the article makes clear, Pardhan's interactions with her participants undergo many more changes after this first, less than ideal, encounter.

'P' for Participants

Participants can be divided into four sub-categories: Speaker or Sender, Addressor (speaker/writer), Hearer (incidental hearer/reader), Addressee (intended hearer/writer) (Hymes, 1974: 56). An interview between the researched and the researcher can often be mediated by a translator or, as in the reflective piece that follows this chapter, by a mediator who may become an incidental hearer. I shall deal with this issue in more detail in the sections below.

'E' for Ends

Ends can be defined as 'purposes, outcomes and goals' (Hymes, 1974: 57). The goals of an event may not always match those of the participants. In a research context, for example, the researcher's expectations may not be identical to the purposes of the researched. This mismatch between the researcher and participants was most pertinently illustrated by a study I recently came across on the impact of educational reforms in the South. Kumari et al. (2011) found that the teachers participating in the research thought their performance was being appraised and, as a result, feared that this 'might have implications for the security of their job or for promotion' (Kumari et al. 2011: 235). In a more light-hearted vein, one of the research students on our PhD training programme reported how surprised he had been at the ease with which he had gained access to the 'mothers' in his study. He had at first put this down to the fact that his topic must be of great interest to mothers . . . It was not until later that he found out the real reason for his success: the mothers in question simply considered him as an eligible bachelor for their daughters.

'A' for Act Sequence

A communicative event can be divided into different parts, i.e. opening remarks, participants taking turns at speaking, and closing remarks. In informal situations, participants may not take turns in a formal sequence, unlike in a classroom setting, for example, where a teacher allocates turns to pupils. This may lead to interruptions and overlaps between speakers.

'K' for Key

This refers to the 'tone, manner, or spirit' of the speech act (Hymes, 1974: 57). Key is so central to the message that it can 'override' (Hymes, 174: 58) the content of an act as in sarcasm. Key can also be signalled non-verbally with a wink, for example, or style of dress. Such non-verbal features are often ignored by linguists, but can be crucially important in a research context across cultures. Although non-verbal features of context are stable and tend to determine the interaction before it takes place, what they mean can be difficult to ascertain in some contexts. As Trompenaars and Hampden-Turner (1997: 24) observe, somebody winking at you is a stable feature of the physical context, but it is the meaning ascribed to it by observers that is important, i.e. is the wink 'a physical reflex from dust in the eye, or is it an invitation to a prospective date?' (Trompenaars and Hampden-Turner, 1997: 24). Such a psychological dimension may be difficult to interpret and adds dynamism to the interaction, especially so in a different cultural context where a wink may 'mean' something completely different from that in your own culture. Indeed, effective communication *crucially* hinges on the speaker's *intentions* matching the hearer's *interpretation* (my emphases).

'I' for Instrumentalities

By instrumentalities, Hymes (1974: 58) refers to channels, i.e. the choice of speech transmission: written, oral, telegraphic or semaphoric, and we could now add electronic. To the concept of 'channel' can be added that of 'modes of use', i.e. the oral channel can be used to sing, to pray or to speak. Hymes (1974: 59) also refers to forms of speech as speech styles or registers which look at the way linguistic features are organised and determined 'in relation to a community or other social context' (Hymes, 1974: 59).

'N' for Norms of Interaction

These are rules which govern speaking, and the participants' behaviour that relates to them, e.g. one may or may not interrupt in certain situations. In a research context, the researcher's contributions or interruptions in the interview process may skew the interaction in a particular way. The problem of *norms of interaction* is referred to by Hymes (1974: 60) as a familiar one when it comes to assessing communication cross-culturally. He illustrates this by referring to interactional norms between Arabic students who reportedly 'confront each other more directly when conversing' than American students (Hymes, 1974: 61). As we will see in Chapter 3, dealing with politeness, a great deal of caution must be applied to how these so-called 'norms' are interpreted in order to avoid over-generalised and essentialist claims about culture.

'G' for Genre

The word *genre* refers to 'categories such as poem, myth, tale, proverb, riddle, curse, prayer, oration, lecture', etc. It is important to bear in mind that the same genre can be referred to in different settings: a sermon conventionally takes place in a church, but properties of the sermon genre can be invoked, for humorous purposes, for example, in other situations. Hymes (1974: 62) reports that women's chanting in the Bihar state of India recurs in different situations such as weddings, family visits and complaints to one's husband. Drawing on Bakhtin's (1986) understanding of speech genres as something we can predict on hearing others speak, linguists (see Kotthoff, 2009; Günthner, 2009) have picked up on the importance of the notion as a means to construct social reality according to conventions which then enable speakers to 'compose talk or texts and recipients to interpret it' (Günthner, 2009: 129).

In the area of fieldwork across cultures, interviewing participants is a genre which is used as a means to develop an image of a particular social reality for particular purposes. The ethical dimension of interviewing as a genre is increasingly being addressed (Kvale, 2006; Shamin and Qureshi, 2013). A dominant narrative emerges from my own participants engaged in cross-cultural research (see examples below), namely that the very concept of being researched by means of interview can be perceived as suspect in some cultural contexts other than the Western academia. This is because, as Kvale (2006) argues, interviews can be a way of 'making the private public', and in certain contexts, 'intimate qualitative interviews with strangers provide a *via regia* to the consumers' experiences and desires and the subsequent manipulation of their consumption' (Kvale, 2006: 497). In some cultural contexts (see Shamin and Qureshi's (2013) analyses of educational research in Pakistan), the researcher's motivations can be misinterpreted in a context where participants, e.g. teachers, fear that the publication of findings may lead to their employment being terminated by the all-powerful authorities/gatekeepers.

So the very concept of interviewing as a genre needs to be problematised, and a distinction should be made between two genres of the research interview, i.e. one that displays an asymmetry of power between the researcher and the researched and 'serv[es] the interviewer's instrumental knowledge interests' (Kvale, 2006: 497), and another which is a form of philosophical dialogue 'with an ideally symmetrical power relation in an egalitarian joint search for true knowledge' (Kvale, 2006: 497). Of course, in themselves, interviews are neutral. It is the way in which they are used by individuals that makes them either a powerful tool of oppression or a contribution to the empowerment of oppressed minorities. Kvale (2006: 497) has the last word here: 'A key issue concerns who obtains access and who has the power and resources to act on and consume what the multiple interview voices tell the interviewing stranger'.

Preliminary concluding remarks

It is clear from the above categories that much of context can be perceived as predetermined in advance of the interaction, and the interest for discourse analysts as well as ethnographers often lies in how a current utterance may be interpreted in light of preceding utterances. In E. M. Forster's (2002: 61) famous example 'the king died, and then the queen died of grief', we, as speakers and hearers, try not to overpopulate discourse, i.e. most people without having to be told recover the meaning that the king and the queen live in the same place and time, that they are married, that she died of grief after he died and that she died soon after he died, not months or years. In other words, we bring our previous similar experience to bear on our construction of context in an *ordo naturalis* (natural order). But the *ordo naturalis* goes only so far, especially when the interpretation is carried out in contexts where the psychological make-up of the participants has been seriously damaged by an oppressive regime of fear, for example. Levinson's (1983) canonical situation of utterance, where each participant knows that they are participants in a conversation between one speaker and one listener face to face so they can see each other, where both participants think they are in a normal place and they are having a normal sort of time, can be disrupted, as we shall see below, to interesting effect. And this naturally leads to a discussion of the dynamic features of context.

Dynamic features of context

Context and the Principle of Relevance: assumptions and the 'context of enmity'

I have so far focused on elements of the context which could be perceived as more or less stable, and could be captured with relative ease. I now turn to a way of construing context as dynamic and constantly enriched in the course of interactions. This is where 'Relevance Theory' as originally expounded by Sperber and Wilson (1986) provides us with a framework within which to account for context from a cognitive internalist perspective. When we communicate with others, we often overestimate our hearers' ability to recover the context to which we refer. Suppose I were on the phone to a French friend in Paris and said: 'Can I ring you back later? I'm going to miss Corrie' As a speaker, I would clearly be assuming that my French friend could recover the meaning of the highly idiosyncratic and culture-bound abbreviation 'Corrie' which stands for 'Coronation Street', a series on British television. This is not to say that when we communicate we always give our hearers access to knowledge which we assume they share with us, also known as mutual knowledge. For the requirement of mutual knowledge, i.e. the knowledge that I know that you know that I know . . . and so on, if applied to communication, can soon lead to an infinite regress. Indeed, as Blakemore (1992: 20) astutely points out, even if some amount of mutual knowledge is required for successful communication to occur, speakers rarely wait until they have a 100 per cent guarantee of mutual knowledge before they carry on with the business of communicating. In point of fact, the prerequisite for successful communication is not so much that a static context is accessed in advance of communication. It is rather that we are able to access background information, i.e. our old, existing assumptions, our 'initial context' (Wilson and Sperber, 2004), and consequently to derive conclusions that *matter* (my emphasis) to us (Wilson and Sperber, 2004: 608). These conclusions,

Wilson and Sperber (2004: 608) refer to as 'positive cognitive effect', i.e. any input that makes 'a *worthwhile* [my emphasis] difference to the individual's representation of the world: a true conclusion, for example'. Some cognitive effects are easier to access than others. Information that can be left implicit in situations where the speakers know about each other's cognitive environment and encyclopaedic knowledge often has to be made explicit in contexts where an addressee cannot possibly be familiar with the speaker's assumptions. Example (1) taken from Blakemore (1992: 173) illustrates the extent to which a speaker can overestimate a hearer's ability to process the meaning of an utterance:

(1) The river had been dry for some time. Everyone attended the funeral.

A hearer of (1) would fail to understand the utterance since its cultural assumptions have been left implicit, and an 'explicature' would need to be provided, namely that:

(2) When a river dries up a river spirit has died. When a river spirit has died there is a funeral. The river had been dry for some time. Everyone attended the funeral.

The important point to note here is that for speakers of Sissala, a language spoken in Ghana, the conversation in (1) could quite happily take place without the explicature in (2) being added. No contextual effects would be generated for them by doing so. By contrast, someone from a very different background would have needed that explicature in order to recover the full meaning of (1). There is then a greater need for explicatures of the kind I have outlined in situations where participants come from different cultures. Wilson and Sperber (2004: 610) then conclude that, 'aiming to maximize the relevance of the inputs one processes is simply a matter of making the most efficient use of the available processing resources' and so the 'Cognitive Principle of Relevance' is formulated as 'Human cognition tends to be geared to the maximization of relevance'.

I would now like to offer an analysis of an interview I carried out with one of my participants, Eleni Konidari, from the internalist perspective of Relevance Theory, looking at how context can be constructed dynamically during the course of an interaction. Eleni conducted research in a region where a dominant majority culture had oppressed a minority culture. Despite being herself a member of the majority culture, Eleni assumed that her research would be welcomed by the minority community since it was so obviously 'in their interest'. This set of assumptions constituted her initial context (Wilson and Sperber, 2004). However, it soon became clear that the community she was researching was very reluctant to be interviewed. This was because she had stepped into what she called eloquently 'a context of enmity' (Eleni Konidari, interview notes 2014). At that point, Eleni was so distraught that she considered 'giving up on her research altogether'. She gradually realised that she herself was under suspicion and that the community members she was researching had experienced many researchers like her from the 'majority culture' who had betrayed their trust and reported 'findings' to the majority government; these findings were then used to manipulate the political situation. This cancelled the previously held assumptions of her initial cognitive environment. When she realised that she could be suspected as a spy even by her own friends, Eleni had to give up on her 'old' assumptions since the new realisation so obviously cancelled them:

> I found myself in this context of people getting tired of researchers going there and I was from the dominant culture. I was guilty until I was proved innocent. I think the main problem for me and my assumptions is that I have a guilty nature. This was a problem. I'm very supersensitive to people and I don't want to make anyone feel uncomfortable. So I went there and I started hearing about how suspicious people were and they were afraid of people my nationality [. . .] so I was walking, speaking to people doing everything, thinking that they think I am a spy and I work for the Foreign Ministry and I am there to gather information, so I could see it was like a double mirror so I could see myself in the way that I was assuming people would see me [. . .] so in every encounter, what first came to my mind was what does this person think of me, then I had to turn it over and prove the opposite.
>
> *(Eleni Konidari, interview notes, 2014)*

We can see clearly here the process by which previously held assumptions are dynamically cancelled by her new experience of the context. As a member of the majority state herself, the greatest challenge for Eleni was, therefore, to build trust within the minority community. The reason why I am referring to the dynamic nature of context here is that researchers frequently present context as if it is rigid and unchangeable even though during the course of interactions in the research site, assumptions can be cancelled and replaced by other assumptions which may lead to entirely new situations taking place. After Eleni changed her perspective, she could connect from a different standpoint that altered her experience.

In Relevance Theory, the most important feature of human cognition is the act of ostensive-inferential communication. Such an act makes the communicator's intention to communicate something obvious. Žegarac (2009: 34) in an article on Relevance Theory and inter-cultural communication illustrates this point in an example which says a great deal about the risk of not recognising somebody's informative intention. He mentions the case of a British family who had lived in an African country for many years. On being forced to leave suddenly because of civil war having broken out, they asked local people to try to rescue some of their 'special things'. They were surprised some time later to find that their TV and video recorders were the main rescued items. Their surprise, argues Žegarac (2009: 34), was to do with the fact that the British family had not taken the cultural context, i.e. the set of assumptions, in which the local people would interpret the phrase 'special things'. Their communicative intention had not been

34 Alain Wolf

recognised. Unrecognised communicative intentions are often at the centre of miscommunication, and especially so in contexts which involve communicating across cultures. I'll now turn my attention to cases of miscommunication across cultures and reflect on their ethical dimension, especially in the context of multilingual research.[4]

Contextualisation cues: failing to recognise communicative intentions

We saw earlier how explicatures are often needed to give us access to assumptions which are not readily accessible in our culture. Our utterances, quite apart from encoding inaccessible cultural content, can also contain structurally ambiguous forms such as personal pronouns, or any phrase with a particular stress. These operate as a *contextualisation cue*[5] (see Gumperz and Cook-Gumperz, 2009: 19) by which hearers can assess what others intend to communicate, i.e. recognise others' communicative intentions. Consider the example below:

> Imagine that Bill had just observed Tom talking to Fred, and Bill asked Tom what he and Fred had been doing. Tom then might answer: 'I asked Fred if he was FREE this evening'.
>
> *(Gumperz and Cook-Gumperz, 2009: 19)*

The word 'free' is stressed by Tom (indicated by capitalisation), thereby causing Bill to infer that Tom is using stress as a contextualisation cue which generates a *conversational inference* (Gumperz and Cook-Gumperz, 2009: 19), possibly that Tom intends to engage in a particular activity with Fred that evening. Bill would need to rely on past communication with Tom, i.e. background knowledge, in order to recover the correct inference.

As far as communication across cultures is concerned, it is important to note that contextualisation cues are not always picked up by interlocutors. In this respect, Gumperz (1982) discussed the prosodic features used by Pakistani women. The women, who worked in a cafeteria, were systematically perceived as surly and uncooperative by British speakers of English. When customers were offered gravy with their meat dishes, the women would ask 'gravy?', but instead of producing the standard rising intonation of native speakers, they would use a falling intonation 'gravy ↓'. This falling contour was interpreted as a statement, or worse, an order, which in this context seemed rude. For the Pakistani women, however, using a falling intonation was a conventional way of asking questions in service transactions. Similarly, an Italian friend of mine kept saying 'goodbye' to me with a falling intonation. The first time this happened I failed to pick up on the contextualisation cue and inferred that he was, at the very least, not in a very good mood. My background in linguistics, however, soon prompted me to ask, when it happened again: 'You weren't annoyed with me just then, were you?', to which he replied 'Well, of course I'm not.' It was with a great deal of incredulity that he finally accepted my explanation that his falling intonation on 'goodbye' would automatically lead native speakers of English to infer that he was displeased with something. As for producing a 'goodbye' with a rising intonation, well, this was beyond him for a quite a few weeks after our linguistic exchange. His response was: 'Are you sure? I can't possibly say "goodbye" with a rising intonation like you, it sounds so effeminate to an Italian man.' As Verschueren (2008: 29) puts it, 'Inferences [. . .] can never unthinkingly be connected with intentions'. In other words, the inferences you derive based on what you think somebody's intentions were in producing an utterance can be deceptive and lead you astray. And it is this knowledge, which Gumperz and Cook-Gumperz (2009: 23) call 'contextualisation conventions', which contributes, as a precondition, to conversational cooperation between interlocutors.

Unthinking and precipitous judgements about what others have said in a cross-cultural context can have serious ethical consequences. Indeed, the Asian dinner ladies in the example above may have had their contract of employment terminated for seeming rude to customers. This is where I shall now turn my attention in the context of multilingual research.

The ethics of context and tolerating the ambiguity of communicative intentions: concluding remarks

First, let me say a few words about truth in the research context. Researchers are often enjoined 'to strive for honesty and openness in the relationship formed and to guard against the misrepresentation of the setting or individuals within it' (Professional Guidelines on Ethics BSA, 1993, cited by Welland, 2002: 141). But pressure to depart from the ideal when one is faced with real life relationships is as common in research as in everyday interactions. Indeed, when engaging with others on a daily basis, we have a presumption of what I shall call approximate truths. That is, we would not represent someone who said 'I got there at 2' as having lied to us, even if they actually got to the place at two minutes past 2, unless, of course, the context required that kind of precision. Often, the messiness of morality is to do with the ambiguity of our communicative intentions. Welland (2002), for example, who explored the life of a theological college, reported how he was asked by two members of staff to give information on a student he had interviewed. While this would have clearly been in breach of confidentiality – and in this case, Welland did not infringe the ethical guidelines – he could clearly see how alienating and displeasing powerful members of staff would not be in the interest of his research. But could he have pleased them by just summarising the information required without going into personal details? As he concluded (Welland 2002: 142, quoting Grills (1998: 165)): 'there is a disjunction between formalised codes of conduct and the messy field situations where some accommodation may be required'. But whilst researchers frequently refer to chaotic events in the field, they rarely focus on the language style needed for such 'accommodation' to occur. For this reason, let us consider an example given to me by Eleni which I think perfectly

36 Alain Wolf

illustrates the way we tolerate ambiguity. She recalls the occasion when she was taken to a mosque by a male friend from the community she was researching. On arriving at the mosque, she was taken to the female side. When the women saw her there, they started chatting to her and as a kind of ice-breaker mentioned the fact that she was a Christian:

> 'So you're a Christian,' they said. 'Yes, yes,' I said evasively, 'my parents are, I come from this kind of family.' I hate to lie but I could not say I was an atheist because that would have been shocking.
>
> *(Eleni Konidari, interview, 2014)*

What makes Eleni's utterance in this context relevant to the Muslim women is that it matches with background information that is available to them, and the conclusions that they generate *matter* (my emphasis) to them (see Wilson and Sperber's 'Relevance Theory', 2004: 608). In other words, her utterance, in order to be judged relevant by the Muslim women, needed to yield a 'positive cognitive effect' (Wilson and Sperber, 2004: 608). In the above example, Eleni, on being asked if she's a Christian, could truly tell the women any of the three following things: (a) I come from a Christian family (b) I'm an atheist (c) Either I'm an atheist or $(7^2 - 3)$ is not 46 (example adapted from Wilson and Sperber, 2004). All three utterances would be relevant to the Muslim women, but (a) would be more relevant than either (b) or (c). It would be more relevant than (b) because the context in which the utterance is made is religious and as Eleni herself acknowledged, to say that she was an atheist in this context and at that time would have been irrelevant, and even shocking. It would be more relevant than (c) for reasons of processing effort, i.e. it is more difficult to process (c) than (a) and so (c) is less relevant than (a). We can see how dynamic the mechanisms for accessing context are in this approach and how they take place 'online' as it were during the interaction. Eleni in this instance reported feeling that she had not told an outright lie and had not, as a result, been unethical. This analysis of the context from a Relevance theoretical perspective places the focus on the individual's, here Eleni's, cognition where all the individual has to bother about is to achieve a balance between the interlocutors' rewards and processing cost.

Yet, this approach seems to me to downplay the inter-subjective dimension of speakers and hearers interacting and second-guessing one another's communicative intentions. It also seems to downplay the ethical dimension of the interaction. The philosopher H. P. Grice (1975) notoriously would have given such an interaction a different treatment. He would have proposed that when individuals select certain contexts for understanding a given utterance, they obey a principle of cooperation, the Cooperative Principle (CP):

> *Make your conversational contribution such as is required, at the stage at which it occurs, by the accepted purpose or direction of the talk exchange in which you are engaged.*
>
> *(Grice, 1975: 45)*

Under this principle, four maxims are subsumed[6], which, if violated by a speaker, alert the hearer that implied meaning is being generated. Consider in the example below the deliberate violating of the 'maxim of quality' by a speaker A, talking about his close friend 'X' who has betrayed a secret:

'X' is a fine friend.

(Grice, 1975: 45)

As I have observed elsewhere (Wolf, 2010), it is obvious to 'A' and to his audience that 'A' has said something which he does not believe to be true, i.e. A has violated the maxim of quality which enjoins him to be truthful, and the audience knows that A knows that this is obvious to the audience from the context. So 'A' must be trying to generate implied meaning, which Grice calls a *conversational implicature* of the sort: 'I am trying to convey the opposite of what I am saying.'

Grice's treatment of context, because it includes the possibility of violating the maxim of quality, does add an ethical dimension to how we understand utterances in any given context. In the case of Eleni's utterance, it is clear that in order not to violate the 'maxim of relation' which required her to be relevant and the maxim of quality which required her not to say what she believed to be false, i.e. 'I'm a Christian', Eleni violated the 'maxim of manner' which enjoined her 'to avoid ambiguity'. By violating the maxim of manner and being less than clear about her communicative intentions, the question is, 'was Eleni being unethical?' The ethical dimension of context is crucially important in research that involves different cultures inasmuch as it emphasises the tensions between building trust and respecting the researched in an ideal sort of way and the messy field situations where this kind of ambiguity and accommodation to situations may be required. Here, the entire research enterprise may have been jeopardised by the naked truth, so to speak, being divulged too early in the research process. Indeed, as the research progressed, Eleni was able to be more open with the researched and she reports how some of them occasionally joked ironically, saying:

as we all know, you're a good Christian.

(Eleni Konidari, interview notes, 2014)

The debates raised in this chapter about the role of context as both a stable construct and a dynamic construct subject to change in the course of an interaction have wide-ranging implications for all those involved in carrying out research across cultures. Analysing the stable physical environment of the research, expecting that one's contextual assumptions will be cancelled in the course of interactions, especially when those assumptions are not mutually shared by participants, are all factors which contribute to successful interactions. If anything, this chapter has shown how central to the research process speakers' and hearers' communicative intentions are. Both researchers and researched are called upon to reflect on their cognitive environment and their communicative intentions, to try to recognise them but also to tolerate ambiguity when some communicative maxim is obviously being violated. To aim at relevance is a generous endeavour because it is an attempt to make the best use of all the communicative resources speakers have available to them in a particular context. But the principle that human cognition tends to be geared to the maximisation of relevance needs to be underpinned by a moral requirement, which is never to say that which we believe to be false, unless, of course, we are being ironical.

Box 2

Questions for further reflection

- How do I try to 'get inside the minds' of the people I have researched?
- How do I set out to describe the stable elements of the research context, especially those relating to the notions of 'scene', 'goals' and 'key'?
- To what extent have I considered the ethical dimension of interviewing?
- What set of assumptions have I started with at the beginning of my research?
- Have any of those assumptions been cancelled and why?
- How will I make sure that I have interpreted 'contextualisation cues' correctly?
- How will I accommodate my behaviour to messy fieldwork situations without being unethical?
- How do I tolerate ambiguity?

As we have seen in this chapter, describing the stable elements of a research site may not be sufficient to recover the full meaning of the context as it is being dynamically constructed in interactions. In the following reflective piece, Eleni Konidari reflects on the problems which confronted her as a doctoral student in a Turkish community in Greece. Here, she elaborates on the examples she has already discussed with me and how she negotiated her entry into a 'context of enmity'. This piece is an interesting step towards finding ways of tolerating ambiguity and accommodating linguistic behaviour to messy fieldwork situations without being unethical.

Notes

1 Crudely defined, pragmatics is the study of language as it used, i.e. language in context.
2 I use the word 'utterance' to refer to any sentence (or indeed sections of text) uttered by a speaker in a particular context. The word will be further defined as the chapter develops.
3 I am using the phrase 'context of situation' as used by Halliday and Hasan (1976: 21): 'The term "situation", meaning the "context of situation" in which a text is embedded, refers

Accounting for the richness of 'context' **39**

to all those extra-linguistic factors which have some bearing on the text itself'. By text, I also understand speakers' utterances (see note 2).

4 The notion of 'intention' will be further discussed in Chapter 3.

5 A 'contextualisation cue' is defined by Gumperz and Cook-Gumperz (2009: 24) as 'any linguistic sign which [. . .] serves as an indexical sign to construct the contextual presuppositions that underlie situated interpretation'.

6 1. **Maxim of quantity:** Try to make your contribution as informative as is required: for the current purpose of the exchange, do not make your contribution more informative than is required. 2. **Maxim of quality:** Try to make your contribution one that is true, specifically: do not say what you believe to be false, do not say that for which you lack adequate evidence. 3. **Maxim of relation:** Be relevant. 4. **Maxim of manner:** avoid obscurity of expression, avoid ambiguity, be brief, be orderly.

Reflective piece 2: Dressing with a scarf while undressing the prejudice

Eleni Konidari

I had never been to Western Thrace prior to my fieldwork. I knew of course where it was; far at the north-eastern end of Greece. Only much later I learned that in Western Thrace resides a Turco-Muslim minority group with around 100,000 members. At the end of the last Greco-Turkish war, the Muslims from Western Thrace were excluded from the forced exchange of populations which was specified by the Convention of Lausanne in 1923 as a means of ethnic cleansing. The aim of the Convention was to enhance the creation of homogeneous nation-states; Orthodox Greeks at the one side of the Aegean Sea and Muslim Turks at the other. The Western Thrace minority group remained as a living trace of Greece's Ottoman past. Traces from this past have been muted in the public space because they only create an anomaly to the national rhetoric of the glorious national continuum from Ancient Greece to Orthodox Byzantine till the Modern Greek nation.

I was coming to Western Thrace having been born and bred in the Greek Orthodox national paradigm. I arrived for the first time in Rhodope[1] during Ramadan. The night before I met my first contact from the minority group, I had a long walk through the town of Komotini, where all mosques were lit due to the holy days, and many of the restaurants and fast foods were closed due to the fast. The following morning I took the bus to the next village to meet Mehmet. I was very stressed and excited about it. It was a hot August day but I always had a long scarf covering my shoulders and arms. I would have a scarf on my shoulders for many months, trying to be acceptable and fit in with what I thought were the local Muslim standards. Mehmet welcomed me at his home, and I was surprised that for quite some time he had not offered me anything. In the end he offered me a Turkish coffee with a dessert. I accepted happily and started eating the dessert when I noticed that he had not made a coffee for himself. I asked him 'don't you want a coffee too?' He answered 'It is Ramadan'. My non-Muslim identity flashed as a beacon in my mind. During a phone call that Mehmet received in another room, I ate the whole dessert in two bites feeling so ashamed and disrespectful.

How to bond successfully with a different religious culture was an issue I had to be considerate about all the time during my fieldwork. However, the greatest challenge was how to build trust in the community being a majority Greek. For thirty years[2] the group suffered overt discrimination by the Greek state; a condition which worked to the advantage of the local majority population in economic terms. During this period para-state mechanisms were developed to ensure national security through the means of surveillance. A large network of spies was developed which is in action even nowadays but in a less intensive form.

Since the early 1990s, after the official denouncing of the 'administrative harassment', a research boom occurred in the area. Western Thrace was the 'exotic' research destination in Greece, and also the field where crucial national policies had to be built backed by research evidence. Mistrust was the least that could characterise the relationship between the minority community and the researchers.

On a cold November night, I was introduced to Cenk. When he asked what I was doing in Komotini and I said that I had come to conduct research, he started laughing out loud! Very surprised, I asked why he was laughing, what was so funny about it. He said 'I am laughing because nobody in this area is going to open his mouth to you'. I asked again why and he said 'because people are afraid; you say that you are a student, you are doing a PhD in England but how can we know that you do not work for the Greek National Intelligence Service?' As a majority Greek researcher I needed to prove myself before getting access to a closed community which is largely a Turkish one.

'The magic word if you want to enter the world of the minority is *kefil*, look up for it.' It was in July that a young person from the minority told me, while I was thanking him for his amazing help; after many months in the field it seemed finally that I was getting some good data for my research. He had brought me in contact with many participants who were all extremely willing and happy to take part in my research. He said 'let's say that there are many people who like me and trust me'. *Kefil* is a word in Turkish, which is all about credibility and trust. It means the one who guarantees for someone else; he or she is the person who is the key to convince a third party that someone is indeed a person to be trusted.

Imagine a scheme of three people: A is the kefil, B is the potential research participant and C is me, the researcher. For A to be a kefil for me, he or she needs to trust me and be absolutely sure about me, my identity and intentions and, at the same time, he or she also needs to be trusted absolutely by B. If this is the case, then A (the kefil) guarantees for me to B that I am OK and he/she should talk to me, B because he/she trusts A decides to take part in my research. Sometimes a kefil may not know me well but because someone else knows him/her and said that he/she is the kefil for me then he/she also takes the role depending on how much he/she trusts the other person who guarantees for me. It is a chain of trust.

It was thanks to my kefils that I managed to conduct my research. For an ordinary person in Thrace, to talk to a researcher means to put him/herself into the risk of getting in trouble. Consequently, the word of a kefil was necessary in most cases to give me access to people. When people are asked to participate in a research study, the questions that come up are: 'Who is this researcher?', 'What kind of research is this?', 'How it will be used?', 'How can they be sure that indeed confidentiality and anonymity will be ensured?'. Nobody in the field who did not know me well enough could take at face value my claims: 'I am a student, I am doing my PhD. Everything will be anonymous and confidential'. I could not assure anyone as my own word was of no value in a place where people did not know me and everyone was over-suspicious about everything. However, a kefil could do this on my behalf and also answer all the above questions that people who are very kind and polite would not ask me.

It was such a case once when a kefil who wanted to bring some people to participate in my research, called me on the phone and said: 'Eleni, this person

42 Eleni Konidari

agrees to talk to you but he needs to know beforehand if you are going to ask him about identity issues. If you will, he does not want to participate'. The potential participant, for example, would hesitate to have this kind of discussion with me in advance but could openly share his concerns with his friend who in turn could openly talk to me about it. So, a kefil would also be the mediator in this kind of negotiation between me and the participants.

Being a kefil, however comes with a huge responsibility. For example, a common context where a kefil is employed is in the banks. If someone needs a loan from a bank then he/she needs to provide a kefil, someone with a good credit score, to guarantee that he/she could pay that money back and in the case of his/her failure the kefil will pay that amount on behalf of the person. My Turkish friend, Cansu, explained to me: 'If you can't keep up with your kefil's word, your kefil would face the consequences maybe even more so than yourself at times. Your wrongdoing could destroy their credibility and reputation'.

I had kefils from very different strands of life and political positions from both within the minority and the majority group, and this helped me extremely to reach different sorts of people. The people who were far from the poles of local power were much more open and interested to take part in my research with the guarantee of a kefil whereas, those closer to these poles were always more hesitant as they would risk more if something went wrong. A typical example for this was a very dear friend of mine from the minority group. He acted as a kefil for me in different situations and helped me in my research not only morally but also in making the chance for me to conduct some very rich and in-depth interviews. However, he was very different to me in private when we would meet at my home or his home for lunch or coffee and very different when he would meet me in public, in one of those events where all the influential and powerful people of the community were present. My dear, warm, supportive friend was transforming to a distant kind acquaintance. He was a young person building his career around the local power poles, so the risk for him was very high, I concluded, and I could understand it.

Coming from the National Road from Thessaloniki and entering Rhodope, the first sign you have showing that you are in Thrace is the impressive mountain range that unfolds before your eyes. My fieldwork lasted for one year, during which I needed to take some short breaks. Every time I was coming back to Komotini and looking through the bus window at the Rhodope mountains I was feeling my heart aching. I had internalised the image that I was assuming everyone had of me as a potential spy. I was returning to the place where I had to be very considerate of how to dress, to talk and to perform – remembering all the particular religious and cultural codes and proving myself in every moment and every interaction.

The field was the space where my assumed Orthodox background and my Greekness had to merge with the Muslim Turkish community who I was asking to help me. It was only at the very end that being exhausted of carrying my stigmatised Greek researcher identity I decided to be myself. It was during my last break when I found I could be myself and I realised how this internalisation had harmed me. I decided that I did not have to prove anything, as there was not anything wrong with who I was. I returned to the field and it was the first time that my heart opened in the view of the mountains while the bus was entering Komotini.

Notes

1 Rhodope is one of the three administrational prefectures of Western Thrace, the one where most of the Turkish population lives. Its capital Komotini is considered to be the centre of the Western Thrace region.
2 The 'stone years' were from the late 1950s until the early 1990s, with the worst period being the 1980s.

3

THE PRAGMATICS OF DOING RESEARCH ACROSS LANGUAGES

Inferences and intentions

Alain Wolf

Introduction

We have seen in previous chapters how pragmatics was able to give an account of the mechanisms by which researchers and the researched understand one another in context. The explanations I have offered have aimed to show that language as code, often referred to as sentence meaning, was not by itself able to generate meaning; an appeal to the context was needed if full meaning was to be recovered by researchers and their participants. Following on from this discussion of how context influences intercultural research, this chapter offers an overview of some basic aspects of intercultural communication styles from the early beginnings of cross-cultural research to the more recent perspectives of linguistic pragmatics on the role of intention in multilingual research. I will first briefly review examples of early research which I consider to be misleading, if not plainly misguided, in the field of what is known as cross-cultural pragmatics. I will then present three principles – intention recovery, a certain type of inference known as implicature, and performativity – drawing on interdisciplinary theoretical investigations spanning linguistic pragmatics, narratology and theology. These are intended to inform the data which come from interviews with PhD students involved in intercultural research in the fields of education, international development and applied linguistics. My aim here is to show how meaning is arrived at by researchers and the researched through forms of interaction which involve the use of diverse, and at times strange, even unexpected strategies. This prompts a later discussion of a number of questions further to demonstrate how understanding is arrived at. What role do researchers and participants' intentions play in data collection? And when misunderstandings occur, how are they resolved?

Cross-cultural pragmatics and the myths of cultural difference

The majority of the early work carried out in the area of cross-cultural pragmatics aimed to tell a narrative, the main plot of which was a comparison across seemingly stable and identifiable national cultures. Researchers studied the different ways in which speech acts, or for that matter any other language devices the researcher felt like investigating at the time, were realised across national cultures. There are many early examples of such studies (see Blum-Kulka and Ohlstain, 1984; Pomerantz, 1978; House and Kasper, 1981; House, 2000), all of which tend to ascribe fundamental characteristics to national cultures. Pomerantz (1978), for example, finds that Chinese speakers respond to compliments by denying them. Even studies which analyse the production of talk between participants in an intercultural exchange still focus on differences derived from putative national traits. House (2000: 148), for instance, analyses misunderstandings between German and American speakers and puts their conflict down to 'differential weightings given to small talk by German as opposed to Anglophone speakers'.

The problem with such studies is that they tend to focus on static, universalist and essentialist comparisons between homogeneous national cultures, as we discussed in Chapter 1 in relation to Hofstede (1991). Blum-Kulka and Ohlstain (1989: 196), for example, perceive the aim of their research as 'essential in coping with the applied aspect of the issue of universality', and their claim is based on a two-phase process: first, one attempts to specify 'the particular pragmatic rules of use for a given language', then one lists the 'rules which second language learners will have to acquire in order to attain successful communication in the target language'. But the rules of use of a particular language are variable rather than universal, and it is never too long before someone comes along and finds acceptance routines for compliments to be common among Chinese participants (see, for example, Ye, 1995). The misguided assumption, then, is that an intercultural context is the sum of two opposing national cultures, rather than the creation of a new one. The main objective of a pragmatic approach is not to analyse and compare participants with different cultural 'essences' or traits, but to show how a new context has emerged and the way in which meaning has been generated in the interaction. As Verschueren (2008: 25) justly argues: 'a static comparison of cultures seems the worst possible basis on which to approach intercultural communication'.

In this chapter, I will apply the findings of contemporary linguistic pragmatics to focus in more detail on the dynamic nature of the researcher and their participants' intercultural interactions. This will, I hope, allow me to explore the multiple identities of both researchers and the researched in the context of divergent interpretations (see Bhabha, 1994; Holliday, 2010; Haugh, 2008). It is in this sense that analyses of material can no longer just focus on failures in communication, presenting only the part of the data which shows things going wrong in terms of simplistic binary oppositions between national cultures, e.g. individualistic vs. collectivistic,

46 Alain Wolf

egocentric vs. sociocentric cultures. It must be pointed out that the kind of research paradigm I am about to present has often been accused of being unsystematic. The accusation must be combated as it is, eloquently, by writers such as Holliday (2010) and Bhabha (1994). Holliday (2010) does so by establishing the principles of 'decentred research' which, he argues (Holliday, 2010: 11 citing Bhabha, 1994), allows vernacular realities 'to emerge on their own terms'. I will apply such a methodology here, focusing on the individual experiences of researchers, attempting to 'mak[e] visible the unexpected for the purpose of revealing deeper complexities that counter established discourses' (Holliday, 2010: 11). But before doing so, I would like to revisit certain notions about speaker meaning which I alluded to only in passing in the previous chapter.

Speaker meaning: the role of intention in multilingual research

Earlier, I outlined Grice's well-known concept of conversational implicature, and I would like now to take a closer look at his notion of 'meaning$_{nn}$' and speaker meaning presented in his seminal paper 'Meaning' (Grice, 1957). Here, Grice remarks that if I were to utter:

(1) Those spots mean measles.

(taken from Grice, 1957: 377)

I could not then follow with 'but he has not got measles', so that in a case like (1), x means that p entails p, i.e. the fact that p. Indeed, we can re-state (1) as 'the fact that he has those spots means that he has measles'. Contrast this with the example below:

(2) That remark, 'Smith couldn't get on without his trouble and strife', meant that Smith found his wife indispensable.

(taken from Grice, 1957: 378)

Here, unlike in (1), I can go on to say without fear of contradiction 'but in fact Smith deserted her seven years ago'. In this case then, x means that p does not entail p. Grice speaks of the sense in which (2) is used as the non-natural sense of the expression and uses the abbreviation 'means$_{nn}$' to distinguish the non-natural sense of the utterance. This kind of meaning is the one that pragmaticists should be concerned with. This is because it is defined exclusively by a speaker's intention and the recognition of that intention by an addressee. And so, Grice (1957: 385) defines meaning$_{nn}$ thus:

'*A* meant$_{nn}$ something by x' is (roughly) equivalent to '*A* intended the utterance of x to produce some effect in an audience by means of the recognition of this intention'

This view that speakers' intentions and how they are recognised by an audience are central to successful communication is the touchstone of pragmatics. For as Bach (2012: 64) says, there is something special about the intention recognised by the audience insofar as speakers intend their audience to recognise the effect they are trying to produce in them, i.e. one intends to produce an effect 'by means of the recognition of this intention'. That intention, says Bach (2012: 52) is 'in a certain sense reflexive', i.e. the speaker must intend the audience to recognise his or her intention.

Now seems an appropriate time to outline the characteristic principles of Grice's theory of implicature. An implicature is defined as the meaning intended by a speaker. So what is implicated by saying something goes beyond what one says. One can say after going out for a meal, 'It didn't make me sick' (taken from Bach, 2012: 55) and implicate that the meal was not very good, but this is not implied by what one *says*, since a meal that does not make you sick can still be excellent (see Bach, 2012: 55). Another characteristic of implicatures is that they are cancellable, i.e. in the meal example one could add 'I don't mean to say that the meal was awful'. In fact, there are contexts in which the implicature that the meal was not very good would not have arisen, i.e. if the context was related to a hygiene inspection of the restaurant and you said: 'the food didn't make me sick'. A common misconception also noted by Bach (2012: 60) is that implicatures are inferences. This happens because what is implicated by a speaker is confused with what is inferred by the hearer. Implicatures are generated by speakers in saying what they mean; it is the hearer who works out what is meant and that requires inferencing. Yet another misconception is that linguistic expressions implicate things:

(1a) Some of my friends like choral music.

(1b) Not all of my friends like choral music.

(2a) A Turner was stolen from the National Gallery.

(2b) A painting by Turner was stolen from the National Gallery in London.
(constructed examples)

There is a great deal of debate concerning the status of such utterances, but this is beyond the scope of this present chapter. I hold what I believe to be a Gricean view here, namely that the expressions in (1a, 2a) do not strictly speaking 'implicate' (1b, 2b); it is speakers using these conventionalised sentences (Grice refers to them as 'generalised conversational implicatures') who implicate. Their intentions can be worked out by hearers on the basis of their understanding of the conventional linguistic properties of the sentence and as we saw in Chapter 2, the intended content can also be recovered on the presumption of a particular context.

In the context of researching across cultures, much that is communicated when researchers collect data is often implicitly conveyed rather than actually said. From a Gricean perspective (Grice, 1975) one could say that implicatures arise through inferences about the intentions of the researcher.

48 Alain Wolf

In multilingual research, researchers may use generalised conversational implicatures, for example, to implicate that they are showing respect. Ali Alsohaibani, one of my PhD informants doing research on the presence of religious utterances in everyday Arabic, went back to Saudi Arabia to collect data. Many times during our interview, he recalled how he benefited from his insider's experience of Muslim religious culture (a point we explore further in Chapter 5 in relation to writing up research).

He noticed how all-pervasive religious expressions were in his participants' everyday discourse and how he would have to give in-depth explanations of his data if English readers were not to arrive at the incorrect interpretation that his participants were all intensely religious people. In Arabic, for instance, the uses of *In šā' Allāh* and *Mā shā' Allāh* are nuanced and give rise to conventional implicatures often wrongly translated as if they were synonyms of each other, i.e. both meaning 'God willing'. A speaker using '*In šā' Allāh*' would in Saudi Arabia implicate that, in a particular context, say, before someone is being operated on, that the future outcome of the operation is in God's hand. By contrast, *Mā shā' Allāh* is used for contexts involving reference to past actions — if a speaker, for instance, wishes to compliment someone about passing an exam whilst reminding the hearer that his or her achievements are only possible because of God's blessings on him or her. These different implicatures arise through inferences about the intentions of the researched based on what they say, on shared knowledge and contextual information. The contextual information here is that Islam has a belief system according to which all in destiny is willed by God, including the acquisition of riches, the passing of exams and so on. The implicature which would arise in a Western context directed, for example, at a rich individual may generate very different inferences, namely that, for example, the speaker intends to dampen the frenzied spirit of competition and acquisition by a marked, i.e. particularised, reference to God. It is interesting then to realise that implicatures which are generalised in one culture become particularised in another.

The focus so far has been on speakers' intentions and the ability of hearers to recover them. But research both in pragmatics and in psychology (see Keysar, 2007) have shown that speakers often overestimate their ability to project intended meanings onto addressees, mainly because of our innate egocentric natures (Keysar, 2007). Indeed, as Haugh (2008: 220) citing Mey (2001: 217) notes, in politics as in daily life, interlocutors often fail to understand each other not because the words are not clear 'but simply because the one interlocutor doesn't see what the other is talking about, or because she or he interprets that which the other is talking about as something entirely different (Mey, 2001: 217). Rancière's (1995) distinction between a surface lack of understanding (in French 'malentendu') and a deep misunderstanding (in French 'mésentente'), where understanding because of diverging ideological stances has become impossible, is also relevant here. I will now turn to instances where resorting only to the speaker's intention in determining what is implied gives what Haugh (2008: 224) calls 'an impoverished account of implicatures'. I will show by referring to examples drawn from the experience of

Pragmatics and research across languages **49**

doing research across cultures that it is not enough to account for what is implied by attributing intention to a speaker.

The deep miscommunication of implicatures

As we have just seen, so far there has been a focus on the successful communication of implicatures rather than on their miscommunication which presumably arises when the researcher fails to infer the communicative intention of the researched or vice versa. Now the problem is that the recovery of speakers' intentions, and indeed the very notion of 'intention', is 'murky' (see Haugh and Jaszczolt, 2012: 87).[1] So communicative success between the researched and the researcher may not always be achieved through the simple recognition of a speaker's intentions. Misunderstandings and distrust can still occur even when intentions are recognised.

In this respect, Haugh (2008) refers to an incident which involved the Mufti of Australia, Sheik Taj Din al-Hilali, who in the context of a mosque warned about the dangers of fornication and immodest dress by saying that 'uncovered meat attracts cats'. As Haugh (2008: 206) makes clear, widely divergent sets of inferences were drawn by different sections of the population. The sheik's supporters derived the inferences that Muslims should practise abstinence outside marriage and that dressing immodestly can lead to sex outside marriage. The media, however, and some sections of the feminist movement interpreted the sheik's utterances as implying that women who don't wear the hijab 'invite rape, and so can be blamed for such rapes' (Haugh, 2008: 205).

A model of the communication of intentions must, argues Haugh (2008:1), 'move beyond the received view that it involves "correctly" inferring the intentions of speakers'. It needs to take into consideration the fact that to work out what is implied does not just depend on attributing intentions to the speaker 'but also on which folk interpretive norms are invoked, and what kinds of sociocultural presuppositions are assumed by interactants' (Haugh, 2008: 224). Central to this argument is the notion based on Arundale's (1999, 2006: 196) Conjoint Co-Constituting Model of Communication (cited in Haugh, 2008) that inferences emerge which may be constructed by participants, but are not controlled as such by either the speaker or the hearer (Haugh, 2008: 224). Haugh (2008) ends on a fairly pessimistic note by owning that these sets of divergent implicatures can never be agreed on and that we need to come 'to acceptance that we do not have to always agree about what is implied'. Such a 'let's beg to differ' position implies accepting non-resolution and this may well lead, in some cases, to increasing conflict. We will see later how the principle of 'dialogical co-construction' can help us out of what I consider to be a communicative cul-de-sac. But before doing so, I would like to present two examples of miscommunications derived from divergent implicatures which were generated on the basis of interlocutors' divergent socio-cultural presuppositions.

In the context of researching across cultures, the phenomenon of divergent implicatures can have devastating effects for both the researcher and the researched. One of the PhD students I interviewed for this project, Vera Da Silva Sinha, had been

50 Alain Wolf

studying time intervals with colleagues in Amondawa, a Tupi language and culture of Amazonia. She published an article, the abstract of which states that Amondawa 'has no lexicalised abstract concept of time and no practices of time reckoning'. The media got hold of the research, and soon afterwards a piece appeared in the *Daily Mail* (2011) with the headline: 'No concept of time: the Amazonian tribe where nobody has an age and words like 'month' and 'year' don't exist'. During our interview, Vera, obviously still pained by the inferences created by the media article, felt the need to 'correct' the divergent implicatures in future research:

> I'm very worried about that. I'm going to write about the notion of time. I don't want to write about what people do not have, i.e. clocks, mobile phones. So they don't have birthdays. That's the way they live. My research is not about that. They [the tribe] want to teach me how they see time and I don't want to compare their notion of time with what we have. I published before. People asked me: 'why did you say that these people didn't have time'? I didn't say that.
>
> *(Vera Da Silva Sinha, interview, Amondwa, 2016)*

Of course, the harm done to the researcher is nothing compared to the harm done to the vulnerable researched. We will come back to the participants' response to this because it is central to the dialogue and reconciliation that can follow such hurtful misinterpretations. But one cannot like Haugh just beg to differ. This does not lead to reconciliation but to more rancour. In the example above, Vera did return to the field after the publication of the *Daily Mail* article:

> The participants in my research knew that I was passionate about it. And that's really important. They looked after me all the time. They were very welcoming. They said how important it was that they teach me the right way they live. They were very worried if I'm going to write something that isn't true.
>
> *(Vera Da Silva Sinha, interview, Amondawa, 2016)*

Another example of divergent inferencing often relayed to me by researchers is a deep-seated misunderstanding of the researcher's intentions in conducting the research in the first place. I've looked at this before in the previous chapter where the context needed to be enlarged, so to speak, in order to accommodate the new assumptions developed by both researchers and the researched. Similarly, Ali had something remarkable to say about the reactions of the people he researched:

> My participants expressed their surprise that I was asking them about the presence of religious utterances in their speech. They told me: 'You're a Muslim, you know it is in the Koran. Then they switch to the Koranic verse when they're talking.
>
> *(Ali Alsohaibani, interview: Religious Utterances, 2015)*

Asking your participants about something which they know you already know about is from the perspective of the participants a ridiculous, almost an insulting waste of time. I'll return to this example to show how this was repaired.

As researchers, we approach the research situation with intentions and world views which affect the manner in which we collect data. As we have already seen in other chapters, surprise and frustration can attend the research situation. Ali, again, described eloquently his anticipation of difficulties when he was about to conduct role plays with older relatives from Saudi Arabia:

> I expected I'd have difficulties about the performance of the older participants. But on the contrary, I found them very keen to complete the tasks. I had some concerns with the old participants. It's difficult to ask older 62-year-olds to act. But truly, they were the best in my research. I was amazed. Those participants who were over 60 were the best participants in my research. I was amazed by how they acted. They seemed to me very natural. They were excited.
>
> *(Ali Alsohaibani, interview: Religious Utterances, 2015)*

Probed as to why he anticipated difficulties with that age group, Ali said that he didn't expect them to take research seriously:

> In general in Saudi culture, people show willing to participate because of social reasons, not for the sake of the research.
>
> *(Ali Alsohaibani, interview: Religious Utterances, 2015)*

There is a sense here that researchers sometimes get the data they want in incidental moments when the least expected realities and divergent implicatures emerge to the forefront of research. This is partly why formalising the research process to the extent that it is in countries of the North regrettably misses out on this aspect of data collection as a 'gift' to the researcher.

Dialogical co-construction, bridging the gap between different horizons, submission and emergent realities

In the examples I have just presented, misunderstandings originating in divergent world views led in some cases to breakdowns in communication and the refusal by the two parties involved further to negotiate. Haugh's (2008) view of the matter is to beg to differ which, as I observed earlier, may result in aporia, a lack of reconciliation, and the possibility of future conflict. But further negotiation of the interaction can and does take place between the participants by way of 'dialogical co-construction'. What I mean by the term, which I derive from Ducrot's (1984) theories of communicative polyphony, is a process of negotiation which makes us aware as we interact with others that we weave in several voices within our own. In the act of communication, Ducrot (1984: 193) argues, a speaker controls the

52 Alain Wolf

voices of their addressees and presents us with their attitudes and beliefs. Imagine speaker A arguing with speaker B and saying 'So, I'm a racist?' Ducrot (1984) notices how curious speaker A's use of the first person pronoun 'I' is. This is because even though speaker A uses 'I am a racist', he/she clearly does not agree with this view of himself/herself. Rather, we interpret 'so I'm a racist?' as an echo of a viewpoint expressed by speaker B, in this case the 'entity' represented by 'you'. Language is a strange thing: it gives no other option to Speaker A than to use the first person pronoun, thus integrating the views and beliefs of the Other within his/her own.

Our identity as speakers and hearers, then, is negotiated through a process of acknowledging that within our own discourse, we are able to stage other views with which we negotiate our own identity. This polyphonic negotiation involves accepting that we are not unitary selves, and that we depend on the Other for the disclosure of truth. Similarly, the inter-religious theologian Panikkar (1979: 9) argues that to bridge 'the gap [. . .] between two different *topoi*'[2], we need to place ourselves in a position where we understand the other 'without assuming that the other has the same basic self-understanding and understanding as I have'. This is the meaning of *under-stand*, i.e. 'stand under the same horizon of intelligibility' (Panikkar, 1979: 9). This polyphonic and theological view of the self is particularly applicable to the examples in the research contexts we have been looking at. Take, for example, Vera's understanding of herself as a researcher in relation to her participants. She says:

> They feed you, they put you in their homes, they trust you. You become part of the family, then you get out from there and write things that don't make sense to them. It's really difficult that you're going to formulate things not to break this faith in your fieldwork. Trust, I think trust is the most important thing. The assumption of the media is that these people are inferior. These people do not have a word for 'time' and the media interprets 'tribe without time' Now I try to write without using any negative statements.
>
> *(Vera Da Silva Sinha, interview, Amondwa, 2016)*

In this example, Vera shows how, in Panikkar's (1979: 242) terms, she integrates *topoi* within one person i.e. dialogue is a way of disentangling her own point of view from other viewpoints. She recognises that she is not an autonomous, unitary individual and that she relies on her participants' trust for the revelation of truth. She needs to go back to the field research site, she needs to get them to accept her again. As Panikkar (1979: 243) eloquently observes, 'it is in this sense that dialogue is a religious act par excellence because it recognises my *religatio* to another, my individual poverty, the need to get out of myself, transcend myself, in order to save myself'.

When she met the speakers of 'Huni Kuin' (true humans), Vera was initially impressed that they never seemed to raise their voices, always appearing polite. Vera herself coming from a culture which she would recognise as loud and exuberant,

Pragmatics and research across languages **53**

her assumption was that they would not cooperate and talk. But to her surprise they were not shy and when they started talking, Vera just had to, in her own words, 'calm down' or in Holliday's (2010: 12) terminology, use the principle of 'submission' to express the need for her to 'allow realities which are beyond the initial vision of the researcher "to emerge"' so as 'to enable the unexpected' (2010: 12) in qualitative research to take place.

The pursuance of evidence in qualitative research has to go beyond the mere explanation of inferences because the unexpected emerges out of the researcher 'submitting' fully to the researched, so that two or more topoi may be bridged. Holliday usefully cites Geertz (1993) who demonstrates that two boys winking in a town square can be differently interpreted as one of the boys involuntarily twitching or as one of them winking in parody of the former 'to entertain another group of boys'. 'Getting to the bottom of things' is what pursuing evidence in qualitative research means, and this can be done only through the withholding of 'initial' impressions and submitting to the Other's axiological and epistemological horizon. Holliday (2010: 14) talks about a 'creative exploration' through which the methodology develops which involves researchers 'submit[ting] themselves to the nature of the place and then discover[ing] more than they imagined about their subjects' (Holliday, 2010: 15). That which emerges may be quite different from whatever the researcher started with.

Similarly, emergence as a principle of research is illustrated by Ali in his data collection involving older participants. Ali started off with the thesis that these were going to be difficult participants and that asking them to role play would be an embarrassment. It was only after watching the role plays and talking about them in exploratory conversations with another researcher that he came to an understanding of why they were so successful at acting out a role play:

> Maybe this is because most of them, all of them, knew me. They were trying to give me the best they can. They asked me: 'Have I given you what you want?' They were very excited; because in our culture they don't take research very seriously. In general, in Saudi culture people show willing to participate for social reasons, not for the sake of research.
>
> Maybe here in the West, people participate in projects because this research will help humanity, the environment. But in Saudi culture, they would participate because they know me. They wouldn't ask me questions about how my research is going to be useful. They participate because I ask them kindly. Maybe that accounts for why the old participants did better than the others.
>
> *(Ali Alsohaibani, Religious Utterances, 2015)*

This process of arriving at an emerging thesis (Holliday 2010: 17) is central to how we conduct research across cultures. Emergence as a principle of research is illustrated by the notion of a new thesis being formulated about the meaning of the data. Holliday (2010: 17) refers to a researcher who started off with a 'thesis'

54 Alain Wolf

concerning Chinese students' thinking about the university entrance examination. It was only after much exploratory research on 'private sites' and diaries that the students revealed to him a 'counter discourse' about the examination and he arrived at what Holliday calls 'an emerging thesis'.

These different formulations of the key concept of 'dialogical co-construction', i.e. bridging the topoi, submission, and emergence, form a coherent basis upon which researching across cultures can take place. This dimension of data collection as 'gift' to the researcher (see Ali's older friends and relatives) is overlooked in Western cultures. The corollary notion of researcher hospitality and gratitude is seen by Western university ethics policies as nothing short of corrupt bribery. And yet, for Ali, treating his participants as guests was not only the usual but the required procedure in collecting data:

> I prepared the environment in my house to make the event convenient. I had to deal with my participants as guests. So I had to prepare hospitality, cook for them, etc. At the beginning they were guests, then participants. They expect you to properly thank them, to give something back, to thank them very properly. Just saying thank you would not be enough.
>
> *(Ali Alsohaibani, interview: Religious Utterances, 2015)*

We see here how the concepts of 'trust', 'faithfulness' and 'gratitude' are all involved in the collaboration between researcher, researched and the outside world. A wide panoply of axiological horizons is displayed here which can be difficult to bridge, and yet in our research practices this is what we are enjoined to do: to withhold our initial impressions, to let go of the ethnocentric, unitary self, to orchestrate the views of the Other within ourselves dialogically involving ourselves with the Other. There is a very strong element here of what I like to call performing the culture (see Liamputtong cited in Chapter 1). And this leads me on to a final discussion of another well-known notion in pragmatics required for an intercultural approach to researching across cultures, i.e. that of performativity.

Performativity in multilingual research

An important distinction is made by the philosopher of language, Austin (1988: 105), who argues that we must distinguish between acts that are only attempted, which he refers to as illocutionary acts, and acts that get performed, i.e. perlocutionary acts. This distinction is important because in using a language we may perform an illocutionary act, e.g. by saying 'Please forgive me!' which is quite different from what we bring about by saying something (Austin, 1988: 109), e.g. 'He got me to forgive him': that is the perlocutionary force of an utterance.

As far as researching across cultures is concerned, performativity means not only finding common ground between researcher and researched, it means also changing the world in which we find ourselves, and physically occupying the spaces where cultures overlap (Wijsen, 2007: 245), e.g. worship, food, festivals where the researcher laughs with the researched when they laugh and cry with them when they cry. For Panikkar (1979: 242), it is the concept of conversion which is profoundly performative, inasmuch as it is a realisation of one's 'individual poverty' coupled with the need 'to transcend' oneself, 'in order to save' oneself.

This characteristic of researching across cultures is seldom addressed by researchers, but in my work training student researchers, I have often found that as we 'perform' our research, so we change the world of the research site, and the richer, more fully worked out outcome of the research process increases what Holliday (2010: 26) calls our 'personal knowledge'. We realise as researchers that we were poor, naive and limited about the research site when our assumptions about it are suddenly cancelled in favour of other more valid interpretations on which we are now prepared to act. Although I will look at examples of this below, one example taken from Holliday serves to illustrate the performative nature of research. In his study of Hong Kong Chinese student behaviour, Holliday initially made comments about their tendency not to be on task, expressing surprise when they did the things he had asked them to do: 'some of them perkily looked round to say they were "on-time"'. In a later reflection, he noticed how some of the vocabulary he had used to describe his students indicated a particular 'politics' of his profession which focuses on getting students to achieve things, essentially an objective-led controlling ethos. The word 'perkily' stood out in particular as it seemed to indicate he treated the students as children, almost animal-like, rather than adults. This 'increased personal knowledge about the nature of professional discourse' (Holliday, 2010: 26) is the performative conversion of the individual researcher, i.e. it changes the person ethically and deontologically and leads them to a different, better, cultural place.

Trust, charity and concluding remarks

I shall close this chapter with recounting one last amusing incident, again to do with thwarted expectations, which sheds light on a culture to an extent that it would not have done, had things gone to plan. At the beginning of her research, Vera planned a trip to her research site which involved a boat journey down the Amazon:

> The plan was for the journey to last one and a half days. But we stayed on the boat for four days. So I had to revise all my planning. I had to check all my research questions, and started my interviewing on the boat. And why not? There were so many factors to take into account, the weather, the type of boat. This is when I began to realise I had to conceptualise time differently.
> *(Vera Da Silva Sinha, interview, Amondwa, 2015)*

The beginning of this performative conversion in the researcher can be detected here: Vera wittingly abandons her own Western sense of timing and chronology and immerses herself in other temporal structures. There is no looking back, there is no frustration, no nostalgic harking back to a cultural past that can no longer be.

56 Alain Wolf

The boat effortlessly moving along, however slow its progress in Western time, becomes a metaphor for her research on time.

Performing the culture is illustrated eloquently by Ali and Vera, who both regard hospitality and trust as the cementing glue of the relationships between the researcher and the researched:

> They feed you, they put you in their homes, they trust you.
>
> *(Vera Da Silva Sinha, interview, Amondwa, 2015)*

This unspoken contract goes beyond that laid down by Western universities' codes of practice and ethics policies. This is another realm, more binding because it contains the discourse of the personal, the theological, rather than that of the corporation:

> You become part of the family, then you get out there and write things that don't make sense to them. It's really difficult. How you're going to formulate things not to break this faith in your fieldwork, trust, I think trust is the most important thing. If you're without trust, I can't bring nobody to my house.
>
> *(Vera Da Silva Sinha, interview, Amondwa, 2015)*

Trust is rarely mentioned in research contexts and yet both Ali and Vera express a sense of trust, charity and hospitality towards their participants, freely given on both sides, and often translated in the New Testament as agapeic love. Indeed, I cannot but find echoes of St Paul in Vera's comments: 'If I have prophetic powers, and understand all mysteries and all knowledge, and if I have all faith, so as to remove mountains, but do not have charity, I am nothing' (1 Cor. 11:33).

As we have seen in this chapter, the collection and analysis of data crucially depend on the researcher's interaction with the researched and on a thick, experiential interpretation of their intentions beyond the static context of situation. In the following reflective piece, Achala Gupta addresses a similar issue confronting her as a doctoral student in the UK. She wanted 'to learn the participants' involvement in their children's education' and found that she could not ask direct questions to mothers about their roles and responsibility. As Achala observes, qualitative research in this respect can become 'particularly challenging for it tends to engage in people's thoughts, ideas, and attitudes' and so 'the multilingual researcher must be sensitive to the socio-cultural understanding of the context in which respondents participate'. This chapter is an example of how the relationships between the researcher and the researched cannot be taken for granted and need to be considered critically in relation to thoughts, ideas and intentions.

Box 3

Questions for further reflection

- Have I had misunderstandings with my participants or with my interpreter/ translator, and if so, of what type were they?
- To what extent have my intentions affected data collection?
- Have I read the deep divergent intentions of my participants correctly?
- How have I negotiated conflict, if any, and achieved reconciliation?
- Did I withhold initial impressions in order to get emerging data in incidental moments?
- What world views/beliefs do I have which may have affected data collection?
- How do I perform my participants' culture and show hospitality and trust to them?
- What does the notion of the cultural 'Other' mean to me?

Notes

1 The proliferation of approaches to the notions of intention and intentionality is such that their status in the field of pragmatics has become a challenge for theorists. For a readable review of intentionality see Haugh and Jaszczolt's (2012) article in the *Cambridge Handbook of Pragmatics*.

2 Human topoi are places of understanding and self-understanding between cultures (Panikkar, 1979: 9).

58 Achala Gupta

Reflective piece 3: Cultural connotations in language structures – an experiential account of meaning-making in the processes of translation

Achala Gupta

Amidst the growing interest in pursuing cross-cultural studies and the domination of English as the language of choice in academic writing, translation becomes integral not only to the process of conducting the empirical projects but also, by extension, in the creation of knowledge. The significance of translation at various stages, from conceptualising the research problematic, in developing tools for data generation, to laying out the framework for data analysis, and subsequent dissemination of research findings, create a dynamic in interpreting the everydayness in the social world. Markedly, enhanced mobility of the researcher and the participants adds momentum to the scholarly practice of meaning-making.

Despite plenty of evidence of 'variations in spoken language by gender, ethnic group, social class and nationality' (Bradby, 2002; Wong and Poon, 2010) which suggests that methods of translation are crucial concerns for maintaining the validity of data (Birbili, 2000), sociological research does not seem to pay the required attention to the problematic that the arena of language and translation may offer. This paper discusses methodological issues concerning translation based on my experiential account of carrying out an MPhil research project.

The project aimed at understanding mothers' perception, their engagement, and experience of children's schooling. While most other studies on this theme have emphasised class relations in the processes of parental engagement, my project was an attempt to capture the experience of newly immigrated South Asian mothers in the United Kingdom, and, therefore, was dealing with multiple variables of social stratification. Notably, neither my participants nor I were native English speakers and we had varied levels of comprehending the language. In the course of research, I was dealing with three languages: Hindi, English, and Urdu. While I used Hindi and English in written as well as in spoken form, my understanding of Urdu was restricted to only speech with limited, but sufficient, vocabulary for making everyday conversation. I used translation in developing an interview schedule, during fieldwork and in the phase of transcribing and analysing the data. In all these phases, 'translation involves the transportation of meanings that are already attached to words and concept' (Lutz, 2011: 352), and, therefore, demands the researcher's attention to maintaining the accuracy of expression both in writing and in speech.

As my research problem attempted to understand the perception, experience and engagement of participants with a particular aspect of their lives, I developed a semi-structured interview guide with a majority of open-ended questions. Developing tools for data collection requires a transition from a conceptual understanding of the issue to developing a set of questions that have a potential to address the research problematic. This transition also involves a number of changes in language through not only translating English into Hindi/Urdu, but also by replacing academic jargon with the vocabulary of everyday usage, while simultaneously ensuring that the answer to the question still relates to making sense of the research inquiry.

Also, it is better to write questions in the language/s the researcher expects to be dealing with, because it helps in carrying out an efficient and smooth conversation during the interviews. At first, the questions in my interview guide were written in English but during the pilot interview, I experienced difficulty in accurately translating the questions into Hindi/Urdu during the interview, especially when turning from talking in the native language to following up the conversation with the help of the interview guide. Realising the switches between English and Hindi impeded the flow of the conversation, I decided to write all questions in both languages. This exercise of drafting the same question in two languages helped me to avoid the interruption caused by ad hoc translation and in maintaining the flow of the conversation.

In qualitative research, the relationship between researcher and participants is very crucial during fieldwork as it has serious implications for the nature and the quality of the data generated. While my upbringing in India and experiences of migration to the UK were useful factors in relating well with the participants' narratives, I observed an interesting pattern of switching between the languages during the interviews. As they felt comfortable in conversations, the participants who earlier spoke in English switched to Hindi or Urdu. And as they switched they could explain their experience and thoughts with precision and in greater detail. Notably, participants' expression in their native language was culturally embedded, more informative and incredibly nuanced. Usage of non-English or both (English and Hindi/Urdu) languages may not be very convenient, for it needs translating into one language, usually English, later on. However, code-switching is pertinent in not only developing 'intimacy and solidarity with other bilinguals' (Hoffman, 1991 in Bradby, 2002: 847) but also, as a result, in building relationships in the field and in generating quality data.

Crafting a couple of questions, i.e. selecting words from the general to the particular, usually has the potential to produce rich data. For example, I wanted to learn about the participants' involvement in their children's education. Instead of asking a direct question to mothers about their roles and responsibility, which I thought may not reveal sufficient information, I asked about mothers' role in children's schooling in general and gradually moved on to asking about their particular experience.

As far as selecting words is concerned, it needs pointing out that the two native languages I was dealing with, i.e. Hindi and Urdu, 'are mutually comprehensible in the spoken form' (Bradby, 2002, p. 845). However, while most words in everyday usage in both languages are the same, a few words are exclusive to each language, and, therefore, may not necessarily be understood cross-culturally. For example, the closest meaning of the word 'busy' is 'व्यस्त' (*vyasta*) in Hindi and 'मशरूफ' (*mushroof*) in Urdu. Not all Hindi-speaking Indians and Pakistanis can switch codes while speaking or listening to this word in their respective native languages. Therefore, the usage of the words was crucial to observe during the interviews.

60 Achala Gupta

That is, while most of the conversation provided me with inclusiveness to the South Asian culture, selection of some words over others indicated exclusiveness to the culture (everyday conversation) of a particular country (India or Pakistan). Overall, a crucial element to the interviews was to make sure that I understood what the participants meant, and the participants had a clear idea of what I said.

To avoid this distinction, I used two strategies: to use English words, as they are often considered neutral, and to learn a few Urdu words that are used in everyday conversation. For example, I used 'time' instead of using 'समय' (*samay*) in Hindi or 'वक़्त' (*waqt*) in Urdu. A colleague of Pakistani origin helped me learn the following Urdu words, which were part of my interview schedule.

These subtleties of cultural embeddedness of language and its impact on the vocabulary used between the two languages and the need for switching from one code to another affected the construction of the questions in the interview schedule. I wrote three drafts of the interview guide. The first one was in English, to receive feedback from the supervisors; the second draft was in Hindi; and the third draft was drafted with the help of a Pakistani colleague, which included the Urdu words in required places. One of the questions in the interview guide was:

> What do you think are the roles that mothers should play in their child's schooling?
>
> आपके नज़रिए में बच्चों की पढ़ाई में माँ की क्या ज़िम्मेदारी होती है/ माँ क्या किरदार अदा करती है ?
>
> (*aapke nazariye mein bachho ki padaai mein maa ki kya zimmedari hoti hai/ maa kya kirdar ada karti hai?*)

Having mentioned that, I admit that I could not understand some of the Urdu words that my respondents used during interviews, and also there were occasions when I used certain words which the respondents could not follow. In both cases, the participants and I sought clarification and explanation from one another. It also showed mutual interest and engagement of both the participants and me in fieldwork processes.

TABLE 3.1 Urdu/Hindi translations

English	Urdu	Hindi
Family background	खानदानी पशेमंज़र (*khaandaani pashemanzar*)	पारिवारिक परिवेश (*pariwaric parivesh*)
Parents	वालदें (*waaldein*)	माता-पिता (*mata pita*)
Family	खानदान (*khandaan*)	परिवार (*pariwaar*)
Subjects	मज़ामीन (*mazaameen*)	विषय (*vishay*)
Performance	कड़कड़दागी (*kaarkerdagi*)	प्रदर्शन (*pradarshan*)
Experience	तजर्बा (*tajarba*)	अनुभव (*anubhav*)
Expectation	तवक़्क़ो (*tawaqqo*)	अपेक्षा (*apekhsha*)
Worry	फ़िक्र (*fiker*)	चिंता (*chinta*)

Qualitative research is particularly challenging, for it tends to engage in people's thoughts, ideas, and attitudes. Therefore, along with the competency in languages, the multilingual researcher (and translator) must be sensitive to the sociocultural understanding of the context in which respondents participate in the project. 'The researcher's knowledge of the language and the culture of the people under study' is reflected by 'the autobiography of the researcher-translator' (Vulliamy, 1990 in Birbili, 2000: 2). Being South Asian born, I had the advantage, beyond language, in capturing nuances in participants' narration of migration and their experience with children's schooling. These insights were helpful in understanding the issues in depth.

For example, most mothers mentioned that seeking permission from the parents was one of the most crucial events in making the decision of migration. This information, alone, does not quite capture underlying and culturally rooted ideas and practices portrayed through the dynamics of how parents can affect the personal decision of the family. After marriage, the female participants were answerable to the husband's family and seeking in-laws' consent, which required showing financial and otherwise preparedness, was essential. Also, in making crucial decisions in the UK, the husband's family had a dominating role to play compared to that of the wife's family. This reflects the inherently patriarchal nature of the South Asian community, in which the husband's parents usually have a greater influence not only on household-related issues in general but also on the personal decisions made by couples. Digging into these particulars was insightful in learning about the processes of making the decision of migration and the dynamics of the social network in participants' lives.

When it came to learning the meanings attached to certain relationships, another example was the emotional association with the word 'neighbours'. While describing her experience in the UK, one participant mentioned that her neighbourhood was different now, by which she meant and later explained, the connotation of the word and the social practices associated with it was different in her home and host country. While suggesting a distance in her relationship with her neighbour, she explained, 'neighbours are like, and sometimes more than, the relatives, who are part of the extended family'. Here she refers to the community structure of society, which is different in South Asia and in the UK.

Another crucial aspect concerning the process of meaning-making is of translation and transcription. In my research, the data was collected in a form of a mix of two languages, i.e. while most of the conversation was carried out in Hindi/Urdu, a few exchanges were also made in English, especially with the respondents who had speaking proficiency of both the languages. Such mixed language data required me to translate the data before transcribing it without losing the meaning of the narratives in the process. During translation, therefore, I made efforts to provide 'conceptual equivalence or comparability of meaning' (Birbili, 2000: 2). While it might be a bit tricky if different individuals perform the task of conducting the research, translating and transcribing, since I performed all three roles, I was 'better able to tap into the richness of the research data through multiple layers of interpretation and meaning construction within and across culture' (Wong and Poon, 2010: 152). It was particularly useful whilst analysing the codes and identifying the themes. Thematisation and codification require explaining participants' response by engaging with sociocultural connotations and thus provide an account of 'intimate knowledge' (Frey, 1970) through making the text culturally explanatory and accessible.

Furthermore, at times the words spoken in the native language may have a deeper meaning than the translated versions; in these cases, translation does not serve the purpose of transportation of the idea. In such situations, I used the original words and detailed contextual information and explained the usage of words in the original form.

Thus, the processes of translation are not entirely devoid of problems (Birbili, 2000), but, as this piece tries to demonstrate, there are ways to minimise those issues in empirical studies. Knowledge of the concerns and repercussions associated with the process of translation assists researchers to reduce its effects in presenting the findings and in making sense of the 'everydayness' in the social world.

4

THE ROLE OF THE INTERPRETER/ TRANSLATOR IN THE RESEARCH PROCESS

The ethics of mediated communication

Alain Wolf

Introduction

Researchers in multilingual research contexts often find themselves acting as or through translators. These decisions about whether or how to use a translator influence communicative practices in fieldwork and shape the final published research text. Yet the majority of these decisions are frequently taken on practical grounds to do with how efficiently the data can be collected and disseminated, without much attention being paid to the translation process itself. Further, researchers and their translators can be influenced by ethical concerns about their responsibilities within the research process, with both parties mediating and constructing meaning in different and possibly unrecognised ways. Researchers based in UK, US or Australian universities, for example, are likely to be bound by ethical principles, procedures and practices generated in those contexts, such as requiring individualised written consent. As has become apparent in previous chapters, such practices can influence how researchers negotiate access and develop relationships with respondents in cultures other than their own.

My attention here will be focused on one particular widespread myth about translation, which I hope this chapter will serve to debunk. The myth goes something like this: translating is a simple, unproblematic, almost mechanistic process of turning, say, an Urdu language text into an English language text and translators are neutral channels through which information merely passes (see Chapter 1 on how translation has been discussed in some fieldwork guides). If you are bilingual, not only can you operate this transparent transfer between languages effortlessly, but you can do so automatically, like a machine. We will see later how this view is sadly shared by many researchers, trained and untrained interpreters alike.

My aim in this chapter is to show how complex a phenomenon translation is and how it finds itself at the centre of all communicative and interpretative activities, including those that occur within the same language. The act of translation does rather special things to texts. For a start, it takes an original text out of the context in which it was written or spoken, and places it into another cultural context. Translation effectively changes the world of the original text. So when data, interview transcripts, descriptions of observations are translated, they are subjected to linguistic and cultural interpretations, the processes of which beg for close scrutiny.

In this investigation of translation within the field research context, then, I regard the translators of research data, not as neutral technicians who mechanically decode messages, but as mediators responsibly engaged in representing the values and belief systems of the researched. Such a position, as we will see below, has historically posed wide-ranging ethical issues. And something I shall be keen to explore throughout this chapter is the moral dimension of the translation process in research communities working across cultures. But before I do so, a worthwhile point of departure is to take a brief look at the questions that have concerned translators in the past, as well as the terminology they have generated, in order to gain a clearer understanding of how these ideas still influence current practice in the field research context.

Some terminology and a very brief history of translation studies[1]

Although it could be argued that human beings have for as long as they have spoken different languages felt the need to translate, it is only in the latter part of the twentieth century that a discipline has become established in universities known as 'Translation Studies'. The field has theorised itself around a cluster of concepts and key definitions which can help us to understand the main questions translators have tended to ask. For example, the text or utterance which is subjected to the translation process is referred to as the *Source Text* (ST). Similarly, the original language to be translated is known as the *Source Language* (SL). The language into which the text/utterance is translated is called the *Target Language* (TL) and the resulting text is referred to as the *Target Text* (TT). So Keats' poem *Ode to a Nightingale* represents the ST, and the language in which it is originally written, i.e. English, is the SL. The translation of *Ode to a Nightingale* (*Ode à un rossignol*) would represent the TT and French, being the language it is translated into here, would correspond to the TL. Such a translation would be referred to, following Roman Jakobson's (1959)[2] categories, as an *interlingual translation*, or *translation proper*, i.e. 'an interpretation of verbal signs by means of another language' (Jakobson, 2004: 139).[3] Interlingual translation is clearly what the field of translation studies is mainly about, although it is increasingly found that it is not easy to distinguish between a source text and its target, so that what we mean by 'translation' is challenged. Does, for example, the cultural adaptation of an interview transcript into English for a particular audience of PhD examiners (sometimes referred to as 'localisation') differ from translation proper? And if so, to what extent should it differ from translation proper? Are there

The role of the interpreter/translator **65**

ethical reasons why it should? And are there ethical reasons why it should not? Is it impossible to achieve 'translation proper'? One distinction which has sought to address these questions and has dominated and possibly stifled translation theory (see Steiner, 1998), is that between 'word for word' (literal) and 'sense for sense' (free) translation. The distinction can be traced as far back as Cicero (*De Oratore* I: 35 quoted in Lefevere, 1992: 23–4) who, on translating Greek speeches by Demosthenes, wrote:

> By giving Latin form to the text I had read, I could not only make use of the best expression in common usage with us, but I could also coin new expressions analogous to those used in Greek.

Cicero does something here which is still debated in contemporary translation theory: by giving it 'Latin form', he makes the Greek text appealing to the Roman audience, i.e. he adopts a 'sense for sense' approach, thus going against what would have been the traditional 'word for word' approach of Roman translators. And this traditional approach consisted, as Munday (2012: 30) observes, in literally replacing each individual word of the ST Greek 'with its closest grammatical equivalent in Latin' (Munday, 2012: 30). St Jerome (395 CE), the most famous translator of the Christian Bible and patron saint of translators, also took Cicero's advice to translate 'sense for sense'. But, as St Jerome himself found out, translating sense for sense was not without its drawbacks. Having translated Pope Epiphanius's letter to Bishop John of Jerusalem, St Jerome was attacked by adversaries for not translating 'word for word'. In a letter to his friend Pammachius, St Jerome defends his translation which 'shows the sense has not been changed in the least, nor anything added that counters orthodox doctrine' (St Jerome, 2004: 23), and in a statement which has now become the most famous and most often quoted by students of translation theory, he says:

> Indeed, I not only admit, but freely proclaim that in translation from the Greek – except in the case of Sacred Scripture where the very order of the words is a mystery – I render not word for word, but sense for sense.
>
> *(St Jerome, 2004: 23)*

The distinction between translating 'word for word' and 'sense for sense' may, as we have observed, contribute to a sense of stagnation in translation studies, but it is nonetheless foundational. It has been and is still debated by translation scholars and translators alike who have taken positions on either side of it, often giving it different names in an attempt to prescribe good translating. It is beyond the scope of this chapter to provide a comprehensive overview of the many ways in which this distinction has been developed, but some of them have had such an influence on how ideas have been disseminated in Europe that it is worth our while to look at them in detail. This will, I hope, allow me to shed more light on the choices that confront researchers when their data are subjected to the translation process and to

66 Alain Wolf

show how translators' ethical judgements are necessarily involved in opting for one of these two approaches: a 'literal' or a 'sense for sense' approach.

The 'sense for sense' approach: an ethical minefield

It is generally in order to avoid what they see as bad translating that translators have recommended a 'sense for sense' approach.[4] It is for this very reason that Horace in his *Ars Poetica* advises not to strive to render word for word like a faithful translator. The quality of a translation, then, hinges on the creativity of the translator who produces a translated poem from Greek, in the style of Horace. A 'sense for sense' approach in the aesthetic sphere can be accused of bad taste only if things go awry but, as St Jerome warned, when the translation of sacred texts is concerned, for example 'where the very order of words is a mystery' (St Jerome, 2004: 23), a 'sense for sense' approach has had devastating consequences both for the translators and the world which their translation affected. I am thinking here of two prominent translators in the period of the Protestant reformation, Etienne Dolet and Martin Luther, who stand out insofar as their translation strategies caused the former to be burnt at the stake, and the latter to change the cultural map of Northern European Christendom. Etienne Dolet translated the Platonic dialogue *Axiochus* in which Socrates, talking to Axiochus about death, reassured him that it was pointless to worry about death since it has no effect on the living or the dead. Death has no effect on Axiochus because he is still alive, and when he is dead, it will have no effect either: 'attendu que tu ne seras plus rien du tout' (Dolet, 1868) 'considering that you will be nothing at all'. It was the addition of these four fateful words 'plus rien du tout' (nothing at all) which cost Dolet his life. It was argued by the theological faculty of the Sorbonne that the phrase was not in the original Greek and was added by Dolet to imply that he did not believe in the immortality of the soul after death. It could also have been argued that the addition was simply a way of expressing the proposition 'you will not exist' in idiomatic French, i.e. 'sense for sense', and indeed Dolet was an ardent admirer of Cicero. But nonetheless, Dolet was arrested, tortured and finally burnt at the stake. As I often say to my translation theory students, translating sense for sense is a risky business.

Martin Luther's translation into German of St Paul's letter to the Romans (3: 28) in the New Testament also shows his adoption of a 'sense of sense' strategy. The original Greek below is followed by my own 'word for word' translation and the King James Version:

λογιζόμεθα	γὰρ	δικαιοῦσθαι	πίστει	ἄνθρωπον	χωρὶς
ἔργων	νόμου				
We believe	indeed	is justified	by faith	man	without
the works	of the law				

(Romans 3: 28, my interlinear translation)

Therefore, we conclude that man is justified by faith without the deeds of the law

(King James Version)

As is well known, Luther translated this as:

So halten wir nun dafür, daß der Mensch gerecht wird ohne des Gesetzes Werke, allein durch den Glauben

(Luther, 1984 as cited by Nord, 2001: 199)

(Therefore, we conclude that man is justified without the deeds of the law, *alone* by faith)

(Nord's (2001: 199) translation of Luther, 1984)

The word *allein* (alone) was added by Luther (it is nowhere in the Greek original), thus implying that the individual's belief in God was sufficient for salvation, and that good deeds sanctioned by the laws of the Church, i.e. the Roman Catholic Church, were not necessary. Such an implication sparked off a century-long controversy during the Reformation concerning the relationship between faith and Church tradition. Indeed, a great deal of harm was done by Luther's translation to entire communities of believers and Nord (2001), for example, acknowledges that the translation was the result of Luther's theological ideology. Luther countered this by saying that his aim was to produce the kind of German spoken by the people in the street, i.e. he was translating 'sense for sense'. Needless to say, the addition of *allein* in the translation, whether it is on the grounds of producing an idiomatic translation or to serve ideological interests, takes on an ethical dimension, especially when one considers the ravages that Martin Luther's words generated in Christian and, indeed, Hebraic communities, for years after they were published.

The 'word for word' approach: fidelity to the spirit and the foreign

It must be said here that except in didactic situations where it may be helpful to see how structures and words from one language match those of another (see for example my interlinear translation of Greek above), the 'word for word' strategy of translating is rarely used by translators. Instead, the focus is on the truthful representation of the source text and in the case of sacred texts, on fidelity to the word of God. This emphasis on the source text can take many forms. The German theologian Friedrich Schleiermacher (1768–1834), in a seminal lecture entitled 'On the different methods of translating' (Schleiermacher, 2004: 43), proposes that a translator who wishes to bring the original writer of a text and the foreign-language reader of that text together has two possibilities: 'Either the translator leaves the author in peace as much as possible and moves the reader toward him;

68 Alain Wolf

or he leaves the reader in peace as much as possible and moves the writer toward him' (Schleiermacher, 2004: 49). In the first case, which is Schleiermacher's preferred alternative, the translator 'imparts to the reader the same image, the same impression that he [the translator] himself received thanks to his knowledge of the original language of the work as it was written' (Schleiermacher, 2004: 49). In the second instance, the text is made palatable to the reader, thus disturbing the source text, and here we have echoes of the Ciceronian 'sense for sense' approach. Schleiermacher's influence in contemporary translation theory has been considerable. Venuti (1998), for example, has elaborated essentially on the same distinction, albeit with a different motivation[5], between approaches that 'domesticate' the source text rendering it palatable to the cultural values of a target audience (see Venuti's (1998) notion of 'domestication') and approaches that leave traces of the foreign in the target text so that readers are made to leave their familiar surroundings, sometimes painfully, to place themselves in a foreign land (see Venuti's (1998) notion of 'foreignisation'). Venuti has devoted some space to showing how the two translation strategies differ in practice. A domesticating translation is likely to be praised for a style that disturbs the receiving culture least. It is likely to minimise its foreignness, i.e. it makes the process of translation one that is invisible: place names, for example, may be replaced by those of the target culture, the style of the translated text may be 'inscribed with domestic intelligibilities and interests' (Venuti, 2004: 482), especially if the domestic sensibilities are those of a dominant American culture. In this respect, Venuti gives the example of Camus's novel 'L'Etranger' (1942) which, translated by Gilbert in 1946, is endowed with characteristic British sensibilities, i.e. a tone of formality which is not found in the French source text. Further, Venuti (1998) observes that the role of translation is frequently ignored or taken for granted in research contexts:

> The marginality of translation reaches even to educational institutions where it is manifested in a scandalous contradiction: on the one hand, an utter dependence on translated texts in curricula and research; on the other hand, a general tendency, in both teaching and publications, to elide the status of translated texts as translated, to treat them as texts originally written in the translating language.
>
> *(Venuti, 1998: 108)*

This is a point which we return to in Chapters 5 and 6. Giving the example of Anscombe's translation of Wittgenstein's *Denn die philosophischen Probleme entstehen, wenn dir Sprache feiert* as 'For philosophical problems arise when language goes on holiday' (the alternative is: 'language idles'), Venuti (1998: 108) observes that 'no English translation can ever simply communicate Wittgenstein's German text without simultaneously inscribing it with English-language forms that destabilize and reconstitute his philosophy'.

A foreignising translation, by contrast, aims, as we have seen, 'to restore or preserve the foreignness of the foreign text' (Venuti, 2004: 483). This distinction

The role of the interpreter/translator **69**

between domestication and foreignisation is well known, but less often referred to by students of translation theory is the consequence of this willingness to expose the reader to foreignness.[6] Such a shift away from the ethnocentrism of dominant receiving cultures is effectively perceived by Venuti to be the necessary condition for a truly ethical position in translation. It is this ethical dimension of the translation process that I wish to examine in more detail in the context of multilingual research.

Translating in the research context

I would now like to turn primarily to an analysis of a few examples taken from the literature and my own interviews with research students at two UK universities. From the data I have analysed, four areas emerge which raise fundamental issues concerning the translation process in fieldwork. Many researchers report having difficulties with translating the concepts used in their research tools, e.g. their interview schedules and questionnaires as well as their data, and this is an area which is well worth exploring from the perspective of the distinctions I have just outlined. Also reported is the problem of particular grammatical forms which convey different meanings across languages, such as pronouns and forms of address, for example. Thirdly, code-switching, i.e. switching between languages during an interaction (see definition below), is a very frequent occurrence in the context of doing research that involves multilingual data and this will be explored in some detail, here and in subsequent chapters in relation to students' experiences of fieldwork. Finally, I will address the ethical implications of conducting research across languages, looking specifically at the researcher's and the participants' ideological stance in the research process.

Conceptual meaning

One of the thorniest problems which faces researchers writing up an article in a language that is different from that of the research is to find what is sometimes called 'conceptual equivalence' (see Birbili, 2000) between the source texts and the target texts. Many researchers have, as Robinson-Pant (2005: 133) has already observed, tried to find ways to resolve the problem of conveying the meaning of words that do not have an equivalent in English (see also the examples given by students in Chapter 5). In this respect, Birbili (2000), who has an interest in the training of social researchers, notes that connotations do not easily transfer into the language of the write-up. She gives the example of the phrase 'civil service mentality' which in English has connotations of people who are 'very observant of their rights' (Moses and Ramsden, 1992: 102, cited in Birbili, 2000) whereas in Greek, the phrase has extremely negative connotations which would have to be made explicit for an English reader. We came across the need for explicitation by means of explicatures in Chapter 2 and it is worthwhile here to look at the phenomenon in the context of translation. Explicitation is a strategy by which an entity (often cultural, though not always) in the source language but not present in the target language has to be made explicit. For example, the word 'owl' which denotes a nocturnal bird has, in Western culture, connotations of wisdom. Indeed, it is often portrayed wearing a mortar board. The same bird, however, has negative connotations of death in Middle Eastern cultures which would have to be made explicit to a reader from another cultural context. Many researchers (Sechrest et al., 1972; Brislin et al., 1973; Warwick and Osherson, 1973) advise that giving access to comparability of connotative meaning can occur only if the researcher (or the translator) has not only competent language skills but also, as Frey (1970) puts it, an 'intimate knowledge of the culture'. I would go further here. Since language proficiency cannot so easily be distinguished from knowledge of culture, a translator could not properly be called linguistically competent if he/she did not have knowledge of the devices that encode cultural differences, i.e. connotative and affective meaning.

Another example concerning how to translate certain concepts or phrases was mentioned by one of my PhD interviewees, Ali Alsohaibani, who carried out research on the use of religious utterances in Arabic. Translating kinship terms, he found, was particularly problematic:

> For example, the word 'uncle' in English can refer to 'mother's brother' or 'father's brother', but in Arabic they are referred to differently. In Arabic, 'father's brother' is referred to as عم *amm* and 'mother's brother' as خال *khal*. In the same vein, the word 'aunt' in English means 'mother's sister' or 'father's sister', while in Arabic they are خالة *khalah* or عمة *ammah* respectively. However, these kinship terms can also be used as honorifics to show more respect to elderly people, which may stem from religious beliefs and moral codes, or to express rapport and intimacy with friends. It is the latter use that I met in my research. When a participant addresses a friend with 'uncle', I felt compelled to explicate this in brackets and to explain in more detail in a footnote.
>
> *(Ali Alsohaibani, interview notes, 2015)*

What Ali added was that in the patriarchal society he was working in, the uncle on the father's side was often regarded as more important and worthy of more respect than the mother's brother. The important point that can be made here as far as gaining conceptual equivalence is concerned is that responsibilities lie with both researchers and translators. Researchers have a responsibility for explaining to interpreters/translators the concepts they work with, as this leads to the kind of useful dialogue which makes the relationship between researcher and interpreter possible. The interpreters/translators need to be fully cognisant of the various connotations that such concepts convey across the languages concerned. This of course involves a great deal of linguistic knowledge, as we have just seen, in the areas of connotative and affective meaning. In practice, wherever a connotation or a lack of information is noticed by a translator, an addition/explicitation

The role of the interpreter/translator **71**

is needed. In a country, for example, where it is not necessarily known who the prime minister of the UK is, it would not be enough in a translation to leave the following utterance unaltered: 'David Cameron has talked about his idea of the "Big Society"'. An explicitation would be needed by means of stating who David Cameron is, i.e. David Cameron, the prime minister of the UK, has talked about his idea of the 'Big Society'. The source language word can also be quoted in the original language with a gloss explaining the context in which the word is used and the attending connotations. This was the strategy used by Tanu, one of the researchers I interviewed. Tanu was looking at how South Asian migrant parents were engaging with their children's schooling in the UK. After interviewing one of the participants in the project, Tanu realised that one of the expressions used in Hindi, *alag nahi lagta*, could mean different things in English in the given context:

> At one point, I asked the mother how she felt about the head teacher's support and she said: '*alag nahi lagta*'. The literal translation of the word would be: 'don't feel different'. However, in the context of attempting to engage in school activities while simultaneously adapting to the British system of school education, this phrase means more than what it can be translated as. This could mean that she didn't feel excluded from the community in general or that she was made to feel included in the school's environment. Therefore, even though I explained the possible ways of looking at the phrase, I mentioned the term in Hindi in my research report.
>
> *(Tanu, interview notes, 2014)*

Keeping the item in the original language, which 'foreignises' the translation, not only preserves the traces of the original interaction but also, as we have seen, allows the translator to indicate that there is ambiguity of meaning in the data with the resulting possibility of many interpretations (as we will see in the examples given by students in Chapter 5). Indeed, rich communication often involves uncertainty and ambiguity (see Chapter 2 on context in this volume) and it is important in a research context that they are flagged up rather than erased in a fluent but unfaithful translation. Tanu concluded:

> There were loads of times when I had those uncertainties and the fear that translation would lose the meaning, so I kept the item in the original language and would explain the context.
>
> *(Tanu, interview notes, 2014)*

The kind of explicitation that we have just outlined at semantic/conceptual level also occurs in grammar, i.e. languages use different grammatical forms to convey meaning. The lack of grammatical equivalence is as important as the difficulties presented by a lack of equivalence at other levels, and I shall explain why in the section below.

72 Alain Wolf

Form–function pairings across languages

Languages, as I have just observed, use different grammatical devices (forms) to convey different types of conceptual meaning (functions). A lack of form–function pairing between two languages can be very subtle and difficult to detect, especially when grammatical forms exist in both languages, but encode different functions. Let us take as an example the third person singular conditional form of the verb 'to be' in French '*il serait*' which literally translated into English is 'he would be'. As I have observed in an earlier monograph (Wolf, 2005: 43), the conditional form '*il serait*' in French expresses the meaning (function) of 'hearsay' in the context of news reporting. So if a journalist used the form '*il serait*' as in: '*Le président serait malade*', he/she would convey the function of 'hearsay', i.e. that the president has been reported as being ill. The conditional form does exist in English, but a translator who produced 'The president would be ill' would not render the function of 'hearsay' which can be encoded in English only by the use of the adverbials: 'Reportedly/Allegedly, the president is ill'. This kind of obligatory 'modulation' is common in translation, but it requires a very high level of grammatical proficiency on the part of translators. Indeed, the form–function pairing I have described here is a major 'explanatory factor of language acquisition' (Wolf, 2005: 44). Klein (1990: 227), in a seminal article 'A theory of language acquisition is not easy', lists three very important components of language proficiency, namely that in order to communicate, learners, and here I include translators, need (1) to be able to find the appropriate form to express a given function, (2) to realise that there is no one-to-one relationship between form and function, and (3) to know that maximal communication involves using the full range of functions possible for a given form. An example which illustrates the importance of using the full range of functions possible for a given form is given by Pillay (1995: 292) in a case study on the English language curriculum programme in Malaysia[7]. In the comment below, she shows that the translation of the Bahasa Malay form *kita*, in her interview transcripts, involves a range of referential functions:

> Another problem I encountered was in translation. The word 'I' was seldom used in the interviews. One tended to think of oneself as, of, or in a group. This is because the concept of the individual and 'individualism' as understood in Western philosophy is not part of the Malay culture. So in my interviews, interviewees used the word *kita* and I had to decide which sense of the word *kita* was being used – I or we. Also, as I was an educationalist myself, sometimes the word *kita* was used to include me as part of the group.
> *(Pillay 1995: 292)*

Pillay shows here that translation involves a high level competence of language form–function pairings on the part of the translator. The form *kita* changed its function depending on the relationships between participants, and it was the researcher's knowledge of the cultural context and how her respondents interacted with her which enabled her to translate the form competently into English.

Ali, to whom I referred earlier, also reported that the translation of pronouns in forms of address was particularly important. He reported feeling at a loss about the translation of terms of address:

> In Saudi culture, interlocutors sometimes address each other in the daily speech context using entities other than their names. They use a phrase of two components: *um* or *abu*, which means 'mother of' and 'father of', respectively, and the name of the elder son or, sometimes, the elder daughter. For example, people address me as '*abu* Abdulrahman' ('father of Abdulrahman'), as my elder son's name is Abdulrahman'.
>
> *(Ali Alsohaibani, interview notes, 2015)*

Curiously, Ali remarks, this form of address can be used with speakers who are not fathers or mothers at all. The question that he asked himself, therefore, was:

> Should I translate the phrase 'son of' as a name, and the reader would not notice the way that interlocutors communicate using such forms of address? Conversely, should I translate the phrase literally as 'father of X', which may cause confusion to the readers and cause them to think that the addressee is a parent although s/he may not be? If I used the former approach, this would lead the reader to miss the function and illocutionary force of politeness motivation in using such a form, to show more respect and intimacy towards the addressee. On the other hand, employing the latter approach may mislead the reader.
>
> *(Ali Alsohaibani, interview notes, 2015)*

Ali also referred to the use of the plural pronoun in Arabic as in the address:

> *wesh akhbarakum?*
>
> What news-PRN: PL (Pronoun: Plural)
>
> What is your news?
>
> *(Ali Alsohaibani, interview notes, 2015)*

Here Ali observes:

> The domesticated translation 'what is your news?' does not show that the speaker used the plural pronoun when addressing the hearer, while the interlinear translation clearly reveals this. When an Arabic speaker addresses another person with a plural pronoun, as in the above example, s/he actually asks about the addressee and their family. Hence, when the addressee responds with 'we are all fine', this may confuse the reader if s/he is not

given sufficient linguistic context in addition to the cultural context. Such an inquiry about one's family as a greeting speech act reflects the collectivistic cultural context, which perceives the individual as part of an in-group and acknowledges the religious context of the high status of parents in Islam.

(Ali Alsohaibani, interview notes, 2015)

Indeed, as Robinson-Pant (2005: 134) recognises, making the assumptions in the source language explicit in English is an 'extra responsibility' for the student or researcher working in another language. In this case, omitting the plural reference of the pronoun in a one-to-one form of address involves ethical and religious considerations of respect and status to which I will return in the section below. For the time being, I advise the researcher to reflect on the form–function pairing as the interviewees above have done and to find as many ways as are possible without impeding meaning and coherence to give readers access to cultural differences. So just using a domesticated version of a name, or a domesticated rendering of a form of address would risk losing the force of politeness and respect and would be, as Ali realises, an ill-advised translation strategy. His preferred strategy is a combination of a sense for sense approach for the sake of preserving the illocutionary force and elegance of the original utterance and a foreignising approach which gives readers access to the source text:

A sense-to-sense translation does not always enable the reader to trace the beliefs and values represented in the interlocutors' discourse. As a translator, I will likely find it more efficient to employ a foreignising approach as well and explain to the reader the sociocultural context of my research. This explication can be in a footnote or in-text. In my case, and since my research is a sociopragmatic study concerning the interaction between culture (particularly religion) and language use, it is sometimes more appropriate to include the explication in my discussion, as it will show the social and religious references of language.

(Ali Alsohaibani, interview notes, 2015)

Code-switching

Code-switching is a form of borrowing between languages and is described by sociolinguists as a communicative switch in which bilinguals or multilinguals are able to introduce a particular topic in a different language from the one they started using. The reasons for doing this have been extensively researched into (see Hoffman, 1991; Heller, 1988; Miller, 1983; Haugen, 1987; Rampton, 1995; Wolf, 2015) and include, for instance, showing intimacy with other bilinguals (Hoffman, 1991), and managing conflict through humour (Heller, 1988). The first example I would like to explore here comes from Bradby's (2002) studies of wellbeing among Glasgow Punjabis. These studies are an eloquent illustration of how code-switching is a 'means through which identities and support networks

The role of the interpreter/translator **75**

are negotiated and affirmed'. So, for example, speakers could avoid being identified as Pakistani/Muslims by employing 'busy' as in *maiñ kaafi busy hun*, instead of the Urdu term *mushroof*. Similarly, they could avoid drawing attention to their Indian/Sikh or Hindu identity by using 'busy' instead of the Hindi term *mushgool* (as in *maiñ mushroof/mushgool hun*).

One of my interviewees, Joanna Nair, found that code-switching revealed yet other aspects of her participants' identities. Some would start the interview in Nepalese but code-switch into English to show off their knowledge of another language. Indeed, English has such a dominant status that speakers created English expressions not used in English-speaking countries. Such an expression frequently encountered by Joanna was 'out-knowledge' which in the context in which she worked referred to any knowledge acquired outside the rural village in which her participants lived. The expression 'climate change' was also used to refer to the seasonal change in weather, the local word for climate and season being the same.

> And so a fair-weather road which flooded during the monsoon season was described as being impassable because of 'climate change'.
>
> *(Joanna Nair, interview notes, 2014)*

Code-switching then is used by speakers for the purpose of conveying an identity with which they feel comfortable. This identity usually depends on their perception of the status of the language they switch into. Joanna explained to me that one of her participants switched into Hindi which he perceived to be a higher-status language than Nepali:

> When I asked what he considered necessary for his personal well-being, contentment, he used Indira Gandhi's slogan, using the exact Hindi words rather than expressing the idea in Nepali: *roti, kapada aur makkan*. This literally means 'chapati, clothes and building/house' and connotes 'bread, clothes and house', i.e. 'food, clothing and shelter'.
>
> *(Joanna Nair, interview notes, 2014)*

This was to demonstrate not only that he had a certain level of education, but also that code-switching transcends the monocultural self (see Wolf, 2015) and gives access to a world beyond that of an oppressed minority. On another occasion, the same man again switching into Hindi from Nepali talked about how grateful he was to the UK:

> He expressed his gratitude to the UK (the word *bilayat* can also mean 'England' in the sense it is used by some in English, conflating the UK and England) again using Hindi, by saying, '*Bilayat ka maine bahut namak khaya hain*'. Literally, this means, 'England/UK of I have a lot of salt eaten' i.e. 'I've eaten a lot of UK salt', meaning 'I have been a recipient of UK's munificence'.
>
> *(Joanna Nair, interview notes, 2014)*

76 Alain Wolf

This kind of navigation across languages can be a central, compelling and creative aspect of multilingual research. The outcome of code-switching is a form of hybridisation, two languages coming into contact with each other, which has the effect of liberating the speaker from the monocultural language self. This echoes Bhabha's (2011: 20) call for translations that 'creat[e] the conditions through which newness comes into the world'. The purpose is, he argues (ibid.: 40), citing Rudolf Pannwitz, 'not to turn Hindi, Greek, English into German [but] instead to turn German into Hindi, Greek, English'.

Domesticated vs. foreignised translations in research

We saw earlier (see the section on a 'word for word approach') how a foreignising translation can help to restore the foreignness of the source text (Venuti, 2004: 483) and contribute to a shift away from ethnocentrism. This willingness to expose the reader to foreignness was perceived as the necessary condition for a truly ethical position in translation. In a research context, it is also often the first step towards restoring the authentic nature of the data, thus giving a more loyal and ethical representation of the original message. The need for foreignised translations in research is illustrated by a very interesting study of transcultural nursing (Wong and Poon, 2010). Here, three translators were given the task of translating an interview transcript from Cantonese into English. The researched had given his views on gender role within marriage. When he used the Chinese idiom 相夫教子, which is a common expression used by Chinese people who have conservative views on gender roles, three different translations were produced. Two of the translators found a domesticated equivalent for the idiom, translating it as (translator 1): I would want to marry a woman who 'looks after the husband and kids' and (translator 2): I would want to marry a woman 'tending to the needs of the husbands and bringing up the kids'. The third translator opted for a foreignised way of translating the Chinese idiom 相夫教子 as: My ideal 'female will be home the whole day, eh, taking care of household chores, "facing the husband and teaching the children"'. The translation of the third translator alerted the researchers 'to explore further into other meanings beyond the expression "looking after the husband and the kids"' (Wong and Poon, 2010: 154). After consulting the Cantonese idiom more closely they found that it contained historical elements which were of significance to the interview. The word 相 represented the title of 'the adviser to the emperor' in historical China and while the adviser's role was to give the emperor information on how to act, the adviser had no 'real' power, and decisions were made by the emperor. The use of the idiom by the researched then implied that women play the role of advisers to their husbands, but do not have any real decision-making power. The researchers later consulted the researched and he confirmed that he did mean that women have no decision-making power and that husbands have the final say. The important point about the idiomatic and domesticated translations of the kind produced by the first two translators is that their apparent fluency in English concealed relevant information in the analysis of data. As the researchers concluded (Wong and Poon, 2010: 155), the 'word for word' translation allowed them 'to further examine the historical, social, and political contexts of a dominant discourse on gender relations among Chinese people'.

The ethics of mediated communication

The ethics involved in communicating through a translator have much to do with representing the source text or person, the foreign Other, justly. This interest in anything to do with ethics in translation is shown in the proliferation of articles on the subject. In a special issue of the journal *The Translator*, Pym (2001: 129) proclaimed the return of 'Translation Studies' to ethics, arguing that this is now a 'very general social trend' related to decision-making beyond the individual and national level. While Pym admits that few translation scholars agree about how to define the field of ethics, he provides a discussion of Chesterman's (2001) proposal for a 'hieronymic'[8] oath based on five ways of talking about ethics in translation: the ethics of representation, the ethics of service, the ethics of communication, a norm-based ethics and the ethics of commitment. I would like to focus on three of these categories here as I have found them to be a useful starting point from which to evaluate current debates in research about the role of ethics in translation. First, the *ethics of representation* concern the responsibility of the translator in representing the source text or the source author. Representation can also be understood in terms of the translation rendering a service to a client, the *ethics of service*. This is Christiane Nord's (2001) understanding of ethics as a translator's loyalty to authors' communicative intentions and their readership. Here it is easy to see how representation of the Other goes beyond mere textual representation. This emphasis on treating the foreign text as a person, i.e. focusing on a 'relation with people rather than texts' (Pym, 2001: 133), Chesterman refers to as the *ethics of communication*. This ethics of *alterity* (Pym, 2001: 133) is seen by many (Gouanvic, 2001; Laygues, 2001; Nord, 2001) as going beyond a notion of ethics as a professional code. Pym (2001: 136) thus derives four ethical principles from the articles in the special issue of *The Translator*:

1. The concerns of linguistic fidelity from target text to source text are broadened to include higher levels of fidelity between individuals.
2. Ethics is a 'contextual question dependent on practice in specific cultural locations and situational determinants'.
3. The researcher's positionality is taken into consideration.
4. There is a greater emphasis on universal values and general causes.

These principles which Pym (2001) uses as concluding remarks to his article beg to be developed, I think, in a discussion of what it means to take an ethical stance with regard to translation in a research context.

78 Alain Wolf

Being faithful to people rather than to utterances: principles 1 and 2

What strikes me as particularly interesting is that translators' concern with representing people rather than texts (see principle 1) sometimes requires that strict fidelity to content be abandoned in favour of faithfulness to individuals. An example which usually leaves a lasting impression on my students of 'Translation Theory' is that provided by Clifford (2004) in his attempt to illustrate the failings of the conduit model of interpreter training.[9] A female patient is described as having recently moved to Canada with almost no English. A few months after arriving in Canada, her husband becomes ill with what he tells his wife is leukaemia and he passes away three weeks before the medical appointment, which required an interpreter. A short time after her husband's death, the patient is told that her husband had been having sexual contact with other men, and that he had died of an HIV-related disease. At a previous meeting, a blood sample was taken from her, and when she arrives at the surgery waiting for results, she is in a state of bewilderment and fear. As the physician enters, the interpreter is sitting with the patient. The physician sits down at his desk, picks up a printout and abruptly says: 'Yup, you're positive'. The interpreter at that point feels that if she conveys the physician's words directly, the patient may enter a state of shock. She then alters the physician's choice of words and produces: 'I'm afraid that the tests are positive'. Clifford (2004: 91) notes that when the interpreter told her trainer what kind of strategy she had adopted she was severely reprimanded by him. He maintained that the interpreter 'should never do anything other than repeat, in the other language, everything said that is said, exactly as it is said. To do otherwise, he continued, is not ethical.' (cited in Clifford, 2004)

Clifford (2004) is critical of the conduit model of interpreter training which is used in conference interpreting where interpreters have very little opportunity to engage with the individuals for whom they interpret (Wadensjö, 1998). The conduit model can be seen as a reaction to the 'helper model' used in interpreting for the deaf, where friends and relatives made decisions, sometimes unwelcome, on behalf of the deaf. The helper model had such problematic consequences that the personal involvement of the helper was rejected so that the interpretation remained neutral and 'uninvolved' (Clifford, 2004: 94). The conduit model is also based on older theories of communication, according to which a message is encoded by a speaker and decoded by a hearer without taking non-linguistic contextual factors into consideration. Clifford is critical of fidelity to the original message and claims that community interpreting is better suited to an 'ethics of communication' (see Chesterman, 2001) which stresses the needs of the Other and concerns itself not so much with fidelity as with understanding. The interpreter's working relationship with the healthcare practitioners is looked at from the perspective of developing trust and of interpreters acting as cultural informants.

These concerns spring from a deeply felt concern for the Other. Indeed, I have found that an understanding of this example from an ethical perspective which involves theological considerations sometimes yields insights which the approaches of contemporary writings do not. Responding to the Other in the theological sense is not an empty phrase. It is to be aware of our neighbour's nature as being the image of God. And it is to be aware that we are commanded to love (the primary command to love one's neighbour as oneself) that image (see Tillich, 1963). In other words, what the interpreter did by attenuating the physician's message was to respond with her whole person to the complexity of the situation, adapting her response to a context that required her to suspend the professional rule of the 'conduit model' precisely because in this event, it had become unserviceable. This kind of moral situationism where professional codes of fidelity to the message are suspended in favour of the primary command is central to any discussion of the role of ethics in translated communication. As Joanna Nair explained to me, she, too, was confronted by the demand to suspend fidelity on occasions when it was unclear what the source utterance was meant to convey:

> The secretary of the village Development Committee, who was in a very powerful position, used an expression which I could have translated as 'a robust programme'. I resisted using the word 'robust' because of the associations the word has in the UK with political jargon. But I don't think he meant it like that, so to translate the expression he used with the word 'robust' might make the reader think he was a phoney. And that would be unfair. This is a debate I had with myself.
>
> *(Joanna Nair, interview notes, 2014)*

This higher level of fidelity for the individual rather than the text in this instance does not mean a wholesale rejection of the source text. On occasions, however, translation is unethical because, as we shall see below, translators knowingly betray the source text for the sake of conveying their own ideology.

Faithfulness to the source text: resisting attempts to domesticate for ideological purposes – researcher's positionality (principle 3)

Recent contributions to discussions of ethics have perceived the morality of a translation as a kind of compensation 'for a defect in the translating language and literature, in the translating culture' (Venuti, 2004: 483), i.e. when the target translating language wilfully domesticates the source in an attempt to erase its sensibilities. The kind of moral compensation I am thinking of was illustrated quite frequently by the researchers I interviewed. One of my interviewees, Sylvia Woolfe, conducted research in how museums translated the labels of the artefacts presented to the public. Her original hypothesis was that:

> Anglo-American museums influenced other countries in their use of interactive texts, inclusive language, a style that engages the public.
>
> *(Sylvia Woolfe, interview, 2015)*

80 Alain Wolf

On finding out that this was not the case, she reported a temptation:

> I was tempted to incorporate the source text in my research, the temptation is for it to tell you what you'd like to hear. Sometimes you have to be very respectful of what is actually in the text and let it speak instead of letting your wishes speak. It's quite a temptation; there are subtleties in language and a little alteration and you could have something quite different.
>
> *(Sylvia Woolfe, interview, 2015)*

This example speaks volumes about the importance of being able to identify not only the ideological stance of an interpreter/translator but one's own ideological preferences and assumptions as a translator of one's own data. In this case, the possibility of a moral defect in the translated text of the PhD research compelled the researcher to respond with her whole person to the complexity of the situation. Sylvia's positioning of herself within that particular context is manifest here. Her in-depth knowledge of the source language and its nuances enabled her to realise that something could be amiss if she translated it in a particular way. Her intervention, however, was an attempt to ensure fidelity to her source utterance in order to preserve the perceived needs of the Other – and by Other here I mean the museum translators.

Some important 'tips' for translation in fieldwork and concluding remarks

Although I am often called upon by researchers and students to give a simple list of techniques for translation-related problems, I have been reluctant in the past to do so. This is because there are no easy 'techniques' to overcome some of the questions I have addressed in this chapter. Also, the advice given to researchers can sometimes be misleading, arising out of a lack of training in languages and, more specifically, in translation studies. One such piece of advice is given in Birbili's (2000) article on translating from one language into another. The technique of back translation is put forward as 'one of the most common techniques used in cross-cultural research'. This involves 'looking for equivalents through (a) the translation of items from the source language to the target language, (b) independent translation of these back into the source language, and (c) 'the comparison of the two versions of items in the source language until ambiguities or discrepancies in meaning are clarified or removed' (Ercikan, 1998: 545; Warwick and Osherson, 1973: 30). This tortuous exercise is based on at least two unexamined assumptions, namely that translators can and should produce mechanically equivalent renderings of a source text, and that 'discrepancies in meaning' are an indication that something has gone wrong. But as we have seen, when two translations of the same text are produced by two translators independently, they can never be 'equivalent' inasmuch as they necessarily convey different facets of interpretation which it would be wrong to call 'discrepancies'. When translated back into the source language, the two translated texts would obviously display 'discrepancies' at all levels, but this would not be an indication that the translators had misinterpreted the original text. The technique also raises the question of who, in the final analysis, is the judge of the 'discrepancies'. And supposing that such an individual exists who can distinguish between a 'correct' and an 'incorrect' translation, why not then use him or her in the first place?

Much more important, as Bradby (2002: 852) advises, is that a good working relationship between the researcher and the interpreter be established. This cannot be prescribed but is more likely to happen if the relationship is collaborative, i.e. if the researcher perceives the interpreter's role as 'actively participative'. What this means is that the interpreter has to take responsibility for the fact that his/her translation is a reading of a particular situation providing rich details about participants' motivations and intentions rather than a simple matter of transferring information from one language to another. This kind of consultation with bilinguals and teams of translators and researchers is much more useful than the type of exercise I have just described. The King James Bible was arrived at through the collaborative efforts of a team of translators and has become one of the literary masterpieces of English literature. Translation is often best done by means of collaborative discussions between translators with researchers explaining what kinds of theoretical frameworks they are dealing with. This is in the end the strategy Birbili (2000) rightly advises, i.e. a joint involvement by researchers and translators from the language backgrounds concerned in the construction of the research instrument and the research design. In this respect, Joanna Nair reported that she would have missed important items in interviews if one of her interpreters, a close relative, had not been at her side ready to intervene when he felt that she had misinterpreted an utterance:

> A man I interviewed used the 'garden' as a metaphor, comparing his community to an unspoilt garden and how flowers could be made to blossom. And because there'd been a big farming project there, I misinterpreted what he was saying, thinking he was referring to development and farming. But actually he was developing this metaphor to emphasise the idea of well-being in the community. But my interpreter put me right.
>
> *(Joanna Nair, interview, 2014)*

Pre-testing interview schedules or questionnaires with the target culture is also an efficient way of avoiding translation problems, as we saw earlier. In this respect, the researched can be called upon to give an interpretation of the meaning of the test items.

Researchers then need to provide a clear and transparent account of the context in which translation occurred and be prepared to justify the strategies they used during the process of translation. Does the translation represent the Other and avoid an ethnocentric bias? In what way is the vulnerable Other represented? And when the research involves the use of translators/interpreters, information

82 Alain Wolf

about who was used, i.e. untrained local community interpreters or professional translators, and their role in the research process need to be included.

Naturally, none of these 'tips' are in themselves sufficient to guarantee against the production of data that once translated are less than valid. It is the combination of all these strategies coupled with a sustained attention to language issues which will guard against the pitfalls of unreflective intercultural research.

As we have seen in this chapter, the translation process and issues of fidelity can crucially affect not only the analysis of data but also the relationship between the researcher and the researched. In the following reflective piece, Gina Lontoc considers the issues that confronted her as she observed English language classes with multilingual research participants in the Philippines. As Gina observes, relying on a translator meant 'not only translating the words per se but also keeping the meaning and authenticity of the original text'. Her analysis of classroom transcripts is an illuminating example of how difficult it is, in her words, 'to capture the freshness of interaction, and how I can translate into writing the reality of the actual conversations'.

Box 4

Questions for further reflection

- What writers in 'Translation Studies' have influenced my translation strategies?
- How did I decide on a choice of translation strategies, e.g. foreignisation? domestication?
- Did I use a translator/interpreter to translate the data, or did I act as a translator myself: how will this affect data collection and the analysis of findings?
- Did I represent the source data justly/ethically?
- How will the 'foreignness' of the source data be preserved in the final published text?
- Have I used 'explicitation' as a translation strategy, and how?
- Have I come across examples of connotations and form–function pairings which were difficult to translate into the target language?
- Have I encountered examples of code-switching in my data and how have I preserved it in the final published text?
- Have I been faithful to what the research participants implied rather than to what they said?
- Does my translation represent the Other?
- What form of dissemination will I conduct and will it take translation issues into account?

Notes

1 This is not meant to be a history of translation. A number of writers have done this well in the past and for further reading, it would be advisable to consult, for example, Jeremy Munday's (2012) *Introducing Translation Studies* or Lawrence Venuti's (2004) *The Translation Studies Reader*.
2 Roman Jakobson wrote a seminal paper 'On linguistic aspects of translation' (1959) which is essential reading for anyone intending to find out more about the interface between linguistics and translation.
3 The other two ways in which a verbal sign can be interpreted are: *Intralingual translation:* 'an interpretation of verbal signs by means of other signs of the same language' and *Intersemiotic translation* or *transmutation:* 'an interpretation of verbal signs by means of signs of nonverbal sign systems' (Jakobson, 2004: 139)
4 It must be said that the literal approach is also advocated for the same reason, albeit with the added concern of faithfulness to the source text.
5 Whilst Schleiermacher wanted translated texts to keep traces of the German source in order to give readers a chance to appreciate German culture at a time of rising German nationalism, Venuti's foreignisation approach is intended to apply to all translated texts irrespective of their source.
6 This could be seen as offering opportunities for intercultural learning; see Chapter 6.
7 This study (Pillay, 1995) was carried out as part of a PhD at the University of East Anglia and further details can be found in Robinson-Pant's (2005: 134) *Cross-Cultural Perspectives on Educational Research*.
8 Chesterman uses the word 'hieronymic' to refer to St Jerome's Latin name: Eusebius Sophronius Hieronymus.
9 The conduit model of interpreter training perceives the interpreter as a mechanical filter through whom information is intended to pass unaltered, i.e. the interpreter should just repeat in the other language everything that has been said, including obscenities, for example, exactly as it is said. The interpreter should never report, i.e. use the third person, but always speak in the first person.

84 Gina Lontoc

Reflective piece 4: Transcribing language, translating culture? Transcription convention and issues on translation in educational research

Gina Lontoc

My study explores how teaching and feedback practices in ESL (English as a Second Language) writing (re)construct students' linguistic, social, and cultural identities in the context of state schools in the Philippines. The three case studies in my research represent the three biggest state secondary schools in the three major islands of my country – Luzon, Visayas and Mindanao.

For my data collection, I observed English classes and conducted informal interviews with teachers. I also collected students' written essays and conducted individual sessions with them to record their think-aloud protocols. This technique provided me with insights into how they responded to the feedback of their teachers.

The process of transcription: convention and issues

To capture the idiosyncrasies of utterances, transcription should be taken as a systematic process. Failure to do so will result in simple 'transcribed data'. This evokes several concerns that I addressed in my study, such as the organisation on the page, the balance between efficiency and accuracy, the paralinguistic and non-verbal behaviour to be included, along with the conventions to symbolise them, and the basic units of transcript such as utterances, turns, tone units, and so on.

According to Lapadat and Lindsay (1999: 66), choices about transcription enact the theories researchers hold 'because the process of collecting, transforming, and analysing language interaction data are in themselves theoretical, they have implications for the interpretations and theories that can be drawn from the data'. Thus, in transcribing the conversations, I incorporated the transcription conventions formulated by Ochs (1979) and Ochs, et al. (1996).

The sample transcript that follows illustrates how paralinguistic cues such as sighs, laughs, whispers, pauses, intonations, inflections, audible breathing, overlapping of utterances, etc. add more meaning to intentions that the participants convey. For instance, the underlined words in lines 1–4 indicate the importance that Paul attached to the words as he gives more emphasis to them. This is combined with rising in intonation (*kami* ↑) and a sudden rise in intonation in some words (*kami?* and *at?*) which suggest a greater degree of preference to the concept.

I hold the view that standard orthography cannot capture the idiosyncrasies of these instances, for speakers' intention is foregrounded not only in pauses but also in the lengths of these pauses, not just on utterances but specifically on the overlapping of these utterances, not just on intonation but in every audible breathing the participants produce.

```
 1 Paul: kami↑ (.) ay matalino↓ dahil marunong kami? umintindi↓
 2       ng ininglish↓ ay (.)
 3       ((students laugh))
 4       english↑ at? (.) tagalog↓ at?
 5       (Tr: We are intelligent because we can understand English,
 6          Tagalog, and . . .)
 7 Beth: SPANISH↑
 8 Paul: Spanish↓
 9 Beth: BISAYA↑
10 Paul: at? sa bisa[ya]↓ (Tr: and Bisaya)
```

FIGURE 4.1 Sample transcript

Translation: of words, meaning, or culture?

In Visayas and Mindanao, my research participants are multilinguals having Cebuano – a language I am not familiar with – as their lingua franca. This creates the need for me to have someone who can translate to English some of the sentences which contain Cebuano words. However, translation entails not only translating the words per se but also keeping the meaning and authenticity of the original text. Nikander (2008) points out that there is a range of practical and ideological concerns involved in translating data extracts. In this direction, I face a constant battle in deciding which aspects of interaction I should focus on, how the transcription convention I follow can capture the freshness of interaction, and how I can translate into writing the reality of the actual conversations.

The excerpts that follow are from my transcription of a classroom observation in Visayas. The three sample transcripts are representations of challenges I confront as I translate utterances from Cebuano to English.

Because teachers code-switched during class discussions, I decided to look for someone to translate Cebuano to English. I never thought that translating short utterances would be complicated due to considerations of culture as reflected by various shades of meaning. In some instances, there might be a need to witness the actual situation where the conversation took place. This is illustrated in the following extract:

```
S: Unsa man photocopy, Sir?
T: Okay, I will leave one copy then just photocopy for the
   person. I will leave one copy, Joan. Then guys have a
   photocopy so that you have a copy of the poem as well as
   the song. Are we clear?
S: Yes we are.
```

FIGURE 4.2 Extract conversation

86 Gina Lontoc

Filipino	English
(1) Ano ang ipa photocopy, Sir?	What will be photocopied, Sir?
(2) Ano'ng photocopy, Sir?	Which photocopy, Sir?
(3) Alin dito ang ipa-photocopy, Sir?	Which one (here) will be photocopied, Sir?

FIGURE 4.3 Extract translation

The first issue in translation the extract raises relates to the most accurate way of translating the utterance to English. There are possible ways of translating the utterance and the dilemma of choosing the best option cannot be resolved unless the one translating has witnessed the actual situation in which the utterance was used. To arrive at the closest translation, I have to go beyond the literal level of the utterance and consider the deeper meaning intended by the speaker. This brings to light the second issue in translation which deals with translating the meaning of the speaker.

It can be said that none of the three translated versions above fits the message the student was trying to convey. The student was not asking a question nor expecting a factual answer from the teacher; rather, she asked the question to compel an action from the teacher and that is, to give her her own copy of the text. Therefore, the utterance can be translated as, 'What about my photocopy, Sir?' or 'Where is my photocopy, Sir?' This relates to the notion of indirect speech act (Searle and Vanderveken, 1985) which asserts that a different propositional content can be conveyed from what is directly expressed by the speaker. Therefore, what complicates the process of meaning-making here is the unfolding of the three layers of meaning of an utterance which are the literal meaning of words, the actual intention of the speaker, and the hearer's (mis)understanding of the speaker's intention.

The final issue in translation that I would like to raise deals with the use of sentence structures in Philippine English and their effect on how an utterance is translated from Cebuano into Filipino, and then into English. Since I can work only in Filipino and in English, it is imperative that all utterances in Cebuano be translated into Filipino first so that I can translate them into English. In this process, my English translation of utterances is influenced by my first language and my cultural orientations which are embedded in language.

I share with other Filipinos the language features of the kind of English I use which is a nativised variety of American English. Bautista (2000) argued that the grammatical features distinct to the Standard Philippine English follow D'Souza's (1998: 92, as cited in Bautista, 2000: 33) criteria for the standard: 'the usage should be widespread, systematic, rule-governed, and used by competent users in formal situations'. Therefore, my English is characterised by restructuring of some grammar rules as illustrated in option (3) of the extract.

| *Filipino:* | Alin dito ang ipa–photocopy, Sir? |
| *Translation:* | Which one (here) will be photocopied, Sir? |

In literal translation, *alin* means 'which' and *dito* means 'here'. The hyphenated *ipa-photocopy* is a way of transforming a noun to a verb in Filipino and adding the word *ipa*-facilitates verb conjugation denoting future action. So, *ipa-photocopy* means will be photocopied. The resulting sentence structure, 'Which one here will be photocopied, Sir?', can be understood by Filipino readers, but will be found vague by some members of the international community who may not take the existence of other varieties of English into consideration. In the field of 'World Englishes', this is what Matsuda and Matsuda (2010) address as the complex push–pull relationship between standardisation and diversification. Consequently, this cautions me to develop a certain degree of awareness of the privileged status of Standard English and the possible consequences of not using this dominant variety.

On a final note, the way I write my research in English has a direct consequence on communicating the results of my study because writing conventions which privilege Standard English will have an impact on how the academic community will read my research – a concern I share with other researchers who are using other varieties of English. Therefore, in conducting a research in an intercultural environment, one has to constantly navigate around the issues on language and the social, cultural, and political ideologies they constitute.

5

WRITING ACROSS CULTURES

Reader expectations and 'crises of identity' (Ivanic, 1988)

Anna Robinson-Pant

Introduction

The phrase 'writing up' research gives a hint of the implied hierarchy between oral and written texts, and the privileging of written knowledge over visual and spoken modes of production. This chapter explores such assumptions, through looking at the question of what counts as knowledge and who has authority over it. By taking a perspective on writing as a social practice, constructed in response to specific cultural and institutional contexts, I discuss the challenges of writing across cultures and languages. The analysis draws on interviews conducted recently with postgraduate students based in universities in the UK, Nepal, Korea and Iceland in order to investigate the decisions and strategies they adopted in relation to writing research. In the case of international students, they may already have learned to adapt their writing style and the ways in which they construct an argument to respond to the expectations of their UK or Korean university teachers. When writing about data collected in contexts unfamiliar to their audience, such researchers face additional challenges. Not only do they have to identify and explain differing cultural values and practices, but they also have to develop their authorial voice in relation to the voices of their respondents. This also relates to Alain's points about 'explicature' ('to make a hearer aware of the cultural assumptions of an utterance') discussed in Chapter 2.

Questions around 'whose knowledge and whose voice counts?' are integral to this process of developing an academic text that carries weight in (say) a UK university, yet also responds to and reflects ethical and methodological concerns in the fieldwork context. Decisions about when and how to reference knowledge are part of this process – for instance, 'common sense' knowledge about kinship structures may have to be accompanied by citations to anthropological literature in a thesis for a foreign audience unfamiliar with the context. References to research literature published by non-Western publishers and in an indigenous language may not be considered appropriate by some UK doctoral supervisors and examiners.

This chapter expands on the theoretical concepts from academic literacies research introduced earlier in Chapter 1 to suggest ways of addressing the questions that arise when writing across languages and cultures. These include: how can a research text based on bilingual or multilingual fieldwork incorporate or simply acknowledge such diversity of voices? Will the reader be aware of all the texts (published and unpublished) shaping ideas in the final book/article and practices in the fieldwork? Such exploration can enable the writer to share with the reader the experience of writing across cultures and languages, in terms of her or his multiple and shifting identities. However, such accounts are rarely made explicit in the final thesis, even within a chapter on methodology.

Writing across cultures in the academy: two starting points

A doctoral student conducting fieldwork and writing up their research can be regarded simultaneously as an 'expert' in terms of their understanding of the cultural context (and possibly languages) in the field, and as a 'novice' in relation to academic literacy practices (particularly thesis writing) in the academy. This tension is not always evident in the final text (thesis) but certainly influences many decisions taken around identity, voice, language choice and style during the writing process. Setting out to explore the relationship between fieldwork/er and text, I realised that ethnographers over the decades have offered insights on their experiences of 'textualising culture' which are relevant to idea of the doctoral student as 'expert' fieldworker. In order to look at the specific context of the doctoral student writing a thesis based on empirical research, I also turned to the literature on academic literacies and academic discourse in higher education, where the student is more likely to be positioned as 'novice'.

I will begin by looking at each of these starting points in turn. This is partly to identify some valuable conceptual tools, but also to make my ideological assumptions about writing across cultures in the academy more explicit. This is a necessary step in a chapter arguing that a writer should share openly the values, practices and identities underlying their text! A major dilemma for me is that whilst I recognise that the issues faced by doctoral students writing across cultures and languages are in essence the same as for many other doctoral students, I have decided to frame my analysis around this sub-group as 'different' in some way. I hope that this chapter will help to explain why writing across languages and cultures is both the same as and different from the challenges faced by all researchers engaged in the writing process.

90 Anna Robinson-Pant

(i) Constructing knowledge through written text: learning from ethnographers

Van Maanen (1988: xii) recounts how his supervisors advised him to: 'simply "write up" what I had "discovered" in the field as if what was then in my head (and field notes) could be uncorked like a bottle and a message poured out'. As Holliday (2007: 122) points out, this notion of writing up as 'simply a matter of reporting' has been institutionalised within British universities in the form of a 'writing up year' (without supervision) after the end of a doctoral student's period of registration. These ideas about writing up field research have been strongly contested within many qualitative research traditions, particularly within ethnography. Of course, debates around writing as constructing rather than delivering knowledge are not unique to cross-cultural or multilingual settings. However, since the ethnography (meaning 'the text') has been seen as central to ethnography (meaning 'the research approach'), critical ethnographic writing can provide particular insights into what actually happens during the process of 'writing up'. Clifford and Marcus (1986: 6) emphasise in their seminal book, *Writing Culture*: 'The making of ethnography is artisanal, tied to the worldly work of writing'. We can then begin to identify what Van Maanen (1988: x) calls the 'taken-for-granted tricks of the trade'.

Arguing that 'ethnographies join culture and fieldwork', Van Maanen (1988: xi) lays out four aspects that need to be considered in relation to methodology:

> (1) the assumed relationship between culture and behavior (the observed); (2) the experiences of the fieldworker (the observer); (3) the representational style selected to join the observer and observed (the tale); and (4) the role of the reader engaged in the active reconstruction of the tale (the audience).
> *(Van Maanen, 1988: xi)*

In this analysis, the writing process cannot be considered separately from the methodological approach adopted, particularly the role of the researcher and relationships developed in the field. Van Maanen (1988: ix) describes ethnography as resting 'on the peculiar practice of representing the social reality of others through the analysis of one's own experience in the world of these others'. In other words, questions about methodology are also questions about textual representation – and about culture.

Holliday's (2007: 34) notion of all qualitative research settings as 'cultures, where research is essentially culture learning' offers a way of analysing what happens when data is constructed through fieldwork. He discusses field research in terms of an intercultural encounter – where the researcher enters a setting 'bringing her own cultural baggage and discourse' and the setting 'thus becomes a culture of dealing between this and the culture of the people there' (ibid.: 163). Understanding of 'culture' can thus provide 'the network of meaning for the social phenomena found as data' (ibid.: 34). Analysing Holliday's and Van Maanen's work, we can see a strong emphasis both on culture as meaning-making and research writing as being part of this process – and on ensuring that researcher relationships and texts are more visible. Holliday (ibid.: 163) discusses how to show 'the workings of the study': this does not stop at the point of just explaining what the researcher did and why.

The need for reflexivity has emerged particularly through postcolonial theory and decolonising research methodology. As Sikes (2006: 354) suggests, critical personal narrative is necessary when Southern authors 'recount what it feels like to have one's own people officially described and analysed in an othering fashion'. The decision about how to present the participants' voices is similarly acute when participants are speaking a different language from that of the final text. However, as Temple and Young (2008: 96) argue: 'speaking for others in any language is always a political issue that involves the use of language to construct self and other'. These multiple complex identities are more visible in the case of a multilingual researcher than for a researcher working in one language.

The idea that writing is central to constructing research knowledge is not specific to multilingual settings nor to research (such as ethnography) that involves crossing cultural boundaries. However, in such settings, it may become more obvious that decisions around representing voice and identity in text have to be made. The relationship between fieldwork, empirical data collection, and the resulting text is also made more complicated in the context of multiple audiences with differing values, languages and priorities. Regarding writing from an epistemological perspective can lead to exciting new developments, particularly methodological innovation. Examples include Gonzalez and Lincoln's (2006:7) discussion of the 'conversational and dialectic' characteristics of Participatory Action Research and Bradby's (2002: 852) observation that the 'hybridising process of language mixing opens up new world views'. Liamputtong's (2010) discussion of reciprocity and the possibility of 'giving back' findings in more creative forms that participants can access responds to the issue of the academy valuing written above oral texts. In the next chapter, I will also be looking at some of the strategies that doctoral students are developing in this regard.

This section has focused on the relationship between fieldwork and written text, with the aim of providing a framework for analysing how knowledge is constructed through the process of 'writing up'. Of particular significance to this chapter are the ideas from ethnographers about:

- how culture is portrayed in terms of 'the Other' and the process of 'learning culture';
- how writing involves negotiating and mediating different values, practices and identities in recognition of multiple audiences/readers (including research participants);
- making the transition from fieldwork to text (which can be oral/audio recording or visual text as well as written text).

(ii) Writing in the academy

My second starting point is more specific to students writing within the structure and expectations of a PhD course and draws on academic literacies research into power, authority, voice and identity. The plural form ('academic literacies') recognises the multiple and often hierarchical cultural and social practices around literacy in academic institutions. As I discussed in Chapter 1, academic literacies researchers view writing and reading as ideologically constructed and shaped by context, rather than as a set of neutral skills. The notion of one homogeneous academy has also been challenged through analysis of how academic texts and practices – and the idea of what makes 'good' writing – vary across disciplines and between different institutional and cultural contexts. The concept of a continuum from oral to written practices is particularly helpful in this chapter to explore the interconnection and transformation of fieldwork data into text and the power relations involved (including between academic institution, supervisor, researcher and participants).

The expert/novice frame informs much academic literacies research – with regard to both non-traditional students and international students entering an unfamiliar academic context. Holliday's (1999: 5) concept of 'small culture' is useful here, defined as 'a different paradigm through which to look at social groups'. Putting the emphasis on 'culture' as an analytical (and therefore potentially transformative) tool, he suggests that: 'a "small culture" approach attempts to liberate "culture" from notions of ethnicity and nation' (Holliday, 1999: 237). In the higher education context, students may be unfamiliar with the dominant culture in their university department because they come from industry or commerce, not necessarily because they come from another country or ethnic group. Ivanic (1988) identified a 'crisis of identity' as students encounter such unfamiliar literacy practices and much research has looked at the strategies they adopt to manage this transition. For instance, in South Africa Paxton (2012) used the concept of 'interim literacies' to analyse how students from diverse cultural and linguistic backgrounds engaged with this process of learning and mediating familiar and dominant academic discourses.

Hyland's (2009) analysis of how students are inducted into unfamiliar academic discourses highlights the dangers of essentialising culture and developing cultural stereotypes. Like Holliday, he takes a broader view of culture, suggesting that:

> Seen ethnolinguistically and institutionally, culture implies an historically transmitted and systematic network of meanings which allow us to develop and communicate our knowledge and beliefs about the world.
>
> *(ibid.: 126)*

He points out that cultural experiences help to shape schemata, 'influencing our intuitions about language and expectations about appropriacy and correctness; our sense of audience and ourselves as text producers' (ibid.). Hyland's analysis of students' essays revealed shared characteristics – such as Hong Kong students using more assertive language than UK students (who used 'hedges' such as 'probably' or 'suggest'). However, he warned against adopting a 'normative, essentialising stance which leads to lumping students together on the basis of their first language' (p. 127). The idea of multiple identities shaped by diverse experiences – only some of which are related to ethnolinguistic culture – is important to note.

Taking academic literacies as a starting point shifts our focus onto examining the learning process and looking at student writing as not just writing across languages, but across institutional cultures too. The expert/novice frame is useful in terms of distinguishing the differing values, expectations and practices adopted by the student during the process of transition, and also for investigating power hierarchies constructed through academic texts. Central to academic literacies discussions are questions about audience and readers – as Ivanic (2005) argued, an academic text is not written in a vacuum and is shaped as much by the reader as the writer.

This section has explored the relationship between the doctoral student writer and the academy as a way of looking at how writing (and reading) practices in and beyond the fieldwork setting may be shaped by academic hierarchies and discourses. In this chapter, I will draw on the following ideas from academic literacies research:

- positioning the doctoral student as a 'novice' in the academy (which many students can experience as an unfamiliar culture);
- micro level analysis of academic writing processes and expectations within the academy;
- a focus on induction and how students make the transition into new ways of reading and writing, yet also respond to multiple audiences;
- an understanding of academic knowledge and writing as constructed through local and global power hierarchies.

By bringing together the two starting points of critical ethnography and academic literacies, I set out to develop a theoretical lens for analysing the experiences of doctoral students writing across languages and cultures. Both areas of research explore how unequal power relations shape the construction of knowledge through texts – whether between Northern researcher and Southern research respondents or between doctoral student, supervisors and university examiners (or journal editor and author, as I will discuss in Chapter 6). However, the research process and particularly academic writing can also provide a means to challenge and transform such inequalities – rather than simply reproducing conventional research texts. I turn now to focus on particular aspects of the doctoral writing process to investigate how students have addressed such challenges – starting with writing during the fieldwork process and ending up with the thesis.

94 Anna Robinson-Pant

Textualising data: the initial process of transforming fieldwork into text

Van Maanen (1988: 95) refers to Ricoeur's (1973) term 'textualization' to describe the process 'by which unwritten behavior, beliefs, values, rituals, oral traditions and so forth, become fixed, atomized and classified as data of a certain sort'. Now that the use of video, camera and digital recorders is commonplace, the concept of 'textualization' can be expanded to include visual and oral material 'fixed' in this way too. Van Maanen argues that 'only in textualized form do data yield to analysis' (ibid.) and suggests that the analysis relies on a 'second-order, textualized, fieldworker-dependent version of events' (ibid.). Taking this notion of 'textualization' into the context of doctoral researchers working across languages and cultures, I found that the process was even more complex. For instance, students' decisions about which language to take notes in or how (or whether) to transcribe interview data were influenced not only by their understanding of the fieldwork context, but also by institutional expectations and, in some cases, an awareness that their supervisor might later read and comment on fieldnotes.

For students engaged in participant observation, the first challenge was around how to capture what they were experiencing and discussing fast enough and in sufficient depth. Sara, a student in Iceland who conducted her fieldwork in Burundi in French and Kirundi, an indigenous language, conveyed a sense of the pace: 'I just tried to write everything down, get it out there' (Interview, 2016). Though she kept her notes mainly in English, as this was the language she had used most in her academic and professional life, she sometimes 'wrote a word here or there in Icelandic [her mother tongue], sayings for things that came more easily in Icelandic for instance'. In addition, she noted down some direct quotes in French and included certain words in Kirundi, such as those related to ideas of masculinity: 'They say that a boy turns into a man when they are married, whatever the age, so the words for boy and man do not mean the same if I used Icelandic or English'. Sara's notes were in a mixture of languages – responding to her need to take notes fast and in detail, capturing meaning in the most accurate way possible. Significantly, at this stage, she was writing for herself so did not have to take account of any other reader, and this was reflected in the spontaneity of her decisions around language.

Monika, originally from Poland and now researching in Icelandic schools, described a similar mixture of languages in her fieldnotes. While following a child respondent throughout one day, she explained: 'I used a diary to record this. My diary is in Icelandic and afterwards I added some reflections in Polish. I think in Polish and it is sometimes easier to put words in Polish. But when I am thinking about issues in theory, I use Icelandic' (Interview, 2016). It is interesting that Monika distinguished different aspects of her fieldnotes in relation to the two languages: the ongoing description of what was happening to the child was in Icelandic, whilst her thoughts on the account were written in Polish and any theoretical connections explored in Icelandic. Like Sara, her decisions about when to write in which language drew on her previous educational, personal and professional language experiences (she had been a teacher using Icelandic) and what worked for her as a reader and writer.

Sanjek's (1990: 92) distinction between 'headnotes' (memories) and 'fieldnotes' is particularly relevant to this discussion of how researchers slip between different languages in their accounts of 'the field'. He explains: 'Fieldnotes are meant to be read by the ethnographer and to produce meaning through interaction with the ethnographer's headnotes'. Hrefna (the Icelandic student quoted in Chapter 1) explained how this 'interaction' worked for her in terms of the sound of the language evoking vivid memories and feelings:

> Sometimes I would sit in the beautiful rose garden of the Greek university while I was listening to lectures from Iceland on visual ethnography . . . So when listening, I could almost go home and feel the fresh wind from the North, even if I was in a Greek garden. Now this happens the other way round. When I am listening to the notes and interviews in Greek, I get pulled back to the place. And I feel a longing to go back there, to the food, to the people and to the singalong of the Greek language.
>
> *(Interview, 2016)*

Hrefna took notes 'all the time' during fieldwork, often recording her thoughts in Icelandic through talking into an audio recorder. She would transcribe the recordings later. This had been particularly important when taking part in protests with activist groups that she was researching as she could record aloud when walking home without anyone understanding her Icelandic reflections. Unlike Sara and Monika, Hrefna would also write (and sometimes translate) her notes into English to share with her supervisors, one of whom was based in Greece and did not understand Icelandic.

Transcribing audio recordings and translating fieldnotes is a time-consuming task, especially if some of the data is not eventually useful in the analysis. Dinesh, a doctoral student at a university in Nepal, explained how his approach changed during the course of his fieldwork:

> The problem is what to transcribe or not transcribe as it takes such a long time to build up trust. My first conversations with them [participants] were very formal and later I didn't transcribe it at all as they weren't saying much. When it was meaningful data, then I noted in my diary. I transcribed so much but it was not meaningful data. I slightly changed my methodology from having intended to transcribe everything – this was with the consent of the supervisors . . . I began to question the purpose of transcription – is it necessary or not?
>
> *(Interview, 2016)*

Dinesh had interviewed young people in the Nepali language for his study and explained that he transcribed the recordings using Roman script since he lacked the typing skills in Devanagari script (which is usually used for Nepali transcriptions). He then translated extracts into English for his thesis. As he mentioned above, he discussed his decisions with his supervisors about what and when to transcribe from the data. Partly because of the issues he faced around transcription (much surplus and not 'meaningful' data) and the difficulties of translating 'youth culture' into English, he began to question his overall approach to analysis and writing. From having relied heavily on transcriptions of formal interviews, he explained: 'now my transcription is blended with other fieldnotes and my journals and it is more creative with different ways of thinking'. Now that he is writing the thesis, Dinesh is also experimenting with that form and described some chapters as 'semi-fictional ethnography'. The experience of textualising spoken data and translating (youth) culture seemed to have led Dinesh into methodological innovation – supporting the ideas around constructing knowledge through text discussed in section (i) above.

Dinesh also talked about the fieldwork process in terms of his own learning – both in terms of learning to understand the youth participants and in attempting to convey the meanings in English:

> Because I am researching youth voices, I try to become closer to them and collect different words in everyday life, try to understand these words. I try to use these words and gauged their reactions. It is difficult to translate their meaning into English.

He explained that the young people spoke a mixture of English and Nepali, and 'different kinds of words, not Nepali or English. Like *langlang* which could mean a very disengaging thing or a very boring thing. There are multiple meanings and you need to know the exact context in which they used the words'. His account is similar to that of the earlier ethnographers cited in section (i), learning to communicate across cultures and how to share unfamiliar discourses with their readers.

In addition, Dinesh and other doctoral students whom I interviewed in a university in Nepal were aware that they were making decisions about how to construct their text – even at the fieldwork stage – in the context of an academic degree. Students in this Nepali university had been advised that they needed to type up their fieldnotes in Devanagari rather than Roman script. They explained that this was because the university required them to and that 'it seems mandatory to transcribe into the original language'. This presented problems for students who could not type in Devanagari, as Indra explained: 'When I had to type up the Nepali data, I did it in Roman script as I am more familiar with English. Then later I found software to put it in Devanagari' (Interview, 2016). Though the students were making decisions about which script to write in on the basis of their own ease and familiarity, they felt the need to transcribe Nepali data into Devanagari script to fulfil university expectations.

Students' decisions about translating data into English were also influenced by discussions with their supervisors, as Meenakshi explained: 'They think some ideas may be lost if it is translated straight into English.' (Interview, 2016) Similarly, Dinesh commented that his supervisors 'are worried about the originality of the data and show their concens whether the meaning of data will remain same as in translation or not'. Here, rather than university regulations, there seemed to be a sense that the data transcribed into Nepali conveyed more 'original' meaning of the spoken interactions than translated fieldnotes. Meenakshi faced an additional challenge as one of her supervisors was based in the US and could not read Nepali:

> I was writing everything in English and sending to my supervisor . . . But for me it was like [refers to Nepali saying] – how can you eat liquid from a leaf plate – as it is always moving around? However I won't question her decision as I am comfortable.
>
> *(Interview, 2016)*

Meenakshi's decision to transcribe and translate all her raw data in order for her supervisor to be able to share in the analysis process was influenced by the recognition that her supervisor was the 'expert' in terms of research experience. Meenakshi's sense of herself as a novice in terms of how to report data and decide how much to translate – as she questioned: 'How can I decide what is useful or not?' – contrasted with her confidence in the field site. She was working in an area in the West of Nepal, using a mix of Awadhi (local language), Hindi and Nepali to interview parents, teachers and children. Like Dinesh, she enjoyed learning to communicate within an unfamiliar community, but she emphasised that it was 'triple work': 'I would make notes in Anwadhi first, then in Nepali then English'.

The challenges described by these students are around transcribing oral data in Nepali into a written form, as well as translating written data collected in Nepali and other languages into English. Ingrid, who was conducting research with Polish migrants in Iceland, identified this point as being both around language and mode of communication (oral or written):

> I use direct quotations from Polish. But I don't know English well enough to reflect what people say, so I am not sure that my writing can really reflect what they say. After all, it is not like a written language. Even when we write it in Polish, we are transcribing an oral interaction into writing and we change thought, the interaction.
>
> *(Interview, 2016)*

The assumption that audio recordings had first to be transcribed had informed most students' and supervisors' approach to data analysis. An exception was Gunnar, who was studying in Iceland and Scotland. Rather than transcribing his interviews with Icelandic musicians, he had conducted analysis directly from the audio recordings. He explained:

> I recorded the interviews in Icelandic, wrote no notes or transcription afterwards. This is the way I did interviews as a journalist. It has to be fast. I wrote comments from the recording, listening and analysing from that. So the written text is in English and the audio in Icelandic. [Gestures to head] It goes in one side in Icelandic and out the other side in English.
>
> *(Interview, 2016)*

Gunnar's previous professional experience as a journalist had also shaped his approach to sharing his written text with participants: 'I am used to running it back with them after interviews . . . it is more informal . . . It's very Icelandic, no paperwork' (Interview, 2016).

The recognition that conducting research in a language other than English could entail a huge amount of extra labour had influenced some students' initial decisions about their research site, as Boyoung (a student in Korea) explained:

> The language issue is influencing my decision about where to do the research and influencing what I do. If I don't speak the local language, it will be a hindrance to find out what is going on, what is in their head. I would rather do it in English than use interpreters again for the sake of efficiency and accuracy of the research.
>
> *(Interview, 2015)*

Sara (from Iceland) had conducted research in Burundi and originally intended to use interpreters to reach a broad range of informants (including non-French speakers). However, she soon changed that and started relying more on one-to-one interviews, even though that meant she could speak only to those who were comfortable with French. She explained: 'Things changed because of the language. It is limiting what in-depth interviews you can do when you have to do it through a translator' (Interview, 2016).

Those students who decided to conduct research in a second or third language were making decisions about what to translate from their fieldnotes partly from their own familiarity with the research site (or the 'research culture', to use Holliday's term). Their confidence in learning and mediating meaning across cultures came out strongly in many of their accounts (as cultural insiders) and their flexible approach to language decisions and code-switching. But some students also suggested that their decision-making was informed and (in the case of Devanagari transcriptions) could be constrained to some degree by university regulations or assumed practices. As 'novices' in the academy, they sometimes looked to supervisors for advice on these practices. However, a contrasting notion of 'pure' language – rather than the students' understanding of code-switching and intertextuality in multilingual situations and writing – tended to underpin university regulations and writing conventions.

Writing up: issues of identity and voice

Within accounts of fieldwork, the complexity of the researcher identity has often been reduced to an insider-outsider dichotomy. As Liamputtong's (2010: 111) typology of cross-cultural researchers suggests, there can be a greater range of positions from 'external outsider' to 'indigenous insider'. Mutua and Swadener (2004: 4) point out that 'the researcher, whether foreign or indigenous, can never be permanently located at either the emic or etic pole'.[1] I have found it useful to conceptualise researcher positionality in terms of a continuum from outsider to insider, to capture the notion of constantly changing and multiple identities (see Crossley, Arthur and McNess, 2016). Considering the researcher as writer too brings even greater complexities – negotiating identities within and outside the text as well as within the fieldwork situation. Holliday (2007: 133) discusses a 'complex of voices' within a research text: the first voice is the personal narrative, the second voice comprises the data, the third voice comments on the data at the time of collection, the fourth voice comments on the first three voices at the time of writing and the fifth voice is the final overarching argument. His analysis is useful to explore what can go wrong as writers can 'get stuck in any one' of these voices (ibid.: 134), such as those who find it difficult to stand back and give commentary on their data (stuck in the second voice). Alongside this analysis of the authorial voice within the final text, there are the layers of intermediate oral and written interpretation, transcription and translation in the field (discussed in the previous section) to be considered.

Van Maanen's account of the different kinds of tales constructed by ethnographers appears at first glance to be comparing narrative styles in terms of writing conventions – realist tales, confessional tales and impressionist tales. However, his analysis of these different kinds of ethnographic texts also tells us much about how the researcher positioned himself/herself in the text and in the field – such as 'the almost complete absence of the author from most segments of the finished text' (Van Maanen, 1988: 46) within realist tales. He suggests that 'closely edited quotations characterise realist tales, conveying to readers that the views put forward are not those of the fieldworker but are rather authentic and representative remarks transcribed straight from the horse's mouth' (ibid.: 49).

Turning to the situation faced by doctoral students, I am struck that the decision about how to position themselves in the thesis is not just about what kind of 'tale' they want to construct, but also what kind of text would be acceptable for the PhD. In this respect, they need to respond to their supervisors' and examiners' expectations around form, style and voice, as well as university regulations (such as a requirement to write in the English language). As I discussed earlier, the contested notion of a homogeneous academy means that there is great diversity of genre and style in terms of what is acceptable as a PhD thesis.

Several students whom I interviewed talked about these writing decisions in terms of 'first person' versus 'third person' and said they had made a change in their style and authorial voice at PhD level. Referring to Ivanic's (1998) table showing a dualistic structure of 'ideologies of knowledge-making in higher education', Turner (2003: 39) suggests that the use of the pronoun 'I' is associated with the left-hand side of the table ('relatively oppositional') as opposed to the traditional epistemology of the 'scientific, rational, objectivist, autonomous, "knowing subject"'. This connection between new rhetorical strategies and ideological positions was evident in the way that students discussed their writing too, as Dinesh explained:

> While I was a Masters student, the supervisors prefer you to write in the third person and not write in the passive voice . . . When I came here [to do the PhD], there was such a difference. When I wrote in the third person, the teachers said you became positivist. I thought what is positivist about writing? I thought that was only a research tradition.
>
> *(Interview, 2016)*

Dang, a Thai student in the UK, had similarly associated first-person writing with a certain methodological stance: '"I am", "I am doing". It's as if it is your own diary, not official enough in our country. But I am doing qualitative research so I have to describe myself as "I"' (Interview, 2010). By contrast, Youyi, a Chinese student in Korea, observed that she could write in a more personalised style when in China:

'In English the professor asks us to directly write about the topic. They don't ask us to talk about our personal experiences in English. In Chinese we may use personal experience to illustrate or explain something' (Interview 2015). Boyoung, a Korean student at the same university, also commented that her professors had advised her to write in the third person: 'At first I wrote up term papers in the first person but I was advised later it was best to use third person' (2015).

As Hyland warned, it is sometimes easy to create cultural stereotypes through generalising about writing preferences. The few examples above illustrate that students often talk in polarising terms about first- and third-person writing, whether to relate to the Masters versus PhD, quantitative versus qualitative research or Chinese versus English. What is more revealing are the ways in which they have learned what is acceptable in a new academic context. Gil, a student from Brazil, explained that there were certain practices he could not do back home – such as 'mixing the literature review and the research' – which he found were acceptable in the UK university: 'I realised that my previous academic framework had gone. It was not a conflict, but about changing my ideas' (Interview, 2010). Whilst Gil felt comfortable discussing his writing expectations with his supervisor, other students suggested they had had to work out the rules of the new university on their own. This was particularly so in relation to any language difficulties faced, as Youyi emphasised: 'I never talked about language as I thought this may be personal issues that I should overcome on my own and this is something I need to do' (Interview, 2015). Her stance connects with Turner's (2011) work on languaging in the academy and her suggestion that language becomes visible in the UK university only when it is considered a problem, rather than a resource that multilingual students can contribute to the institution. Several students whom I interviewed saw the doctoral supervision meeting as a contested space – power relations between them and their supervisor meant that sometimes their differing assumptions about writer voice, aims of the research and processes of translation were never discussed or were recognised by the student only (not by the supervisor).

The question of writer identity was very bound up with their mother tongue and country of origin for many of the students I interviewed – and less about their persona within the field. Youyi, as the only Chinese student on her course in Korea, emphasised that:

> When I am writing, I have a different identity based on what I belong to and what I speak against, what groups I am representing. Most of the time I don't represent myself as Chinese. I don't want to do that because the topic is not culturally related.
>
> *(Interview, 2015)*

George, a Nigerian student in a UK university, explained how he had struggled to move from his culture to 'the English culture' in terms of writing expectations, and this was partly because of challenging his identity as a writer and junior scholar in the African context

> It's only when I came to England, for example, that I learned to critique. I mean like there are some things you don't say. Let's take an example – this was written by a senior person, it's difficult for a junior person to critique it, you know in the African culture context.
>
> *(Interview, 2010)*

Again, it would be easy to generalise in terms of the kind of power-distance models that Hofstede (1991) proposed in his cross-cultural research and training for international commercial companies (see Chapter 2), for instance to argue that African and Asian students are 'less critical' than UK students. What is more interesting is to look at how Youyi and George positioned themselves as 'novice' English language writers within the academy.

Gunnar, an Icelandic researcher who had studied in Scotland, summed up the common experience of writing in English as a second language: 'That's the shackles that we international students face – we are always dealing with two languages, not just one like the English students' (Interview, 2016). However, he also challenged the common deficit approach: 'It can be beneficial too as we have to think about the ideas and terms. We get an extra dimension. Instead of just writing "enthusiasm", we have to think, "what is enthusiasm?" We have to think, so it is extra.' Alga, an Icelandic student who was researching museology, shared this ambivalence towards writing in English. She too began by describing a sense of loss and the double burden: 'I lack my individual voice in English and I have to work really hard . . . When I'm writing, I am constantly having to look up words, think of alternatives using the thesaurus so it is interrupting my thought' (Interview, 2016). Although she positioned herself as a novice academic writer in English, Alga was frustrated by what she termed a 'colonial attitude' towards her writing on the part of a member of her supervisory committee – criticising the grammar, rather than engaging with the content. She felt that this kind of feedback from journal editors, too, was 'designed to subordinate me in the world of academics' and emphasised that it was 'not a question of speaking perfectly, but having a voice'. Having worked as a journalist previously, Alga compared her experience of writing in Icelandic, including creating an academic voice where she could 'feel what words were right' and recognised 'it was a different process as you did not lose your train of thought'. However, she also emphasised the 'fun' side of writing in a second language: 'I enjoy trying to create an academic voice in English. I want to keep doing it for that reason. It's a creative process, trying to find your own voice'. In the next chapter, I will be looking more closely at the question of language, identity and knowledge raised by Alga in relation to the geopolitics of academic publishing.

All the doctoral students whom I interviewed in Nepal, UK and Korea[2] were required to write their thesis in English, so they could not make a decision to produce a bilingual or multilingual text. Some talked about how different their style would be if they were writing in their first language: 'If I was writing in Korean, I would bring more styles into the academic writing, like poetry. Even Korean writing has a structure but there is room to put in more nuances, complexity and be more sensitive' (Boyoung, 2015). Dinesh described how he was trying to give 'space to the participants as narrator of a chapter. So it is a kind of mix-up, using their actual words but in English'. He was sharing his writing with participants through 'telling the story orally in Nepali' to get their feedback: 'for instance, I mentioned the father of one participant had a tattoo and long hair. She [research participant] asked why I did that and I removed it'. This interaction with participants around the textual representation of their experiences was taking place alongside discussion (in Nepali and English) with his supervisors.

Thesis-writing can be seen in this section as a balancing act between differing expectations, modes of communication and languages. As well as thinking about how they represent themselves and their respondents in the text, these researchers were acutely aware of their identity as a novice in the academy, constrained to write in English. Questions about voice and writer identity were shaped very strongly by perceived or actual rules within their department about using first or third person and the appropriacy of informal personalised language, and many talked in deficit terms about their experiences of writing in English as a second language. Students spoke particularly about their supervisor or examiners as the main audience of the thesis – as passing the PhD was their first priority. Although they positioned themselves as a novice in this respect, some of the tensions that they described while writing arose from their sense that they were the 'experts' in terms of the field situation and relationships and were conscious of writing for multiple audiences.

Audience: the relational dimension of writing

Ivanic's (2005) four-leaf clover (see Chapter 1) provides a way of analysing four dimensions of writer identity. Her discussion of the 'relational dimension' draws attention to the effect of readers on writer identity:

> the way in which, at the moment of writing, a writer conceives of the reader(s) who will be constructing an impression of the writer (from the socially available resources on which they are able to draw) as they read what has been written
>
> *(ibid.: 398)*

The writer's assumptions about who the readers may be, what values they hold and power relations between them and the writer influence how an academic text is constructed. Ivanic suggests that before the moment of 'take up' by the reader, 'the writer's representation of self exists in a vacuum' (p. 400). Similar to Alain's discussion of the 'dynamism' of context in relation to oral utterance (Chapter 2), the emphasis here is also on the way that a text is shaped by the interaction (or anticipated interaction) with an audience.

Hyland (2009: 48) identifies the idea of community as providing 'a principled way of understanding how meaning is produced in interaction'. I found the three dimensions of context that he cited from Cutting (2002: 3) to be particularly useful when analysing how PhD students talk about their writing in relation to reader expectations:

- the *situational context*: what people 'know about what they can see around them';
- the *background knowledge context*: what people know about the world, what they know about aspects of life and what they know about each other;
- the *co-textual context*: what people 'know about what they have been saying'.

(From Cutting, 2002: 3, cited in Hyland, 2009: 48)

Writing across cultures raises particular challenges around all three aspects of context. In relation to the 'background knowledge context', doctoral students are aware that they need to provide factual background information about the situation where they conducted research. However, the issue about 'what people know about the world' is perhaps much harder to address, especially if the reader has not had experiences of intercultural research. Piti, who had come from Thailand to study in a UK university, explained that though she felt that understanding of situational and background context was key to interpretation of the data, she realised that her supervisors read her work from a different perspective:

> We never discuss the context in detail. My work is about Thailand education and when they write something, I can see they are seeing from the British view and I have to tell them . . . I include the detail in my writing as I need to explain to the reader of the thesis too.
>
> *(Interview, 2010)*

Scholastica (the student from Tanzania quoted in Chapter 1) recognised that her supervisor could not imagine the fieldwork situation she described – 'I realised that when I said a 'town centre' she was imagining Norwich town centre' (from DVD, 2010). Scholastica found that supplementing her written text with photographs helped to bridge this gap with her supervisor and eventually with the reader of her thesis.

In Iceland, Alga was writing up her PhD research as journal articles rather than a thesis, which meant that she had to anticipate who her readers might be in relation to the journal's scope. Writing from a post-disciplinary, post-humanist and feminist approach, she was surprised to be asked to 'provide more contextual information even in conceptual pieces'. She gave the example of a journal in Norway where the editor had wanted 'a lot of empirical examples' which she then had to contextualise in relation to Icelandic culture. As with writing in a second language, Alga saw this as a creative process: 'when writing transculturally, it is difficult having to explain everything but it can enhance it too' (Interview, 2016).

Having a reader from a different cultural background meant that the writer needed not only to give a greater account of the 'situational context' but also to consider Cutting's 'co-textual context'. Several students mentioned the difficulty of knowing what to reference, when and how, as an aspect of writing for an audience unfamiliar with both their cultural context and indigenous knowledge. As Scholastica explained:

> I have been born from Tanzania and I have lived there all my life so there are some things I know as I was growing up. But when I put it in the thesis my supervisor will ask, who says this? You need a reference. I say, I don't have any reference, this is how it is. No one has written about it. So if I don't put it, no one will know, no one will talk about it. There are no books, no research has been done, but that is what it is.
>
> *(From DVD, 2010)*

Scholastica had a strong sense of constructing new knowledge through writing – yet for her this was also the question of what was common knowledge in her home context not being known in the UK. This relates partly to the greater value put on oral communication in that context (see Chilisa, 2012) and the difficulty of transposing such knowledge into an academic context where written texts are dominant.

These issues around different knowledges also relate to global power hierarchies and the geopolitics of academic writing. Whilst Scholastica referred to a situation where there was no written reference, another international student in the UK, Naak, had drawn on Thai journals to support her findings: 'I think it's difficult to find in English journal about Thai study. So most of them are written in Thai language and the supervisor was not happy with Thai references' (Magyar and Robinson-Pant, 2011: 671). Her supervisor had explained that he could not check the rigour of these references as he did not read Thai language but also that these articles were not published in high status academic journals. Naak decided that she should use only 'good' references (i.e. from UK/US journals in English) so said she tried 'to find a journal that talks about Thai culture and try to bring the Thai culture to my supervisor' (Interview, 2010). The 'relational dimension' for these students was influencing not only what kind of information they needed to include in the thesis, but also the literature that they chose to cite to support their claims.

As Alain discussed in Chapter 3, translation involves questions of judgement and recreating context and meaning within a text. Students translating their raw data into English for their thesis were aware of the different assumptions that their readers might bring to the text. Diego (a student from Colombia) found that he was anticipating how an English reader might interpret a word as compared to a Korean reader (he was now studying in South Korea) and whether to use the English word, even within his Korean writing. He pointed to the word 'left' as an example:

> People who study democracy, they use the vocabulary like left and right in English not Korean. When they say it in Korean, they tend to use terms like conservative and liberal, as the word 'left' has such a strong idea regarding North Korea. Left has a very strong even illegal meaning. So they don't use left and right in Korean.
>
> *(Interview, 2015)*

Diego had picked up on these subtleties through reading other research in Korean and noticing that the English words 'left' and 'right' were used rather than the Korean equivalent in survey data. Youyi, also studying in Korea, explained that the word 'crowd' had been important in her course, in relation to the power of the crowd. When she came to write her reflective paper (in Korean), she felt that she needed to explain the broader 'political, cultural and communicational dimensions' of the word 'crowd' in Chinese (Interview, 2015). Hrefna was translating quotations from her respondents into English for her thesis, but retained Greek words which she felt had 'a special importance like *kavla* which means passion for life and is sometimes used in leftist politics, but it also has a sexual meaning' (Interview, 2016).

These writers acknowledged that part of their role as writer involved mediating meaning for their readers within the text – recognising that the reader might understand a word like 'crowd' or 'left' in a different way from that intended. An additional dimension was mentioned by Meenakshi, in relation to Sanskrit words which were used in Nepali academic writing: 'now we are looking at words in Eastern constructs that can't be translated into English like *gyan* (knowledge), some Sanskrit words which can't be translated. You have to think whether "think" means the same as "meditate"'. Meenakshi talked about the rich philosophy in Sanskrit – whereas she felt able to draw on these words when writing in Nepali as her readers would also be familiar with Sanskrit terms, she could not make those assumptions when writing for English readers. This could be seen as Cutting's 'co-textual' dimension associated with community – a shared body of knowledge that has informed thinking and writing. Interestingly, Meenakshi said that whilst she could explain about these Sanskrit terms orally, she would have difficulty writing about the philosophy in Nepali as her higher level academic training had been in English.

The importance of writing for an international or global audience was emphasised by supervisors and institutionalised in some universities through the need to publish journal articles as well as, or instead of, the thesis. Boyoung (in Korea) was writing two academic articles at the time of our interview – one in Korean and one in English. She had made the decision about which language to use partly on the basis of the topic – the Korean paper was based on philosophical analysis ('it is easier to do it in your own language as it is so complex', Interview, 2015) whereas the English paper was about South Korean educational development drawing on UN data. Boyoung had a clear idea about her intended audiences:

> For the Korean paper, I see my audience as people in Korea who are interested in this area, NGOs and academics. For the English paper, it is open to all. It will introduce Korean education and development to other countries, other cases. Koreans think they already know about their own education.
>
> *(Interview, 2015)*

Boyoung's last statement suggested that when writing the paper in English, she considered her audience to exclude Korean readers – she was setting out to share experiences with an external international audience.

Writing a thesis can be seen as more complex than writing shorter journal articles, in that journals usually have a narrower scope and a more defined audience. By contrast, a thesis writer may be setting out to 'speak to' local readers (including respondents) as well as an international readership. In addition to sharing his writing orally with participants, Dinesh explained that he had sought out critical readers who were similar to his research group:

> Another strategy I used is to ask other Masters students who are like youth to read my work and say how they find it. Some commented on the language and the themes. I am sharing it with students I trust as I go along.
>
> *(Interview, 2016)*

Writing across cultures **107**

This idea of informal peer review enabled Dinesh to try out the youth discourse in Nepali that he was attempting to recreate in his English text.

The challenge of writing for a global audience was a major consideration for many of the PhD students I interviewed. The university in Nepal required students to publish in international journals (in addition to the thesis) in order to pass the doctoral course. The sense of an international audience influenced the way students wrote and how supervisors read their thesis too. Indra related the intended international readership issues to measures of quality: 'It could be that the university requires us to write for a global audience in order to meet international standards'. Dinesh explained how the knowledge of a potential global audience had to be taken into account when writing his thesis:

> My supervisor is always asking, how can a global audience understand the meaning of this sentence? Like if I use a local word from Jumla and they ask, what is the meaning for the global audience? I have not written for the global audience but a Nepali audience. I would have to use four pages to explain the local construct, but my supervisor expects this.
>
> *(Interview, 2016)*

Comparing Dinesh's experience with that of Piti (the UK university student from Thailand) cited earlier, we can see that many international students in the UK already have to negotiate meaning and different knowledges orally and with a 'cultural outsider' during their supervision meetings. Although all the students were similar in having to write across cultures and languages, the Nepali students had to imagine an international readership as their Nepali supervisors were already familiar with the cultural context and languages they used in fieldwork. Significantly, their supervisors had previously studied their own doctorates overseas so had considerable experience of interacting with and writing for international readers. Indra saw the potential international audience as a source of new insights and learning for the writer: 'we are reaching to a larger audience and their lenses of looking could give whole new element of knowledge which we may not have thought of or ventured into' (Interview, 2016). By contrast, Janina (a doctoral student in Iceland) did not see 'writing for a global audience as that different from writing for a local audience. It depends more whether it is for academia or practitioners. If academics, it is not different as all the academics here have travelled widely to conferences' (Interview, 2016). The necessity of writing for a global audience remained, however, a source of tension for many students, particularly those who lacked confidence in English so were relying on proofreaders and sometimes editors even at the draft stage.

This section on readership and the relational aspect of writer identity contributes a wider conceptualisation of 'context' as being not simply the background knowledge required to interpret fieldwork data, but also an anticipation of the linguistic, literary and cultural resources that a reader might bring to the text. There are new hierarchies of knowledge to take account of here too – not just the relationship between student and supervisor (see starting point (ii) above), or between

108 Anna Robinson-Pant

researcher and respondent (see point (i)), but also North–South inequalities in terms of academic publishing which influenced what is regarded as a 'good' reference. The concept of a 'global' audience or international readership was closer to home for international students in the UK who were already engaged in an intercultural dialogue around their texts with their supervisors, as compared to students with supervisors from a similar background who had to create an imagined international audience.

Conclusion

This chapter has explored the challenges of writing across cultures – taking the concept of 'culture' and 'cultural learning' (Holliday, 2007) to look at different fieldwork situations and academic institutions. Through the lens of the ethnographic literature, an international student returning to their home country to conduct research might be seen as an 'expert' in terms of linguistic ability and cultural interpretation. They can simultaneously be positioned as a 'novice' within the UK academy, due to their unfamiliarity with dominant conventions and the expectations of the PhD. Students may also (like Van Maanen and other ethnographers discussed earlier) be conducting research with unfamiliar communities and interviewing in a second language or through interpreters. Through the lens of 'small culture' (Holliday, 1999), all researchers could be considered 'novices' in terms of learning to communicate with specific groups in the field and then transposing these experiences into text. In this respect, researchers are constantly engaged in a process of intercultural learning and communication.

However, moving from one country to another for study or fieldwork or writing up for international audiences – as the experiences of doctoral students discussed in this chapter illustrate – forces the researcher to make explicit decisions about identity, voice and audience in their written texts. In more familiar research or academic writing contexts, these decisions may have remained hidden if the contrasts in values, practices and knowledges were less obvious. A student going to conduct research in an unfamiliar language will be aware of the challenge of interpreting meaning for readers from their own background – having gone through that learning process themselves. Similarly, an international student researching in their 'home' country and mother tongue will be acutely conscious of the gap between what they take for granted as knowledge and what their reader or supervisor may find difficult to understand or accept. Writing across cultures thus involves a mediating and bridging role on the part of the writer – whether this is a perceived gap between worldviews of reader and author, or between author and the fieldwork community.

The process of constructing knowledge across cultures relies on the concept introduced earlier of a continuum between oral and written practices – rather than the hierarchical divide between writing and speaking or data collection implied by the term 'writing up'. As the experiences of students in this chapter have revealed, writing research involves a constant movement between oral and written interaction – whether reading out and discussing fieldnotes with respondents, discussing fieldnotes and written drafts with supervisors or peers, or negotiating the translation of texts with others in the community. The accounts in this chapter also point to a dynamic situation of language and code-switching – in writing, speaking and thinking – recalling the discussion in Chapter 4 about code-switching based on speakers conveying an identity with which they feel comfortable. In the multilingual situations described in the current chapter, researchers were drawing on rich resources of literature and shared knowledge, which was not necessarily written down but passed on through the generations. Researchers were also making decisions about how to write down and transcribe interviews on the basis of their own familiarity with writing conventions and university expectations. Many students faced the challenge of conveying this dynamic mix of languages and scripts and recognition of multiple identities through a monolingual (English language) thesis.

Alongside the experience of textualising fieldwork data, doctoral students described how they had learned to write acceptable texts in their academic institution. Interaction with their supervisors and peers was integral to this process as they experimented with form and genre and began to find out the 'rules' for writing in their particular department, including anticipating how their readers might respond to these texts. Their accounts of how they learned unfamiliar academic literacy practices point to the importance of seeing supervision as an 'intercultural encounter' (Turner, 2011). All too often, both supervisors and students can end up essentialising about writing style and voice to suggest, for instance, that all Korean students write in the third person and all English students in the first.

The idea of 'context' shaping interactions – whether in the field or a supervision meeting – is key to the analysis in this chapter. A 'context' chapter is often included in a thesis and consists of background factual information on the institutions, society and culture where the fieldwork took place. However, context needs to be seen as broader and deeper than the immediate fieldwork situation, to take account of the 'co-textual' context and the shared embedded knowledges that students often draw on when writing. The challenge for the writer is how to recreate this context through diverse voices, yet still be understood and recognised by 'international' readers. The questions about how to reference knowledge that is not published in high status journals and 'whose knowledge counts?' relate to power relations beyond the immediate fieldwork context. The tensions that doctoral students described in trying to write simultaneously for local and international audiences are related to global hierarchies influencing academic writing, particularly the higher status of Northern-based English-language publications. This is a problem faced not only by students but also by academics and publishers. The next chapter will focus on this wider community to see how researching and writing across cultures might begin to transform such wider inequalities.

110 Anna Robinson-Pant

In the following reflective piece, Joanna Nair explores some of the issues raised in this chapter around identity and writing in relation to her ethnographic field research in Nepal. She discusses the tensions encountered on returning for her doctoral fieldwork to a community where she had previously worked as a teacher. She reflects on ethical dilemmas faced – particularly around naming respondents – when translating and writing up her data.

Box 5 brings together some questions arising in this chapter that can help to inform decisions about reading and writing within intercultural research.

Box 5

Questions for further reflection

- How do I take notes and keep records during field research and in what language/s? Who do I intend to share these with and how will this influence the language/s or form that I use?
- If recording interviews or observations, do I transcribe these in full and if so, at what point? Do I want or need to translate transcriptions – into what languages, when and why?
- What are the advantages/disadvantages of analysing my data directly from the audio recording, or from summary notes, or from a transcription or translated transcription?
- Who are the intended readers – of my fieldnotes? Of my transcription? Of my final text/thesis/article? How does this understanding of audience influence the form and style of my writing?
- What do I need to explain in more detail for this readership? What ideas, phrases, words and assumptions may be unfamiliar to them? Do they have different ideas about academic writing which I need to take into account, such as a greater focus on empirical data rather than philosophical discussion?
- What are the implications for the language/s I use for these texts? Who will be included/excluded due to my language choices? What am I losing and gaining by writing my thesis in English (or another dominant language)?
- How do I situate myself in the final text? Do I use first person or third person? Whose voices will I include within the text? (See Holliday's 'complex of voices' and Van Maanen's realist, confessionalist and impressionist tales.) How do I construct my identity in relation to my differing roles as 'cultural insider' or outsider, doctoral student, researcher, activist?
- What kind of story do I want to tell and for what purpose/s?
- How do I include extracts from interviews and interactions with participants? Should I translate these and if so, how do I recreate their voices in another language?

- How do I explain words that have no equivalent in English (or the language of my final text)? Shall I use the original word with a footnote gloss to explain the meaning or find a close equivalent?
- How can I get feedback on my writing that offers an intercultural perspective? What alternative readings could there be?

Notes

1 The etic-emic construct comes from linguistic anthropology and should not be seen as directly equivalent to insider-outsider, as Harris (1990: 49) explains: 'etics denotes an approach by an outsider to an inside system, in which the outsider brings his [sic] own structure – his own emics – and partly superimposes his observations on the inside view, interpreting the inside in reference to his outside starting point'.
2 In Iceland, students could choose whether to write a thesis or publish four articles instead, so had a choice of languages (as will be explored in the next chapter). It is also important to note that the role of the supervisor and doctoral teaching structures differed greatly between the four contexts in which I conducted interviews (Nepal, UK, South Korea and Iceland). In the university in Iceland, a student commented that the English word 'supervisor', suggested someone in charge, rather than a guide or adviser.

Reflective piece 5: Writing relationships

Joanna Nair

This piece focuses on two key issues I experienced during my PhD research, and discusses some ethical dilemmas in ethnographic research during fieldwork and writing up. I first look at some implications of choices made in terms of address, in both face-to-face communication and writing. I then consider what may be lost and gained in translation.

My research explored the understandings of development and of wellbeing in a rural community in Far West Nepal. I initially worked there as a teacher (1993–1996) and later spent nine months for PhD fieldwork (2011–2012). This strongly hierarchical community based on the Hindu caste system has powerful *Brahmans* at the 'top' and powerless and discriminated-against *Dalits* (traditionally 'untouchables') at the 'bottom'. Women are also discriminated against, though non-Dalit women are not normally considered 'untouchable'.

Some implications of spoken and written terms of address

Hari, a Dalit in his mid-fifties, is a tailor. I have always called him *Hari Dai* – 'Hari Elder Brother' – imitating others and considering this normally respectful term unproblematic. However, one day I heard a Dalit man referring to as discrimination the way upper castes call all Dalit males older than them *dai*, while addressing upper-caste men of the older generations as 'uncle' or 'grandfather'. McConnell-Ginet notes that in the mid-twentieth-century southern United States 'it was very common for White people to use *auntie* or *uncle* to (condescendingly) address Black people' (2003: 78). The fact that the term *dai* can be understood to be both respectful and disrespectful within the same community demonstrates that 'the significance of particular forms of address lies in . . . the connection between addressing and other aspects of social practice that build social relations and mark them with respect and affection or with contempt, condescension, or dislike' (ibid.: 79). As McConnell-Ginet also states, 'address forms are . . . often socially required and . . . are always socially loaded' (ibid.: 77).

The Dalit man, seeing my shame and discomfort, immediately assured me that Hari did not consider my calling him *dai* an insult. Nonetheless, I began to ask myself why it had never occurred to me that I may have shown disrespect in addressing Hari as *dai* while addressing upper-caste men of a comparable age with titles or with the respectful suffix *ji*. I concluded that it was partly due to the identity which I was assigned, and which I admittedly adopted willingly, while working in the village twenty years previously. Lodging with an upper-caste Brahman family, and as the only Westerner in the village, I was perhaps insecure about my 'outsiderness', and overly anxious to be liked and included. I was happy – unaware of castist undertones – when my hosts commented on my 'Brahman' facial features. Albeit inadvertently, I may have colluded in this process of inclusion which excluded me from valuable insights about Dalit life in the village, which I gained only later during my fieldwork for a PhD.

Thus, I found myself in a quandary when I wrote up my research. I wanted to be respectful to Hari, and to all Dalits. However, I also wanted to be faithful to the way things were in the community. Therefore, although I used pseudonyms in my thesis (as I do here) in order to maintain participants' anonymity, I found myself deliberating how best to name Hari in my writing, recognising the ethical dilemma in options that 'ask you to choose between a "right" and a "right"' (Goodall, 2000: 158). Both *Hari Dai* and *Hariji* involved an ethical compromise, aligning myself to one truth and not another, but I reassured myself that, by mentioning the alternatives, I alleviate the damage. I also believe that discussing these issues brings transparency to my research. In that 'address forms . . . represent a special aspect of relational language' (Mehrotra, 1981: 121), my changing dyadic with Hari reveals much about the 'socio-cultural setting' (ibid.), my place in it and my research journey.

The various identities an individual may have in different contexts, as well as the different identities individuals attributed to me, also complicated my decisions over how to refer to people. As Qureshi notes about her research in Pakistan, in Nepal also the 'cultural codes governing human interactions are relational', meaning that the local 'ethical environmental standards bind researchers in many ways', limiting researcher choice and freedom (2010: 90). An example is my former relationship with Pushkar and his family; it meant that I, as their ex-lodger turned researcher, was exposed 'to what Roberts and Roberts (1999) have identified as "relational vulnerability"' (ibid.: 91).

Sometimes speakers deliberately avoid using any form of address because they are fearful of inadvertently insulting the addressee by according them the wrong degree of status (Mehrotra, 1981). I often avoided addressing Pushkar during conversations, an option not open to me when writing. Bearing this in mind, I named him *Sachivji* in my thesis. Pushkar is the *Sachiv* or Secretary of the Village Development Committee and the *ji* suffix denotes respect.

As McConnell-Ginet notes about Nepal's Tamang community, the community I researched also often labels adults 'in terms of their parental roles . . . or other kinship terms' (2003: 75), known as 'teknonyms'. I found it difficult to name a village woman to whom I had rarely spoken until I interviewed her. Villagers are aware that I do not know her sons, now emigrated from the community; therefore, when speaking to me, they do not talk about her as 'mother of . . .' Instead, they refer to her as 'Chuggy's wife'. I adopted this term with some qualms. By identifying her only in relationship to her husband, was I implicitly colluding with the male-dominated society of the village and demeaning her? It would appear so, based on McConnell-Ginet's statement that teknonyms label people '*only* through their relation to someone else' and that 'Chinese women . . . receive *nothing* but such relational forms' (2003: 75) (my italics). On the other hand, even males of the

114 Joanna Nair

community are frequently referred to by teknonyms, and this participant's identity in relation to the male members of her family did confer status on her. 'Chuggy's wife' may therefore be understood as a positive form of address. Whichever the case, my choice to name her thus is the more honest reflection of our relationship, and of the society.

Lost or gained in translation?

It was relatively unproblematic to name 'Dutt Sir', my ex-colleague at the local school, by respectfully according him the title by which he is known in that context. However, translating his interview was less straightforward. Dutt Sir, a Brahman, said this about Hari:

> If he went to Dhangadhi from time to time . . . it would be an advantage to him but he has to do other outside work here and there, he doesn't have the time.

The Nepalese language has several different versions of 'he/she', showing different degrees of respect. In this case, although they are of a similar age, Dutt Sir referred to Hari with the pronoun reserved for small children, animals and Dalits, although earlier he had stated his opposition to the caste system. The translation above fails to reflect the fact that Dutt Sir was in fact using language which demeaned Hari, and I was tempted to convey this by substituting the pronouns with pejorative terms in the translation. However, I may have then coloured Dutt Sir's words with greater castism than he felt. Rather than being deliberately castist, Dutt Sir may be unaware of the extent to which castism is embedded in the language. I therefore decided to mention the issue in a footnote.

This explanation may be understood as an 'explicitation'; it could be interpreted as an 'obligatory explicitation' resulting from 'lexicogrammatical differences between the source language (SL) and the target language (TL)' (Klaudy, 2008 in Becher, 2010: 4). I, however, would not classify it thus, taking Becher's point that 'explicitation is observed where a given target text is more explicit than the corresponding source text' (ibid.: 3). As Séguinot states, 'the term "explicitation" should . . . be reserved in translation studies for additions in a translated text which cannot be explained by structural, stylistic, or rhetorical difference between the two languages' (1988: 108). In this case, the lack of status differentiation in English pronouns forced me to be less explicit in the TL text, necessitating an explanation in a footnote. Though this could be considered an explicitation if one interprets Klaudy's words to include footnotes also, I was being only as explicit as the SL text had been.

Meanwhile, my explanation of another participant's use of a pronoun could, I believe, belong to both Klaudy's classification of 'obligatory explicitation' (as described above) and of 'pragmatic explicitation', it being 'motivated by differences in cultural . . . knowledge shared by members of the SL and TL communities'

Reflective piece 5 **115**

(Becher, 2010: 4). In this case, I found it difficult to decide how to translate the female participant Devi's use of the term *wahaa*, which means both 'he' and 'she', in the following paragraph of her interview transcript:

> Because of the political parties – Nepal's are the worst . . . They are all bad, I would say . . . Before most people didn't say much, they showed respect for their superiors. Now everyone says I am bigger than you, he/she is bigger than him/her, sir is bigger than him/her etc. Everyone says we are big, we are big.

My husband, who was assisting me with translation, used 'he/she' and 'him/her' – the direct translations of *wahaa* – when transcribing the above passage for me; however, I was for various reasons unsure about this translation. Given the political influence mentioned, Devi was perhaps talking only about men, who, in the community referred to, are those most affected by the political parties. However, I was not sure enough of this to translate using masculine pronouns only. On the other hand, were Devi an English speaker, she might have used 'he/she' and 'him/her', or even 'they' and 'them', as someone in her equivalent social milieu in England probably would. However, given the male-dominated culture of Nepal, I considered it unlikely that she would position herself as sufficiently feminist to write 'he/she'. Nor could I have used the third person plural pronoun, as it would have been confusing in this excerpt. Could I have asked her? Would I then not have been putting words into – or removing them from – her mouth? Séguinot states that, 'to prove that there was explicitation, there must have been the possibility of a correct but less explicit or less precise version' (1988: 108), as is the case here. I ended up choosing to write 'he [she]' and 'him [her]' to indicate the gender Devi most likely intended, as well as the possibility that she also had women in mind.

A matter of ethics

I considered it an ethical imperative to refer in my thesis to the dilemmas discussed above, since an 'ethnographic text . . . helps to construct the social phenomena it accounts for' (Hammersley and Atkinson, 2010: 202). Moreover, a researcher who can, by 'acknowledging individual agency', restructure 'the power relationship between the researcher and the research participants', has a responsibility to present the research as reflectively as possible (Ashraf, 2010: 121–122).

My own identities and understandings, as well as how I identified others and how they identified each other and me, played a major role in my portrayal, as reflected in this exploration of just a couple of the ethical concerns involved in writing up research across languages and cultures. My writing is therefore never a neutral account. Compromise, a dilemma of ethnographic writing, is inevitable. The best I can do is to attempt to be as faithful as possible to myself, to those whom I portray and to those for whom I portray.

FIGURE 5.1 University educated tea shop keeper at work in the local bazaar

6

RESEARCH IN A MULTILINGUAL CONTEXT

Joining an international community of researchers

Anna Robinson-Pant

Introduction

> It is exciting to pursue ideas, experiment, share perceptions and become a member of a community of knowledge-makers.
>
> *(Skillen and Purser, 2003: 17)*

The theme of the doctoral student joining a new community, contributing to knowledge and learning new skills like an apprentice, permeates much of the literature on the PhD process. As Skillen and Purser (2003: 17) suggest, however, 'the thrill of research seems to end when it comes to writing' as the student is faced with the challenges discussed in my previous chapter around meeting the academic writing expectations of the institution. Many students and supervisors understandably view a doctoral thesis as the end product of a course of study, and the emphasis becomes how to learn and reproduce the genre successfully. We can, however, take a broader perspective by looking at the PhD as one step on a research journey, not just in terms of career progression, but also as intensive engagement in a process of learning how to interact with, challenge and influence wider research communities. Those students who have the option to publish journal articles instead of writing a thesis for their PhD – as in the case of some Icelandic students quoted in this book – may have already engaged intensively with editors, reviewers and publishers in addition to their supervision committee. Whilst supervisors and examiners may tend to emphasise the 'future contribution' of a PhD thesis or student's work, I suggest that the doctoral experience in itself can contribute in the here and now – particularly through doctoral supervision meetings – to innovative developments around researching across languages and cultures. The strategies described by doctoral students in this book are not just

118 Anna Robinson-Pant

around how to conduct research in multilingual and intercultural situations, but also about how to communicate and share their learning from those experiences with colleagues, particularly their supervisors.

This chapter looks at the international research community and the geopolitics of academic publishing to explore the broader implications of supervisors and students engaging in this initial intercultural research dialogue. As I discussed in Chapter 1, Canagarajah's (2002) ethnographic study in Sri Lanka suggested that the qualities of academic writing that were prized in his former US university context were dismissed as 'aggressive individualism' (p. 141) by his colleagues in Jaffna. His account of his return to academic life in Sri Lanka after studying in the US gives an unusual insight into how academic literacy practices from different contexts may be seen as in collision – presenting difficult decisions for the academic who wants to bring their new learning into their home institution. In this chapter, I draw on interviews with former UK international doctoral students who are now working as academics in universities across the world, in addition to sources of data cited earlier. The focus is less on these researchers' practical adaptation back home, than on the ways in which they position themselves ideologically through bringing alternative research and writing practices into their academic institution or cultural context.

Turner (2003: 50) described the PhD as having 'a life of its own as an institutional rhetorical practice' and her interviews with supervisors suggested that they saw real risks in experimenting with the conventional structure and style of a thesis, as an 'inherently conservative genre'. For this reason, the doctoral student may decide to postpone any experiments with authorial voice, hybrid or multilingual texts until a later stage, as Turner (ibid.) argued in relation to PhD writing in the humanities: 'it is predominantly at the micro level rather than the macro level that changes are occurring'. This chapter is concerned to look at the potential role of the doctoral student as a change agent at the macro level too – in terms of challenging and aiming to transform cultural and linguistic hierarchies that often appear to be solidified and reproduced through the geopolitics of publishing. Although this may be regarded as too unrealistic and aspirational – on the part of students and Alain and me as authors too – we consider that taking the broader lenses (such as decolonising methodology) introduced in this book involves addressing these more ambitious aims. This chapter deliberately addresses some of the larger decisions that the doctoral student may have put on hold but which are the focus of decolonising-methodology writers – such as the choice of language, forms of reciprocity and alternative ways of writing up research.

Constructing knowledge for multiple audiences

In Chapter 5, I discussed the difficulties of writing for audiences with differing expectations of both research and academic writing. A doctoral student might want to represent the voices of their research participants in ways that their

Research in a multilingual context **119**

fieldsite community would recognise and approve of. However, uppermost in their mind is probably how their supervisor and eventual examiner would read and judge the final text. In many ways, the experience of writing the thesis with several audiences in mind (and juggling writer identities within the text) is good preparation for future academic writing where the researcher will need to take account of journal editors, peer reviewers, close colleagues, research participants, as well as local, national and international readers. What is different, however, is that the researcher may now have to decide where to publish, what language to use and even which research question would be of more interest to these various audiences – rather than being guided by PhD assessment criteria or their supervisors' advice. This means reflecting on questions like those raised in Lillis and Curry's book: 'What kinds of texts and knowledge "travel" across national and transnational borders?' (2010: 2)

Icelandic university students who had chosen the article route for their PhD revealed in our interviews that this could be for career reasons. In particular, they wanted to have the publications necessary to apply for university posts immediately after the degree so as to contribute directly to their professional development through co-authoring articles with an established academic. As Ingrid pointed out, the journal doctoral route was also beneficial for supervisors as 'it all counts towards the point system . . . it is good for the supervisors if they participate [in co-authoring with their student] as they get points for publications' (Interview, 2016). However, the student's choice to write articles rather than a thesis was also influenced by issues around audience. Ingrid had switched from writing a thesis in the knowledge that 'only five or six people would read it', whereas journals had the potential for a broader international audience. She was researching Polish migrants in Iceland and hoped that the articles would reach scholars of migration in Poland too. As she explained: 'I was not thinking much about audience when I was doing a monograph but I am thinking about it now as there are more implications, doing articles' (Interview, 2016). Monika, originally from Poland, explained that she too had chosen an article-based PhD in order to 'do different articles for different audiences' (Interview, 2016). Her concern was both to bridge the practitioner-academic gap, through writing for Icelandic teachers, and to reach a Nordic audience.

My interviews with international doctoral students who had returned to their home context from UK universities revealed that they were aware of having to adapt back to both the academic culture and the specific audience that they wrote for. In some cases, this led to them choosing to publish on a different topic after returning to their home country, rather than writing articles based on their PhD research. In the Saudi context, Mohammed explained that he was actively discouraged by his university from writing on the same topic as his PhD: 'I have to confirm that the article is not taken from your [my] PhD or MA. I would not benefit when I apply for promotion' (Interview, 2012). In order to choose a new area of research, he did an internet search to see which subjects were currently being addressed in Western journals and were likely to appeal to an international audience:

> I search through websites and get up-to-date topics [in the West] and then I concentrate on those. That's how I found 'bullying'. I teach on a diploma for those appointed as teacher counsellors in the Ministry and I keep asking them about bullying. Their understanding is about physical bullying, not verbally. But at UK universities, they have a system [to prevent bullying] for the staff and students. We will just ignore it in Saudi. I prefer to go through the English websites to see the topics. Not all are suitable, some are too sensitive.
>
> *(Interview, 2012)*

He went on to explain that as well as avoiding 'sensitive' topics such as homosexuality or sexual abuse, he had to observe strict rules about direct communication with women, which constrained his research approach:

> My work is like a circle, I have to go around. I can't go inside. There is no way to interview girls. I can't go out of the boundary. So I do quantitative research with the males only. I can't do face-to-face research, so I can't go deeply to understand her point of view.
>
> *(Interview, 2012)*

Having previously worked in the Saudi context, Mohammed had quickly adjusted back to such constraints and referred to the greater freedom that researchers in the UK had to determine their topic and methodology. However, he also saw his current role as introducing a new subject such as 'bullying' to his colleagues and informants – discussing the differing interpretations by Saudi informants, as compared to the work he read about in English. Mohammed used his earlier doctoral experience of literature searches on the internet and mediating different concepts between his UK and Saudi readers to extend the reach of his current research and writing. He emphasised particularly how he shared his research through oral interaction with respondents and local colleagues – including how he was introducing this different understanding of 'bullying' to his students. The written output of his research was intended for international audiences as he had decided to publish in English. He explained that he continued to work with his UK supervisor, partly to 'keep my English language alive', and emphasised that there were tangible rewards for publishing his research in English rather than Arabic:

> They [his university in Saudi Arabia] also give you something, they add financially to your salary for English publications, in an English journal . . . Every time you get published in English, you get 20 per cent increase on the salary. I am trying to write about my project on bullying for an English journal.
>
> *(Interview, 2012)*

At the time of finishing his PhD, Mohammed had had a strong desire to translate not only his thesis, but also some of the key theoretical books, into Arabic to help disseminate the new conceptual understanding he had gained. However, as he now realised that he would not gain any points for promotion by publishing in or translating into Arabic, he had this earlier project on hold. We can see from Mohammed's story that the larger questions around research topic and form of publication were very much influenced by practical and instrumental considerations about career prospects. Whilst Mohammed seemed to have accepted the dominant values in his university (such as needing to publish on a Western topic in English), he was also using his intercultural learning to introduce new ideas around bullying into his teaching and university policies, a different form of dissemination. In his published journal articles, he was keen to speak to Western English-speaking audiences rather than Arabic, but perhaps this was in recognition that knowledge was constructed and developed in different ways within the Saudi academy. This was also related to a lack of research literature in Arabic. Mohammed explained that it was difficult to find up-to-date articles in Saudi journals online, because they did not put the most recent research there in case authors cut and pasted extracts. He saw this as a great advantage of using Western-published research on topics that were of current interest in the West.

Academics' writing is often assessed by the quality and status of the journal in which they publish and Mohammed, like many others, accepted this practice as a reasonable way of evaluating his work and determining career progression. An exception was Karim Sadeghi, a former UK student who is now working in an Iranian university, and who became so concerned about the indicators used for promotion that he published critiques of the system used (Sadeghi, 2010). Significantly, Karim pointed out the unusually high weighting given to papers published in local (Iranian) academic journals as compared to international journals. As an English Language Teaching specialist who writes in English for local and international journals, Karim now observes that this 'localisation constraint' has intensified, with the introduction of a new promotion system in Iran in March 2016 that requires academics to publish at least two articles in the Persian language (from email communication, 2016).

His (2010) journal article offered an insider view of the ways in which academic literacy practices can restrict a researcher's progress – relating a discussion with the panel judging his work who refused to consider his article for promotion because the abstract was 100 rather than 300 words long. Karim gave an unusual insight into the ways in which Iranian academics are being evaluated and the differing assumptions about academic writing quality, such as rigid conventions around length and form. His article is a combination of a rich auto-ethnographic account of the experience of being nominated as 'researcher of the year' in his university (which could be analysed as a literacy event since it was based on discussion of submitted texts), followed by a more conventional analysis of questionnaire data collected from other researchers in his situation. At another level, his article demonstrates how a researcher returning from the UK to his home institution recognised the need to engage with differing institutional values around academic literacy and publishing. By meshing different rhetorical styles, the author could be seen in terms of 'writing back' (see Pennycook, 1994, on postcolonial writers) to multiple audiences in Iran and internationally.

Writing for multiple audiences is not just a question of adapting one's style or genre, though this is certainly part of the process. Janina, who had moved from the Czech Republic to Germany then to Iceland for her studies, was acutely aware of the adaptations she had had to make in response to differing educational and writing practices in each context. She felt 'it was like moving between worlds really' and commented that in academic writing: 'Germans take a historical approach and go into the background. Whereas the Anglo-Saxon tradition here is about essays, going into the text' (Interview, 2016). In Ethiopia, Tesfay Tsegay had drawn on a similar understanding of differing rhetorical conventions when publishing after his PhD:

> When writing and presenting research papers, I usually have Ethiopian and foreign audiences in my mind. But usually the biggest audiences are Ethiopian. In some instances when I need to publish for international audiences, the submission guidelines maybe require me to adhere to new writing styles and ways of presenting an academic paper. But this has seldom caused me serious problems.
>
> *(From email correspondence, 2012)*

Identifying micro-level rhetorical differences in academic writing came easily to Tesfay as a language specialist and from his earlier experience of learning to write in a UK university for his PhD. Significantly, a greater challenge was around his role as an academic in constructing and disseminating knowledge in Ethiopia and he ended up moving outside academia to translate and write philosophical literature for the public in Amharic, the national language. In a similar move, Judith Castaneda Mayo – an academic in Mexico who had earlier studied in the UK – decided to share her research through a national newspaper column in order to reach a wider Spanish-speaking audience. She also later graduated with a second PhD from a university in Spain on the same topic, enabling her to 'adjust my thoughts into my L1 [first language] with all the theories and feminist philosophies' (from email correspondence, 2016).

These accounts reveal how even beyond the PhD, unequal relationships around knowledge construction and dissemination influence researchers' writing and publishing decisions. Within the specific context of the PhD, we tend to see power relationships in terms of hierarchies between the student and supervisor or between the international student and the Northern university. However, after the PhD and when publishing articles, the researcher still has to make decisions around whose knowledges and whose values to prioritise (such as Mohammed's decision to prioritise Western audiences or later in this chapter, Monika's aim to write for practitioners). It is striking that some researchers chose to challenge these hierarchies – whether directly through the subject and form of their writing (as with Karim's example) or through moving outside academia to write for national and local readers through alternative genres (Judith and Tesfay). We also need to avoid conflating dissemination or construction of knowledge with written texts (as discussed in Chapter 5) since researchers may be writing for Western audiences in centre[1] journals, but simultaneously introducing new ways of thinking to local communities through their other research activities, teaching and oral interaction. Sara (from Iceland), who conducted her research in Burundi, suggested that 'giving back research to respondents – sending drafts does not make sense'. She was considering going back in person to Burundi to present her research, explaining 'this is not about writing for academics, more about sharing findings'. As a former aid worker, Sara's concern about the gap between academics and practitioners had led her to do the PhD: 'I know both worlds and try to keep the needs of both in mind' (2016).

The ways that researchers chose to position themselves in relation to global hierarchies of knowledge production can be analysed at an individual level – in terms of their ideological position and values. As the next section will explore, the dimension of resources also needs to be taken into account, particularly in relation to the dominance of English-language research publications. Canagarajah (2002) pointed out the irony of Southern scholars having to read in English to find out about the situation in their own country: 'Due to the one-sided nature of publishing, we are forced into a position of understanding ourselves through center eyes' (ibid.: 237).

Publishing in English: a political decision?

> How is English related to cultural forms and practices? Does its global spread now make it a culturally neutral language? Is the spread of English part of the gradual homogenisation of the world? Is the world getting smaller? Or is English part of the greater diversification and heterogenisation of the world?
>
> *(Pennycook, 2007: 5)*

The decision to write in English is usually taken for practical reasons around career progression and intended audience. However, the consequences can be far-reaching in that other knowledges and research literature have become increasingly marginalised through the dominance of centre journals published in English. As Pennycook's questions above suggest, the spread of English can be seen in positive terms as a 'culturally neutral language' or as part of a homogenising process where indigenous languages and cultural practices are overwhelmed. These two differing perspectives suggest that the choice of language medium for publication may be one of the most 'political' decisions a multilingual researcher has to take. As I discussed in Chapter 5, most doctoral students do not have a choice about which language/s to write their thesis in – but after the PhD and in writing journal articles, the researcher can position themselves differently. However, as Mutua and

124 Anna Robinson-Pant

Swadener (2004: 258) emphasise in their edited book on decolonising research, this decision is not at all straightforward:

> Many of the authors in this volume are constrained and caught up in the use of English as the language of research representation – a very colonizing endeavor – from which, though they are aware of the dangers of English, they cannot extricate themselves.

To take a step back, it is helpful to interrogate our assumptions about language so that the debate is not simply polarised as for or against English. Pennycook (1994: 29) argues for a conceptualisation of language not in terms of a 'pre-given system but a will to community'. The notion of 'community' has been disputed as too static (see Chapter 5 in relation to Hyland's discussion of academic community) but significantly here it takes on a different function as a verb. The emphasis is on what people do with language and 'the cultural and ideological positions in which people use language' (Pennycook 1994: 31). Within the context of this chapter on the multilingual research community, we can take this understanding of language to change the kind of questions we ask – not just, 'do they write in English or not?' but 'how does the researcher develop her/his identity and ideology through English?' The idea of one English (or 'a' language) is also contested by Pennycook (1994: 6), through his exploration of the 'worldliness' of English, 'embedded in multiple local contexts of use'. In relation to written texts, these 'contexts of use' can refer to the specific academic discourses and communities (such as journal editors, reviewers and readers) that shape the final publication.

The question of resources available to researchers writing across cultures and languages is not just limited to practical issues, such as lack of access to journals or distance from high status academic networks. It is also about what Pennycook (1994: 291) termed the 'conditions of possibility for writing' in a particular context. Comparing the experiences of literary writers in Africa who were 'speaking back' in English in quite different ways from those in South East Asia, Pennycook analysed the production of and constraints on language use in these different situations. This is about understanding the shifting position of English in relation to other languages in a specific community and how such language hierarchies are influenced by politics, economics and social change. In all these cases, the researcher can move away from the idea of 'pure' language to consider 'which English' and adopt strategies such as Michael-Luna and Canagarajah's (2007) 'code meshing' approach to develop hybrid texts.

Many of the doctoral students I interviewed in Korea, Iceland and Nepal recognised tensions around choosing to publish in English, yet felt that they would not have other feasible options after finishing their thesis or for publishing articles. Boyoung, like Mohammed, related this decision to the system for career progression: 'In Korean higher education, they give credits for research publications.

But if the publication is in English, the credits are double'. She recognised the implications for the quality of writing and teaching through observing the experiences of her teachers at the university:

> As a Korean I feel bad about this as lots of professors feel comfortable writing in Korean and teach way better in Korean but they are pressurised to teach in English and the whole system encourages this. When I read their publications, I feel bad for them sometimes. They know the ideas so well but they can't express the whole idea because they have to write in English.
>
> *(Interview, 2015)*

Boyoung described how some professors wrote their articles in Korean then had them professionally translated – though this was not an option for most students in terms of the cost and the time needed to read and revise drafts. This sense of compulsion around writing in English seemed to lead to a situation where the content and argument became somehow detached from the expression of the ideas through English. This could be related to Pennycook's (1994: 26) distinction between views of language as a 'passive reflector of rather than active agent in social relations'. A strong deficit discourse came through my interviews with some doctoral students, in relation not only to a lack of confidence in the English language but also expressing a sense of loss that they could not draw on resources in their mother tongue.

Several students expressed unease about the decision to publish in English, recognising that their actions were contributing to the current lack of literature in their mother tongue or other indigenous languages, and what they saw as a downward spiral. Dinesh explained how difficult he had found it during his PhD to obtain or refer to research literature in Nepali:

> I can say that 99.9 per cent of [my] reading is in English. The first thing is that you don't get publications in Nepali, except newspapers . . . But no academic publications in Nepali. Even in the Sanskrit universities, they publish in English. All universities publish journals in English. Most schools use English-medium instruction. In fifty years' time, no one will speak Nepali.
>
> *(Interview, 2015)*

Dinesh's account suggests that the dominance of English in academic publications in Nepal has a direct impact on the diminishing Nepali research literature. Placing this trend in the wider societal context, he sees the shift towards English-medium schooling in urban centres like Kathmandu as exacerbating this problem in future, through decreasing the number of Nepali speakers. This point was emphasised by Meenakshi too, as she described how the Awadhi community, with whom she researched in a rural area, wanted to use English even at preschool stage.

Faced with this situation, Dinesh felt that there was little option but to publish in English too:

> I thought if I lament on loss of language I'll be alone. So I will now celebrate the changing pattern. Sometimes I become more critical and think, let's preserve our language or I try to flow with the same current.
>
> *(Interview, 2015)*

The 'changing pattern' that Dinesh refers to connects with Pennycook's notion of the 'worldliness' of English – that English is becoming integral to Nepali life in this context, particularly in academic institutions. In Dinesh's field research, he described working with young participants who code-switched between Nepali and English, and read more fluently in English than he himself. Through the youth discourse that he was recreating in his thesis, he seemed to be engaging with these other Englishes and 'speaking back' through the linguistic resources available in this context.

As an international student from Colombia in Korea, Diego was working in English, Spanish and Korean. Though he had to write in Korean and English for his current course, he recognised that he would have a wider choice in future: 'I would like to publish in Spanish as not much is in English in Latin America.' His hope was that he would be able to contribute more to the academic community in Colombia through publishing in the dominant language there (Spanish) but was aware that he was losing confidence now: 'I don't write at all in Spanish now. I help those who are translating from Spanish to English . . . I write it again in Spanish for them to explain what it means well but that is not real writing'. Partly because of his sense that he was no longer used to academic writing in Spanish, Diego concluded that he was more likely to write in English in future: 'Most knowledge is produced in English everywhere' (Interview, 2015).

In the university in Iceland, doctoral students had more choice about which language to write in for their PhD, but were influenced by the dominance of English-language academic literature in their field and the small size of the Icelandic population (only 300,000). Sara related the decision to her specific research topic that was of more interest to an audience outside the country: 'It is pointless to write in Icelandic, who would care here? It is one thing to be a big fish in a small pond, but this would be a whale in a puddle!' Similarly, Alga commented, 'But if I wrote in Icelandic, I would only have audience of two so it would be stupid to write only for them. There are so few people in my field in Iceland'. In fact Alga was also writing in Icelandic, particularly for practitioner audiences and in the media. Like other students interviewed in Iceland, she did not see this as an either/or decision about English, but rather a question of which language suited which purpose and audience. Monika emphasised that:

> Icelandic research literature is still strong in the School of Education as so much research is practical and for teachers . . . Since not every teacher reads

or is comfortable reading in English, it is important to make sure that the text is reaching to as many practitioners or future teachers as possible.

(Interview, 2016)

After completing her thesis, she also planned to publish a booklet in Polish and other languages for parents (in Iceland where she worked), recognising the importance of engaging with a wider community through her research.

Several international students mentioned the limitations of Icelandic as compared to English – not in terms of their language competency (as second-language speakers) but in relation to the range of vocabulary. Janina explained:

> This is very much about freedom of expression. I have better choice of words in English. Icelandic is limited as a language – there are not enough words. They [Icelandic scholars] are not allowed to use Anglocisms so they have to make new words all the time in Icelandic. Like there is one word for 'mother tongue' in Icelandic, but many in English. People give up on writing in Icelandic because of this reason, especially in the technical subjects.
>
> *(Interview, 2016)*

A desire to preserve and develop Icelandic as a language perhaps accounted for this resistance to introducing English words into Icelandic – but could end up with students switching over to writing for academic audiences in English instead. Ingrid compared Polish (her mother tongue), saying 'we adapt international words [like 'discourse'] even if they get Polish spelling or pronunciation'.

From the students' accounts above, the decision about whether to continue publishing in English seemed to be related primarily to practical concerns around career progression (the 'system' that Boyoung refers to), their competency in English and other languages (including sometimes a lack of academic writing experience in their first language), the likely size of audience (Alga and Sara) and the difficulties of accessing other literatures. In addition, the experience of writing a PhD thesis has (understandably) prepared students primarily for academic writing in English, with few opportunities to explore or develop alternatives. Their accounts point to the significance of resources, particularly the lack of research literature in indigenous languages on which to draw references or to act as models for developing their academic writing. When students mentioned other kinds of writing that they did in their first language – whether editing translated texts (Diego) or writing novels (Youyi) – this was sometimes seen as quite apart from their academic writing – 'not real writing' (Diego). The decision to draw on different languages and literacies within academic publications would be a huge step to take as a new researcher – particularly as this could be seen as an individual act, rather than part of a collaborative enterprise with supervisors. It could be interpreted as 'going it alone' or setting oneself against a whole research community and their established practices. Conversely, publishing in English was often a collaborative enterprise,

128 Anna Robinson-Pant

with students being supported by their supervisors through co-authoring journal articles ('like holding our hand and pulling us up', Dinesh commented).

As a speaker of English as a first language, I am aware that my options as a writer are limited because I lack the fluency in other languages to experiment creatively with form and voice. Ironically, multilingual and bilingual researchers have a richer resource in this respect. Yet this is often overlooked because of the imperative to publish in standard English and high-status centre journals. In the final section of this chapter, I will look at some of the alternative strategies adopted by such researchers and the possibilities of addressing some of the language and publishing inequalities highlighted above.

Finding alternatives

> In the academy, the authority exercised by peers, editors, reviewers and other community figures influence [sic] who gets heard, who gets accepted and whose arguments are seen as persuasive. Such contexts privilege certain ways of making meanings and so encourage the performance of certain kinds of professional identities. They place restrictions on the rhetorical resources participants can bring from their past experiences.
>
> *(Hyland, 2009: 65)*

In this chapter, I have looked at academic communities in relation to higher educational institutions as well as the 'global audience' that research students referred to in Chapter 5. As Hyland suggests, both can be seen as similar in terms of power hierarchies around reading, writing and speaking which influence 'who gets heard, who gets accepted'. Whilst we are familiar with the discourse around valuing students' prior experiences, it is less common to bring this perspective to the international publishing domain – as Hyland does with the recognition of participants' 'rhetorical resources'. Journal editors and reviewers tend to position themselves as gatekeepers with responsibility for ensuring high quality, rather than as mentors whose role is to induct newcomers into the community or to begin to question the journal's dominant values and practices. Researchers writing in English as a second language have found these encounters particularly fraught with tension, as Alga in Iceland commented:

> Some journals/editors/reviewers make derogatory and/or petty remarks about our language. This seems to vary among reviewers/journals where US-based journals seem – to us – to be most lacking in decorum and inclusion in academic writing!
>
> *(From email correspondence, 2015)*

We have suggested in earlier chapters that supervisors and higher education institutions could view the experiences of doctoral students researching across cultures as a source of intercultural learning. Similarly, if editors and reviewers view academic publishing as a game with rules that do not have to be fixed or prescribed (such as the conventional form of the research article), there is the possibility for a space for alternative voices and knowledge construction to open up. This section looks at alternative forms of writing (Canagarajah's (2002) 'discursive' dimension), as well as the conditions that might allow such changes to take place (the 'material constraints', ibid.).

Speaking back: the discursive dimension

Within the postcolonial and decolonising methodology literature, much has been written about the need to 'write back' to the dominant colonial discourse, using alternative languages, indigenous theoretical concepts and marginalised voices. Such writers position themselves as agents of change, and as Pennycook (1996: 266) emphasises, 'writing back produces realities as well as reflects them'. For a novice researcher, this notion of resisting dominant discourses and writing conventions can be quite daunting, not least because they are subject to both North/South hierarchies and also power relations within their own institution.

Turner's (2003) case study of a Korean student writing her PhD in English illustrates the challenges of trying to change accepted rhetorical practices. Turner described how the student resisted her advice (given as an academic literacy specialist) to use shorter topic sentences because she felt this would be closing down meanings – 'I don't want to give the impression that I have absolute knowledge or that there is just one possibility' (ibid.: 44). The student also explained that she wanted to give the reader a choice by keeping in the text words that Turner regarded as tautologies. The student's decisions about how to construct the text were very much informed by postcolonial and psychoanalytic theorising (the subject of her thesis) – 'that conceptual content affects her rhetorical strategies' (ibid.: 41). Turner's micro-level analysis of how the student constructed and teacher (Turner) interpreted the text gives an unusual insight into the 'new and emerging micro-rhetorical features' that the student was developing in order to 'speak back'. However, without this oral discussion between writer and reader, the resulting text could be dismissed as convoluted, repetitive and not clearly argued. The risks of 'writing back' are thus likely to be high – without the opportunity to give a commentary explaining how the text is to be read and interpreted. In this respect, the supervision meeting or one-to-one tutorial can be seen as a safe space to gauge the reader's response to such writing.

Outside the PhD context, Gonzalez and Lincoln (2006) propose 'non traditional reporting forms' which could better serve the needs of indigenous people. They emphasise that the researcher has to 'consider the presence of multiple audiences with different data needs' (ibid.: 9) and suggest that results should be made available in the languages in which it was collected, to 'give the readers the option of the original language of the data along with the "presentation" language' (ibid.: 11). Some of their recommendations have practical implications, such as the need for a longer text length in order to produce bilingual texts and to allow for 'extensive elaboration of issues and concerns in the local context' (ibid.). The changes proposed in their article to address current inequalities in knowledge production are laudable but the authors give little indication as to how to initiate such change; for instance: 'the academy's interest in evaluating only faculty publications which are in . . . high prestige Western journals . . . has to give way to recognition of journal articles which are not normally a part of the repertoire of Western universities' (ibid.: 12).

In discussion with PhD students in Iceland who were already writing articles and papers, I found that decisions about whether to include quotations from interview data or literature in another language were more likely to be taken on practical than ideological grounds. Monika, for instance, included only the translated English text in her papers, and mentioned that she would do this at a forthcoming conference 'to save time'. She was consciously modelling other authors' conventions in this respect:

> I am reading Nordic journals but notice they only put the English. Then there is a note at the end where they say the author translated it. I will not put the original for literature quotes either, only the English. For titles, I see they put the original and then the translation.
>
> *(Interview, 2016)*

Translation was, however, seen as a specialist and additional role of the author. Alga said she would try to avoid quoting directly from the literature in another language: 'because if I did, I would have to translate it myself and me not being a translator, that would not do it justice. I would not like another writer to do that for my writing'.

Gunnar explained that for extracts from an Icelandic article, he would provide the original in the text with the English translation as a footnote: 'I give the reference at the end of the footnote but put the translation in brackets in English as I reckon this is like giving a service to the reader'. He also mentioned that when quoting and translating interview data, he wanted to 'keep the flow' and realised it was 'difficult to keep the same spirit' (Interview, 2016).

Writing multilingual and multivocal texts can be one way of 'speaking back', to use Pennycook's term. As novices in the academy, postdoctoral students may however prefer to conform to dominant academic writing practices in order to get published. It is also possible to combine experiments with form and voice alongside writing conventional articles for centre-based English-language journals (as writers like Canagarajah do). This takes me onto the practical constraints facing researchers who want to begin to transform or engage with dominant discursive practices in the academy.

Material constraints and strategies to address these

The material constraints described by Canagarajah and other researchers based in the South include: access to up-to-date literature, photocopying and printing facilities and marginalisation from influential academic networks due to lack of funding to attend international conferences. Although Canagarajah was writing in the 1990s, many scholars face similar constraints today. The internet has helped to widen access to recent and current research, but irregular electricity and internet facilities remain a barrier for many in the South. Both academics and students have sometimes drawn on the services of professional translators and proofreaders to translate or edit their journal articles to address the difficulty of being outside an English-speaking community. Alga explained that she and other Icelandic researchers used copy editors on a regular basis, and explained how she worked with a copy editor in Canada:

> I have a good relationship with her and she gets that I have to find a voice and reads it through so she is not incorporating her voice. We work together on email, then when I send the manuscripts we have long Skype meetings to discuss them. But it is another cost in time and money.
>
> *(Interview, 2016)*

As Alain discussed in Chapter 3, translation (and proofreading) can be seen as purely technical acts. By contrast, Alga was aware of the copy editor's potential impact on her voice and identity within the text.

There are, however, alternatives to these battles to enter the community of high-status English-language journals and it is possible to present a challenge to accepted genres and voices from outside. Several former UK doctoral students told me that they had decided to publish in non-academic publications, including national newspapers, partly because they could then bypass journal gatekeepers and reach a more diverse audience. Gunnar's aim to share his research on Icelandic musicians more widely had led him to write a book in English alongside the thesis: 'It is for an audience between the academic and general public. They [the publisher] said "wear your journalistic cap, but it's for the academic world too"'. In the academic context, Gunnar had faced criticism that his style was 'too journalistic' but he felt there was space for alternative voices there too: 'My philosophy is that I believe in lively academic text but you have to be scientific too. A little more formal' (2016).

Another strategy has been to establish a national journal with a space for alternative voices and approaches to research. On his return to Iran, Karim Sadeghi founded the *Iranian Journal of Language Teaching Research* (see www. urmia.ac.ir/ijltr). By encouraging centre-level scholars to contribute through the editorial board and to submit articles, he aimed for the journal to gain an international status and reach. Significantly, the most successful indigenous and national journals based in the South often publish in the English language and so are able to engage with a wide audience. To a large extent they appear to have adhered to the form and genre of centre-journal articles rather than providing alternative models of writing.

Developing alternative writing practices can be seen in terms of methodological innovation. A participatory and collaborative approach to research and writing can emerge from adopting a 'social practice' approach to literacy (Street, 1993; Barton, 1994), as contrasted with the more usual image of a solitary, individual writer. An example of collaborative writing support was given by Janina who co-wrote an article for a journal called *Netla*, published in Icelandic for Icelandic researchers. As part of a Nordic research group called 'Learning Spaces' (http://lsp2015.hi.is) with a policy to publish in Icelandic (coordinated by her supervisor), Janina had been encouraged and supported to co-write with PhD students and professors, all researching secondary school education, for an Icelandic academic audience. Her experience demonstrated the importance of such research groups in facilitating collaborative writing and inspired her intention to write about her PhD research in Icelandic at a later stage. Janina was researching children who attended heritage language classes in Iceland and commented, 'I should make use of my background, like I encourage plurilingual students to do here. When I write in Czech it would reach a large research audience across the region' (Interview, 2016).

Rejection from English-language journals – or failing to produce a successful PhD thesis – is often seen in deficit terms on the part of the individual researcher who apparently lacks the appropriate writing skills. This chapter has illustrated how such 'failures' can be seen as part of a larger picture of global inequalities in English-language academic publishing. Recognising the challenges facing a lone researcher in the South in tackling these inequalities – whether through 'writing back' or attempting to set up alternative publishing opportunities – collaborative ventures seem to be a way forward. Doctoral students in Iceland have set up a Facebook group to share their experiences of liaising with centre-level journals. For example, Alga had been working with a journal editor in Norway, and though she had had to rewrite her article, commented that 'she is willing to engage with me about this and support me to get this published, unlike US journals which just reject outright in a negative way'. Alga also favourably compared an editor's method of giving feedback on her writing through tracking changes, to others who had remarked on her English directly: 'Making remarks about language, I find very rude'. Centre-level journals have set up mentoring programmes for 'new' writers, to introduce them not only to the rhetorical conventions but also to the ways in which they need to understand and connect with literacy brokers such as editors and reviewers (see Lillis, Magyar and Robinson-Pant, 2010). Such programmes can help raise awareness amongst reviewers about alternative ways of writing and feedback – to help counter the kinds of prejudice against non-native speakers reported by Flowerdew (2001) based on his interviews with centre-based journal editors.

Conclusion

I began this chapter by suggesting that a PhD could be regarded as one step towards joining and possibly acting as an agent of change within a wider international research community. As a doctoral supervisor myself, I regard the PhD supervision meeting as providing an unusual opportunity for intercultural learning through dialogue. Whilst a PhD remains essentially an individual project (at least in the social sciences and humanities), supervision meetings and interaction around the student's writing can give the sense of a collaborative endeavour. I have talked about the risks of experimenting within the PhD, yet the doctoral supervision process can also provide a safe space for exploring different options around genre, voice and form. As the example of the Korean student in Turner's article illustrates, the individual encounter between student and teacher can provide a source of learning for both – investigating their usually unstated cultural assumptions about writing, reading and knowledge. In this way, the PhD can provide a space for trying out new rhetorical practices and experimenting with form. Even though this exploration takes place only at a micro level and is constrained by the specific requirements of doctoral writing in the student's institution, this is an important learning experience in terms of first-hand engagement with different ways of communicating across cultures and languages.

After the doctoral degree, the researcher has a different and wider range of choices, such as: which language/s to write in, whether to publish in high-status English-language journals, how to decide on a new direction for their research, how to disseminate research findings and to whom. It is worth noting, however, that other factors may come into play which may constrain these choices, such as funding agencies' requirements or academic promotion criteria. How researchers decide to position themselves in relation to North-South relationships around knowledge, authority and identity are all part of this subsequent process of researching across languages and cultures. Whilst some researchers see themselves as agents of change in terms of destablising or seeking to transform dominant research discourses, others see the first step as becoming part of such communities of practice through adopting and replicating dominant practices. Centre-based journals may prove a harsh environment for the lone researcher and the experiences in this chapter suggest the importance of seeking out peer support and mentors for the transition from the PhD into a wider academic community. With diminishing resources in local or even national languages to provide alternative models of theorising, writing and dissemination, the researcher who wants to step outside the mainstream faces an additional challenge. Yet this situation also provides the strongest argument for researchers to seek to initiate such change, thereby making a contribution to strengthening indigenous research literature and pointing to new research directions in the future. The questions in Box 6 provide some ideas for reflecting on the researcher's role, with regard to decisions that may arise in relation to language and culture after the doctoral degree.

134 Anna Robinson-Pant

Box 6

Questions for further reflection

- Which specific audiences do I want to engage with after completing my PhD? What are the best ways of sharing my research with these groups?
- What written publications do I want to produce? How will these differ in form and language for different groups, such as practitioners, policy makers, academics within my country/region, international audiences?
- Do I intend to write in English and what are the reasons for this? How might this decision influence my identity as a writer, which audiences I reach, and my career progression or direction?
- Are there ways that I can 'speak back' to dominant research traditions and discourses? Drawing on alternative knowledges, using minority languages, constructing multilingual and multivocal texts? What are the risks of doing this in my particular context?
- What resources and support do I need to develop my approach as a researcher across languages and cultures? How do I identify appropriate mentors, collaborative writing groups, new academic networks, alternative literature sources, translators, informal peer reviewers, critical friends, copy editors?
- If writing in English as a second language, how do I construct my own voice and identity through the text and what role might a copy editor or translator play in this? How can I draw on different Englishes if trying to publish in 'centre-based' UK/US/Australian journals?
- If writing for specific academic journals, how far should I change my style and voice to fit with their expectations? Do I try to draw on the theoretical and research literature cited by previous writers in that journal? How do I choose my future research topic/research question?

I will end this chapter with Alga's advice to other doctoral students, which sums up both the challenges and the joys of entering this multilingual academic community:

> My advice is mainly to see the process of doing and undoing and doing again and academic voice as an ongoing creative process. It's not just about you. It's relational. It's artistry that you should enjoy rather than see as something you have to overcome, because you never will. Just enjoy it. There is this

all-encompassing fear. But it's just fear, feeling 'I don't want to do this'. Fear goes hand in hand with creativity. You can't be creative without fear. Enjoy – but there will be moments of utter fear.

(Interview, 2016)

Note

1 Reflecting the terminology in the literature on academic journal publishing, I have chosen to refer to 'centre' and 'periphery' here rather than North/South (see Chapter 1 for explanation of terms).

ENDPIECE

Anna Robinson-Pant and Alain Wolf

Our journey so far

At this point, we are faced with a dilemma about how to conclude this book. We set out to write a 'guide to researching across languages and cultures' – as indicated by our title. However, our intention was never to prescribe tools or methods, nor even to provide definitive answers to some of the questions we raise here! In this respect, our readers may consider that the term 'guide' was misleading and this recognition on our part has remained an underlying tension throughout the writing process. Should we conclude each chapter with a summary of the tools introduced and give explicit advice on how to go about the translation of spoken interaction with respondents or how a doctoral student can work effectively with translators? As will now be evident, we opted instead to end chapters with a box of reflective questions emerging from our discussion, followed by an interlude written by a doctoral student about their related experiences of researching across languages and cultures. These reflective pieces might be seen as fitting with the 'critical personal narrative and auto/ethnographic movement' discussed by Mutua and Swadener (2004) in their work on decolonising research. For those readers who have found our approach too open-ended and were frustrated at the lack of 'best practice' lists of advice, we suggest that the need to be flexible, reflexive and responsive to specific contexts is really the only overarching guidance appropriate here. The challenge of researching and writing across languages and cultures can be summed up (to use Mutua and Swadener's (2004: 7) words on decolonising research again) as 'a messy, complex and perhaps impossible endeavour'.

So, at the end of this particular research journey, we have decided to conclude by sharing the unexpected and sometimes hidden aspects of our experiences of writing this book. Coming from different disciplinary and methodological backgrounds, we faced an initial decision around how to construct the narrative and ended up retaining our individual voices in the chapters for which we were the lead author. Reading and contributing to each other's drafts, we were struck by our differences in style – Alain tending to be 'more didactic' (in his words) and Anna 'more journalistic' (in her words). We were not only writing across our disciplinary cultures, but were also affected by our previous professional experiences, identities and roles – Alain as a former trainee/ordinand for the priesthood and Anna as a development worker. This influenced the differing kind of illustrative material we drew on to explain particular theoretical ideas or methodological interpretations (see Alain's discussion of biblical translations in Chapter 4) as well as the research literature with which we were familiar.

We have also been sharing ideas on research methodology and methods for collecting and analysing data that would contribute directly to our separate chapters. In this respect, Anna's experience in participatory development and research shaped many of the practices we adopted in our interviews and the final text. What remain hidden from the reader are the many oral and email interactions with the researchers and doctoral students who were interviewed for this book. An unexpected outcome of this process of sharing the evolving drafts and interpretations of the data (rather than just 'member checking' through sending respondents the transcripts) was that many participants commented on their methodological learning. For instance, two students quoted in Chapter 5 responded on reading the draft chapters: 'I haven't heard about participatory writing and I find it very interesting, to learn about it and to be a part of it', and 'it becomes a great opportunity for me to learn how the interview becomes part of academic writing'.

We were concerned to include multiple perspectives and voices in the book – through interviewing researchers in different parts of the world – but faced inevitable constraints in 'translating' these ideas into written text in the form of a guide for doctoral students. We recognised the potential irony of advocating 'hybridity' or fluidity in format, language and voice, yet producing a book that responded to the expectations of a conventional guide in terms of structure (thematic chapters) and style (authoritative narrative voice). Thus, in some respects, the processes of learning and action research that lie behind this book may offer richer insights into the intercultural and decolonising research approach that we set out to facilitate, than the resulting text.

Researching across languages and cultures: an alternative perspective

Although approaching this subject from differing disciplinary backgrounds, we share a similar ideological stance on knowledge, power and culture, which has informed the overall argument and contribution of the book. At the simplest level, this is about analysing research knowledge as constructed rather than given and involves reflecting on how and whose values, which languages and literatures are prioritised within research. By looking specifically at how knowledge is constructed through translation and writing, we have shown the value of taking a social practice approach to examine communicative practices within fieldwork and writing up research (see Hrefna's critical account of her fieldwork with regard to identities and language in Chapter 1). Rather than seeing translation and writing as academic skills to be learned in a classroom and then transferred, we have proposed a 'situated' approach to exploring in depth what happens in a specific context, for instance, when someone helps with translating in a sensitive situation (see example of the interpreter delivering 'bad news' in Chapter 4).

Rather than seeing 'ethics' as primarily a consideration around gaining access and informed consent at the outset of a research project, we suggest that this perspective implies ongoing interrogation of ethical values and practices throughout the research process, including the writing and dissemination stage. In his capacity as Ethics Officer for his department, Alain has often experienced how both students and academics regard the ethics approval granted to their project as a rubber-stamping exercise, a hoop through which one has to jump before being allowed to get on with the 'real' work of data collection. Our approach in this book has been to challenge this understanding of the process. Our examples often pointed to the need for translators and researchers to take a constant reflective and ethical stance in relation to data collection. The realisation, for example, that individuals often code-switch to negotiate and affirm their identities (see Chapter 4) raises issues in any PhD thesis which may, for reasons of fluency, translate code-switched data into English, thus erasing the participant's claim to a particular identity. Another example (see Vera's experiences of dealing with the media in Chapter 3) showed how dissemination to the non-academic public raises ongoing ethical issues, in this case related to the media wilfully misrepresenting data findings to the detriment of the researched. We have also tried to adopt an ethical approach to writing this book through encouraging participants to respond to and suggest changes to our drafts. This process was in itself a learning experience, strengthening our belief that how researchers interpret the context and import of their participants' contributions can and should be challenged by them, however painful the process may be. This can lead to a more nuanced and ethical interpretation than the one that researchers started with in the first place.

We thus set out to make a contribution to the growing literature on conducting research in intercultural contexts. In some respects, our book could be seen as continuing key debates within the decolonising methodology literature, such as: engaging with the complexity of insider–outsider identities within fieldwork, experimenting with voice, style and code-switching within written texts and interrogating the overall purpose and intended outcomes of academic research. The dimension that we hope to have added relates to our focus on doctoral research and doctoral students within the academy. By starting from the doctoral student as 'expert' in terms of their linguistic and intercultural understanding of a specific field research context and communicative practices, we challenged the more usual positioning of the doctoral student as 'novice' in the academy (particularly in guides of this kind). This enabled us to move beyond conceptualisation of the PhD as a bounded course of study, to consider the doctoral student in relation to

Endpiece **139**

wider communities – not just the academics within their university, but also the communities where they conduct research and those with whom they engage through their current and subsequent writing (the 'global audience' mentioned by doctoral students in Chapter 5).

Adopting this perspective has several implications for the reach and audience of this book. By looking forward and beyond the immediate goal of the PhD, we suggest that doctoral research can be seen as a collaborative rather than completely individualised endeavour that can contribute to constructing knowledge in multiple communities. Not least of these is the academic community where the doctoral student is based, where the student's hands-on experiences of researching across languages and cultures can provide a source of intercultural learning for supervisors, other students and researchers. Our hope is that this book will not be regarded as a text only for doctoral students – or even more limiting, that it may be considered mainly as appropriate for international doctoral students. The main message of this book is that all academics are researching and writing across languages and cultures. However, unlike international students who are more likely to be writing in a second language and for an audience unfamiliar with their cultural context, many researchers may not be aware of the ways in which we all need to mediate meaning, be explicit about our values and reflect on whose knowledge meets whose ends. With increasing academic mobility and globalisation of academic publishing, the experiences of international students and other intercultural researchers will be more relevant than ever and this book is one step towards sharing that knowledge.

Reading and using this book

A recurring theme in the book is the importance of audience and what Alain described in Chapter 3 as the 'dynamism of context'. We do not see this book as simply fitting into a static context, as might be implied above where we related it to an existing body of literature. As authors, the excitement of writing this has been the unpredictability of how the book will be read and used and the recognition that 'voice is not simply a matter of production but of "uptake"' (Lillis and Curry, 2010: 24). As mentioned above, our first readers were the students quoted in this book who gave their time not only for the interviews, but also commented on the draft chapters. We encouraged them to amend our text if their interpretation differed from ours. Their responses made us realise that we were not just writing about researching across cultures and languages, but we were also modelling different methods for doing this with the group of research students involved in the interviews. The immediacy of email meant that we were easily able to share summaries of the interviews and later the draft chapters with participants from around the world.

At this stage, our focus was on facilitating interaction about our text – trying to counter the usual hierarchies between researcher/researched and student/ academic, though recognising that many of the participants probably viewed us

140 Anna Robinson-Pant and Alain Wolf

as the 'experts' in terms of academic writing and publishing. Through the process of constructing this final text, we have thus been exploring new ways of 'enacting research' that can transcend individual action and texts. Although we set out to reframe the field, in terms of introducing alternative theoretical lenses for analysing intercultural and multilingual research experiences, we did not initially question that the main purpose of our research would be the production of the final text/ this book. Drawing on ideas around reciprocity and cross-cultural collaboration discussed in the decolonising research literature, we note now that whilst the book is the most tangible output of this project, other forms of action and learning have also been facilitated along the way with our 'participant' readers. By sharing the research process through this written text, we hope that a wider audience too will be inspired to share in and contribute to developing intercultural research methodology in future years.

So what next?

Researching and writing this book has given us a broader perspective on our roles as doctoral supervisors, as researchers and as writers in an increasingly globalised knowledge economy. When we set out to analyse the experiences of doctoral students conducting research across languages and cultures, we did not expect to meet such diversity in terms of doctoral routes (such as the choice between articles and thesis), and models of supervision (cross-continent doctoral committees as compared to a single supervisor), all of which influenced academic writing and dissemination practices. Alongside this, we were struck by similarities in the challenges faced by doctoral researchers in very different situations – the most obvious is the pressure to write and publish in English.

The rapid pace of change in technologies, higher education and publishing makes it difficult to envisage the landscape within which doctoral researchers will be making such decisions about language and audience in the coming years. New forms of electronic publication are influencing the way we write and future researchers will need to take into account an even wider range of social media options when working out how to share their findings. As suggested in the last chapter, there are likely to be greater possibilities for doctoral researchers to work collaboratively and interculturally through such channels, and with supervisors/ doctoral committees from outside their immediate institutions. The examples in this book also suggest the importance of developing partnerships with professionals outside the academic sector, who can offer different approaches to translation and ethical accountability. Doctoral students (for instance, those who had been journalists) also commented on how their previous professional skills shaped their research practice. With the increasing emphasis on 'research impact', perhaps professionals from other fields will be invited to join doctoral supervision teams to offer advice on how to design research and engage with audiences beyond the academy.

The strengths of this book could be seen as connected to limitations in its scope: our focus on doctoral students' experiences resulted in a text shaped by their voices and eloquent accounts of their experiences. Although we reflected on the issues arising from our perspectives as doctoral supervisors, the book did not include interviews with established academics, which could have helped to expand our discussion of differing approaches to supervision and doctoral support across cultures. As qualitative researchers, we are also aware of building on the research literature with which we were most familiar and we introduced conceptual debate from ethnography, postcolonial theory and translation studies. This may have given an unintended message that researching interculturally is a qualitative research endeavour. However, we strongly believe that this is an area where a mixed methodology would be enlightening – not just in terms of the topics and research questions addressed, but also the methods used to analyse intercultural research experiences, such as combining corpus analysis of interview data with ethnographic accounts of interview practice.

Looking ahead to the increasing impact of globalisation and commercialisation on higher education and research, we recognise the importance of working with partners outside academia to find new ways of researching interculturally. But this is an ongoing, emergent kind of dialogue, not one that can be enforced, because the demand that dialogue take place is inimical to it. This is why this book does not give easy tips for dialogue across cultures to occur; it merely offers the light touch of creating conditions through which dialogue may or may not emerge in precious ethical moments of trust. In an era where terror and fear often strike at the heart of our communities, it is important to offer a way, however small, of reversing the Babel curse of mutual unintelligibility between cultures. Enshrined in the message of liberation from fear which begins when human beings are united by mutual understanding is the willingness to transcend one's monocultural self and to engage in dialogue with the Other, interculturally, multilingually.

BIBLIOGRAPHY

Andrews, J. (2012) An exploration of researcher–interpreter collaboration in a research study of out of school learning amongst multilingual families in the UK. Paper presented at the AHRC Researching Multilingually Seminar, School of Education, University of the West of England (from Powerpoint presentation).

Arundale, R. B. (1991) Studies in the way of words: Grice's new directions in conceptualizing meaning in conversational interaction. Paper presented at International Communication Association, Chicago, Illinois.

Arundale, R. B. (1999) An alternative model and ideology of communication for an alternative to politeness theory. *Pragmatics*, 9, 119–154.

Arundale, R. B. (2006) Face as relational and interactional: a communication framework for research on face, facework, and politeness. *Journal of Politeness Research, Language, Behavior, Culture*, 2(2), 193–216.

Ashraf, D. (2010) Using a feminist standpoint for researching women's lives in the rural mountainous areas of Pakistan, in Shamin, F. and Qureshi, R. (eds) (2010) *Perils, Pitfalls and Reflexivity in Qualitative Research in Education*. Oxford: Oxford University Press, 101–126.

Austin, J. L. (1988) *How to Do Things with Words*. Oxford: Oxford University Press.

Bach, K. (2012) Saying, meaning and implicating, in Allan, K. and Jaszczolt, K. M. (eds) *The Cambridge Handbook of Pragmatics*. Cambridge: Cambridge University Press, 59–79.

Bakhtin, M. (1981) *The Dialogic Imagination*, trans. Emerson, C. and Holoquist, M. (Emerson, C. ed.). Austin: University of Texas Press.

Bakhtin, M. (1986) The problem of speech genres, in Bakhtin, M., trans. McGee, V. (Emerson, C. and Holquist, M., eds) *Speech Genres and Other Late Essays*. Austin: University of Texas Press, 60–102.

Barton, D. (1994) *Literacy: An Introduction to the Ecology of Written Language*. Oxford: Blackwell.

Barton, D. and Hamilton, M. (2005) Literacy, reification and the dynamics of social interaction, in Barton, D. and Tusting, K. (eds) *Beyond Communities of Practice: Language, Power and Social Context*. Cambridge: Cambridge University Press, 14–35.

Bautista, M. L. S. (2000) *Defining Standard Philippine English: Its Status and Grammatical Features*. Manila, the Philippines: De La Salle University Press.

Bibliography

Becher, V. (2010) Abandoning the notion of 'Translation-inherent' explicitation: against a dogma of translation studies. *Across Languages and Cultures*, 11(1), 1–28.

Bhabha, H. K. (1994) *The Location of Culture*. London: Routledge.

Bhabha, H. K. (2011) Hybridity. *Translation: A Transdisciplinary Journal*, 1, 37–40.

Birbili, M. (2000) Translating from one language to another. *Social Research Update*, 31.

Birner, B. J. (2013) *Introduction to Pragmatics*. Oxford: Wiley-Blackwell.

Blakemore, D. (1992) *Understanding Utterances: an Introduction to Pragmatics*. Oxford: Blackwell.

Blum-Kulka, S. and Olshtain, E. (1984) Requests and apologies: a Cross-Cultural Study of Speech Act Realization Patterns (CCSARP). *Applied Linguistics*, 5 (1), 196–213.

Bradby, H. (2002) Translating culture and language: a research note on multilingual settings. *Sociology of Health & Illness*, 24(6), 842–855.

Brislin, R. W., Lonner, W. and Thorndike, R. M. (1973) *Cross-Cultural Research Methods*. New York: John Wiley & Sons.

Brooks, R. and Waters, J. (2011) *Student Mobilities, Migration and the Internationalisation of Higher Education*. Basingstoke: Palgrave Macmillan.

Brown, G. (1995) Identifying the relevant context in discourse interpretation. *Working Papers in English and Applied Linguistics*. University of Cambridge, 2, 117–128.

Bührig, K. and Thije, T. (2006) *Beyond Misunderstandings: Linguistic Analyses of Intercultural Communication*. Amsterdam: John Benjamins.

Bulut, A. and Kurultay, T. (2001) Interpreters-in-aid at disasters: community interpreting in the process of disaster management. *The Translator*, 7(2), 249–263.

Bush, H., Anderson, A., Williams, R., Lean, M., Bradby, H. and Abbots, J. (1995) Dietary change in South Asian and Italian women in the west of Scotland. *Working Paper 54*. Glasgow: MRC Medical Sociology Unit.

Byram, M. (1997) *Teaching and Assessing Intercultural Communicative Competence*. Clevedon UK: Multilingual Matters.

Canagarajah, A. (2002) *A Geopolitics of Academic Writing*. Pittsburgh: University of Pittsburgh Press.

Chesterman, A. (2001) Proposal for a Hieronymic Oath. *The Translator*, 7(2), 139– 154.

Chilisa, B. (2012) *Indigenous Research Methodologies*. London: Sage Publications.

Cicero, M. T. (1949) *De invention, De optimo genere oratorum, Topica*, trans. Hubell, H. M. Cambridge, MA: Harvard University Press.

Clark, H. H. and Marshall, C. R. (1981) Definite reference and mutual knowledge, in Joshi, A. K., Webber, B. L. and Sag, I. A. (eds) *Elements of Discourse Understanding*. Cambridge: Cambridge University Press, 10–63.

Clifford, A. (2004) Is fidelity ethical? The social role of the healthcare interpreter. *Traduction, terminologie, rédaction*, 17(2), 89–114.

Clifford, J. and Marcus, G. (1986) *Writing Culture: The Poetics and Politics of Ethnography*. Berkeley: University of California Press.

Crossley, M., Arthur, L. and McNess, E. (2016) *Revisiting Insider–Outsider Research in Comparative and International Education*. Oxford: Symposium Books.

Curry, M. J. and Lillis, T. (2004) Multilingual scholars and the imperative to publish in English: negotiating interests, demands, and rewards. *TESOL Quarterly*, 38(4), 663–688.

Cutting, J. (2002) *Pragmatics and Discourse: A Resource Book for Students*. London: Routledge.

Delisle, J. (1988) *Translation: An Interpretive Approach*, trans. Logan, P. and Creery, M. Ottawa: University of Ottawa Press.

Devereux, S. (1992) 'Observers are worried': learning the language and counting the people in northeast Ghana, in Devereux, S. and Hoddinott, J. (eds) *Fieldwork in Developing Countries*. Hemel Hempstead, UK: Harvester Wheatsheaf, 43–56.

144 Bibliography

Dolet, E. (1868) *Le second enfer d'Etienne Dolet suivi de la traduction des deux dialogues platoniciens l'Axiochus et L'Hipparchus*, Paris: Académie des bibliophiles. http://books.google.co.uk/books?id=ydA5AAAAcAAJ&pg=PR7&lpg=PR7&dq=dolet+et+rien+du+tout&source=bl&ots=2SZYzibl2d&sig=gV1y64BhtXodIS (accessed 24 September 2004).

Drugan, J. (2010) Ethics training for translators and interpreters. *MultiLingual: Language/Tech/Business*, December Issue, 38–40.

Ducrot, O. (1984) *Le Dire et le Dit*. Paris: Editions de Minuit.

Ercikan, K. (1998) Translation effects in international assessments. *International Journal of Educational Research*, 29, 543–553.

Fairclough, N. (1989) *Language and Power*. London: Longman.

Fishman, J. (1972) The sociology of language, in Giglioli, P. P. (ed.) *Language and Social Context*. London: Penguin Books, 45–58.

Flowerdew, J. (2001) Attitudes of journal editors to nonnative speaker contributions. *TESOL Quarterly*, 35(1), 121–151.

Forster, E. M. (2002) *Aspects of the Novel*. Electronic edition. New York: Rosetta Books.

Frey, F. (1970) Cross-cultural survey research in political science, in Holt, R. and Turner, J. (eds) *The Methodology of Comparative Research*. New York: The Free Press.

Geertz, C. (1993) *The Interpretation of Cultures: Selected Essays*. London: Fontana.

Gonzalez, E. and Lincoln, Y. (2006) Decolonizing qualitative research: non-traditional reporting forms in the Academy. *Forum: Qualitative Research*, 7(4), Art. 1.

Goodall, H. L., Jr. (2000) *Writing the New Ethnography*. Lanham, MD: Alta Mira Press.

Goody, J. (1968) *Literacy in Traditional Societies*. Cambridge: Cambridge University Press.

Gouanvic, J. M. (2001) Ethos, ethics and translation. *The Translator*, 7(2), 203–212.

Grice, H. P. (1957) Meaning. *The Philosophical Review*, 66(3), 377–388.

Grice, H. P. (1975) Logic and conversation, in Cole, P. and Morgan, J. L. (eds) *Syntax and Semantics, 3: Speech Acts*. New York: Academic Press, 1–58.

Gumperz, J. (1982) *Discourse Strategies*. Cambridge: Cambridge University Press.

Gumperz, J. (1992) Contextualization revisited, in Auer, P. and di Luzio, A. (eds) *The Contextualisation of Language*. Amsterdam: John Benjamins, 39–53.

Gumperz, J. and Cook-Gumperz, J. (2009) Discourse, cultural diversity and communication: a linguistic anthropological perspective, in Kotthoff, H. and Spencer Oatey, H. (eds) *Handbook of Intercultural Communication*. Berlin: Mouton De Gruyter, 13–29.

Günthner, S. (2009) Intercultural communication and the relevance of cultural specific repertoires of communicative genre, in Kotthoff, H. & Spencer Oatey, H. (eds) *Handbook of Intercultural Communication*. Berlin: Mouton De Gruyter, 127–151.

Halai, A. and Wiliam, D. (2011) *Research Methodologies in the South*. Oxford: Oxford University Press.

Halliday, M. A. K. and Hasan, R. (1976) *Cohesion in English*. London: Longman.

Hamid, M. (2010) Fieldwork for language education research in rural Bangladesh: ethical issues and dilemmas. *International Journal of Research and Method in Education*, 33(3), 259–271.

Hammersley, M. and Atkinson, P. (2010) *Ethnography Principles in Practice*. London: Routledge.

Harris, M. (1990) Emics and etics revisited, in Headland, T., Pike, K. and Harris, M. (eds) *Emics and Etics: The Insider/Outsider Debate*, Frontiers of Anthropology Vol. 7. London: Sage Publications, 48–61.

Haugen, E. (1987) *Blessings of Babel: Bilingualism and Language Planning*. Berlin: Mouton de Gruyter.

Haugh, M. (2008) Intention and diverging interpretings of implicature in the 'uncovered meat' sermon. *Intercultural Pragmatics*, 5(2), 201–228.

Haugh, M. and Jaszczolt, K. M. (2012) Speaker intentions and intentionality, in Allan, K. and Jaszczolt, K. M. (eds) *The Cambridge Handbook of Pragmatics*. Cambridge: Cambridge University Press, 87–112.

Heller, M. (ed.) (1988) *Codeswitching: Anthropological and Sociolinguistic Perspectives*. Berlin: Mouton de Gruyter.

Hoffman, C. (1991) *An Introduction to Bilingualism*. Harlow, UK: Longman.

Hofstede, G. (1991) *Culture and Organisations: Software of the mind*. London: McGraw-Hill.

Holliday, A. (1999) Small Cultures. *Applied Linguistics*, 20, 237–264.

Holliday, A. (2007) *Doing and Writing Qualitative Research*. London: Sage Publications.

Holliday, A. (2010) Submission, emergence, and personal knowledge: new takes and principles for validity in decentred qualitative research, in Shamin, F. and Qureshi, R. (eds) *Perils, Pitfalls and Reflexivity in Qualitative Research in Education*. Oxford: Oxford University Press, 10–31.

Holliday, A. (2011) *Intercultural Communication and Ideology*. London: Sage Publications.

Holliday, A., Hyde, M. and Kullman, J. (2004) *Intercultural Communication: An Advanced Resource Book*. London and New York: Routledge.

House, J. (1982) Conversational strategies in German and English dialogues, in Nickel, G. and Nehls, D. (eds) *Error Analysis: Constructive Linguistics and Second Language Learning*. (Special Issue of *International Review of Applied Linguistics)*, Heidelberg: Julius Groos, 135–151.

House, J. (2000) Understanding misunderstanding: a pragmatic-discourse approach to analysing mismanaged rapport in talk across cultures, in Spencer-Oatey, H. (ed.) *Culturally Speaking: Managing Rapport through Talk across Cultures*. London: Continuum, 145–164.

House, J. and Kasper, G. (1981) Politeness markers in English and German, in Coulmas, F. (ed.) *Conversational Routine*. The Hague: Mouton, 157–185.

Hyland, K. (2009) *Academic Discourse*. London: Continuum.

Hymes, D. (1974) *Foundations in Sociolinguistics: An Ethnographic Approach*. Philadelphia: University of Philadelphia Press.

Ivanic, R. (1998) *Writing and Identity: The Discoursal Construction of Identity in Academic Writing*. Amsterdam: John Benjamins.

Ivanic, R. (2005) The discoursal construction of writer identity, in Beach, R., Green, J., Kamil, M. L. and Shanahan, T. (eds) *Multidisciplinary Perspectives on Literacy Research*. Cresskill: Hampton Press, 391–416.

Jakobson, R. (1959/2004) On linguistic aspects of translation, in Venuti, L. (ed.) *The Translation Reader*. London: Routledge, 138–143.

Jankie, D. (2004) 'Tell me who you are': Problematizing the construction and positionalities of 'Insider'/'Outsider' of a 'Native' ethnographer in a postcolonial context, in Mutua, K. and B. Swadener (eds) *Decolonizing Research in Cross-Cultural Contexts: Critical Personal Narratives,* New York: State University of New York Press, 87–106.

Jerome, St (2004) Letter to Pammachius, trans. Davis, K. in L. Venuti, L. (ed.) *The Translation Reader,* London: Routledge, 21–30.

Jones, C., Street, B. and Turner, J. (1999) *Student Writing in Higher Education: Theory and Practice*. Amsterdam: John Benjamins.

Kamler, B. and Threadgold, T. (2003) Translating difference: questions of representation in cross-cultural research encounters. *Journal of Intercultural Studies*, 24(2), 137–151.

Keysar, B. (2007) Communication and miscommunication: the role of egocentric processes. *Intercultural Pragmatics*, 4(1): 71–84.

Khamis, A. (2011) Education for what? Discourses and research in the South, in Halai, A. and Wiliam, D. (eds) *Research Methodologies in the South*. Karachi: Oxford University Press, 53–76.

Klein, W. (1990) A theory of language acquisition is not easy. *Studies in Second Language Acquisition*, 12, 219–231.

146 Bibliography

Kotthoff, H. (2009) Ritual and style across cultures, in Kotthoff, H. and Spencer Oatey, H. (eds) *Handbook of Intercultural Communication*. Berlin: Mouton De Gruyter.

Kouzes, J. M., Posner, B. Z. (2008) *The Student Leadership Challenge: Five Practices for Exemplary Leaders*. San Francisco: Jossey-Bass.

Kumari, R., Mohammad, R.F. and Vazir, N. (2011) The power and politics of studying the impact of educational reforms in the South, in *Research Methodologies in the South*. Oxford: Oxford University Press, 218–244.

Kvale, S. (2006) Dominance through interviews and dialogues. *Qualitative Inquiry*, 12(3), 480–500.

Lapadat, J. C. and Lindsay, A. C. (1999) Transcription in research and practice: from standardization of technique to interpretive positionings. *Qualitative Inquiry*, 5(1), 64–86.

Laygues, A. (2001) Death of a ghost: a case study of ethics in cross-generation relations between translators. *The Translator*, 7(2), 169–183.

Lea, M. (2004) Academic literacies: a pedagogy for course design. *Studies in Higher Education*, 29(6), 739–756.

Lea, M. (2005) 'Communities of practice' in higher education: useful heuristic or educational model?, in Barton, D. and Tusting, K. (eds) *Beyond Communities of Practice: Language, Power and Social Context*. Cambridge: Cambridge University Press, 180–197.

Lea, M. and Street, B. (2010) The 'Academic Literacies' model: theory and applications. *Theory into Practice*, 45(4), 368–377.

Lefevere, A. (ed.) (1992) *Translation/History/Culture: A Sourcebook*. London and New York: Routledge.

Levinson, S. C. (1983) *Pragmatics*. Cambridge: Cambridge University Press.

Levinson, S. C. (2009) A review of Relevance. *Journal of Linguistics*, 25, 455–472.

Lewin, K. (1990) Data collection and analysis in Malaysia and Sri Lanka, in Vulliamy, G., Lewin, K. and Stephens, D. (eds) *Doing Educational Research in Developing Countries: Qualitative Strategies*. London: Falmer Press.

Liamputtong, P. (2010) *Performing Qualitative Cross-Cultural Research*. Cambridge: Cambridge University Press.

Lillis, T. and Curry, M. J. (2010) *Academic Writing in a Global Context: The Politics and Practices of Publishing in English*. Abingdon: Routledge.

Lillis, T., Hewings, A., Vladimirou, D. and Curry, M. J. (2010) The geolinguistics of English as an academic lingua franca: citation practices across English-medium national and English-medium international journals. *International Journal of Applied Linguistics*, 20(1), 111–135.

Lillis, T., Magyar, A. and Robinson-Pant, A. (2010) An international journal's attempts to address inequalities in academic publishing: developing a writing for publication programme. *Compare: A Journal of Comparative and International Education*, 40(6), 781–800.

Lillis, T. and Scott, M. (2007) Defining academic literacies research: issues of epistemology, ideology and strategy. *Journal of Applied Linguistics*, 4(1), 5–32.

Luther, M. (1984) *Die Bibel, nach der Übersetzung Martin Luthers*. Revised edition. Stuttgart: Deutsche Bibelgesellschaft.

Lutz, H. (2011) Lost in translation? The role of language in migrants' biographies: What can micro-sociologists learn from Eva Hoffman? *European Journal of Women's Studies*, 18, 347–360.

Magyar, A. and Robinson-Pant, A. (2010) *International Students: Reflections on PhD Supervision*. DVD and booklet to accompany the DVD. University of East Anglia, Norwich: Centre for Applied Research in Education. (Available for purchase from: edu.reception@uea.ac.uk).

Magyar, A. and Robinson-Pant, A. (2011) Internationalising doctoral research: developing theoretical perspectives on practice. *Teachers and Teaching: Theory and Practice*, 17(6), 663–677.

Matsuda, A. and Matsuda, P. K. (2010) World Englishes and the teaching of writing. *TESOL Quarterly*, 44(2), 369–374.

McConnell-Ginet, S. (2003) 'What's in a name?' Social labeling and gender practices, in Holmes, J. and Meyerhoff, M. (eds) (2005) *The Handbook of Language and Gender*. Oxford: Blackwell Publishing (first published 2003), 69–97.

Mehrotra, R. R. (1981) Non-kin forms of address in Hindi. *International Journal of the Sociology of Language,* 32, 121–137.

Mey, J. (2001) *Pragmatics: An Introduction* (2nd edition.). Oxford: Blackwell.

Michael-Luna, S. and Canagarajah, A. S. (2007) Multilingual academic literacies: pedagogical foundations for code meshing in primary and higher education. *Journal of Applied Linguistics*, 4(1) 55–77.

Miller, J. (1983) *Many Voices: Bilingualism, Culture and Education*. London: Routledge and Kegan Paul.

Morgan, B. and Ramanathan, V. (2005) Critical literacies in language education: local and global perspectives. *Annual Review of Applied Linguistics*, 25, 151–169.

Moses, I. and Ramsden, P. (1992) Academic values and practice in new universities. *Higher Education Research and Development*, 11(2), 101–118.

Munday, J. (2012) *Introducing Translation Studies*. London: Routledge.

Mutua, K. and Swadener, B. (2004) Introduction, in Mutua, K. and Swadener, B. (eds) *Decolonizing Research in Cross-Cultural Contexts: Critical Personal Narratives,* New York: State University of New York Press, 1–26.

Nelson, N. and Castello, M. (2012) Academic writing and authorial voice, in Castello, M. and Donahue, C. (eds) *University Writing: Selves and Texts in Academic Societies*. Bingley, UK: Emerald Publishing, 33–52.

Nikander, P. (2008) Working with transcripts and translated data. *Qualitative Research in Psychology*, 5(3) 225–231.

Nord, C. (2001) Loyalty revisited. *The Translator*, 7(2), 185–202.

Norton, B. (1997) Language, identity, and the ownership of English. *TESOL Quarterly*, 31(3), 409–429.

Norton, B. (2000) *Identity and Language Learning: Gender, Ethnicity and Educational Change*. Harlow, UK: Pearson Education.

Ochs, E. (1979) Transcription as theory, in Jaworski, A. and Coupland, N. (eds) (2006) *The Discourse Reader*. 2nd edition. London: Routledge, 166–178.

Ochs, E., Schegloff, E. A. and Thompson, S. A. (eds) (1996) *Interaction and grammar* Vol. 13. Cambridge: Cambridge University Press.

Panikkar, R. (1979) *Myth, Faith and Hermeneutics*. New York: Paulist Press.

Pardhan, A. (2011) Ethnographic field methods in research with women: field experiences from Pakistan, in Shamin, F. and Qureshi, R. (eds) *Research Methodologies in the South*. Oxford: Oxford University Press, 116–145.

Paxton, M. (2012) Student voice as a methodological issue in academic literacies research. *Higher Education Research and Development*, 31(3), 381–391.

Pennycook, A. (1994) *The Cultural Politics of English as an International Language*. Harlow, UK: Pearson Education.

Pennycook, A. (1996) Borrowing others' words: text, ownership, memory and plagiarism. *TESOL Quarterly*, 30(2).

Pennycook, A. (2007) *Global Englishes and Transcultural Flows*. Abingdon, UK: Routledge.

148 Bibliography

Pillay, H. D. (1995) Fragments of a vision: a case study of the implementation of an English language curriculum programme in five Malaysian secondary schools. PhD thesis, University of East Anglia, Norwich.

Pomerantz, A. (1978) Compliment response: notes on the co-operation of multiple constraints, in Schenkein, J. (ed.) *Studies in the Organization of Conversational Interaction*. New York: Academic Press. 79–112.

Pring, R. (2011) Researching very different societies: an impossible task?, in Shamin, F. and Qureshi, R. (eds) *Research Methodologies in the South*. Oxford: Oxford University Press, 77–89.

Pym, A. (2001) The return to ethics in Translation Studies. *The Translator*, 7(2), 129– 138.

Qureshi, R. (2010) Ethical standards and ethical environment, in Shamin, F. and Qureshi, R. (eds) *Perils, Pitfalls and Reflexivity in Qualitative Research in Education*. Oxford: Oxford University Press, 78–100.

Rampton, B. (1995) *Crossing Language and Ethnicity among Adolescents*. Harlow, UK: Longman.

Rancière, J. (1995) *La Mésentente*. Paris: Galilee.

Renganathan, S. (2009) Exploring the researcher–participant relationship in a multiethnic, multicultural and multilingual context through reflexivity. *Qualitative Research Journal* 9(2), 3–17.

Ricoeur, P. (1973) The model of the text. *New Literary History* 5(9) 1–120.

Risager, K. (2007) *Language and Culture Pedagogy: From a National to a Transnational Paradigm*. Clevedon, UK: Multilingual Matters.

Rizvi, F. (2010) International students and doctoral studies in transnational spaces, in Walker, M. and Thomson, P. (eds) *The Routledge Doctoral Supervisor's Companion*. London: Routledge, 158–170.

Robinson-Pant, A. (2001) *Why Eat Green Cucumber at the Time of Dying? Exploring the Link Between Women's Literacy and Development in Nepal*. Hamburg: Unesco Institute for Education. Available at: http://unesdoc.unesco.org/images/0012/001236/123606e.pdf

Robinson-Pant, A. (2005) *Cross-Cultural Perspectives on Educational Research*. Buckingham, UK: The Open University Press.

Robinson-Pant, A. (2009) Changing academies: exploring international PhD students' perspectives on 'host' and 'home' universities. *Higher Education Research & Development*, 28(4), 417–429.

Robinson-Pant, A. (2016) Exploring the concept of insider–outsider in comparative and international research: essentialising culture or culturally essential?, in Crossley, M., Arthur, L. and McNess, E. (eds) *Revisiting Insider–Outsider Research in Comparative and International Education*. Oxford: Symposium Books, 39–56.

Robinson-Pant, A. and Singal, N. (2013) Research ethics in comparative and international education: reflections from anthropology and health. *Compare*, 43(4), 443–463.

Robinson-Pant, A. and Street, B. (2012) Students' and tutors' understanding of the 'new' academic literacy practices, in Castello, M. and Donahue, C. (eds) *University Writing: Selves and Texts in Academic Societies*. Bingley, UK: Emerald Publishing, 71–92.

Robinson-Pant, A. and Wolf, A. (2014) (eds) Researching across languages and cultures: a collection of reflective pieces providing an unusual insight into how doctoral students engage in multilingual and intercultural research. *CARE Working Paper No. 1*. Available at: https://www.uea.ac.uk/documents/595200/0/CARE+Working+Paper+1.pdf/ e2b7032b-c7e8-4fff-9b0e-f6fb8e10c486

Rogers, A. (2013) The classroom and the everyday: the importance of informal learning for formal learning. Paper presented to the International Conference on The Nonformal and the Informal in Education: Centralities and Peripheries, at the University of Minho, Braga, Portugal, 25–27 March 2013). *Investigar Em Educacao,* 2014, 1(1), 7–34, pdf at: http://pages.ie.uminho.pt/inved/index.php/ie/issue/view/1/showToc

Sadeghi, K. (2010) Metric yardstick: the status of EFL research evaluation in Iran. *The Asia-Pacific Education Researcher*, 19(3), 475–488.

Sanjek, R. (1990) *Fieldnotes: The Makings of Anthropology*. New York: Cornell University Press.

Sarangi, S. (1995) Culture, in Verschueren, J. (ed.) *Handbook of Pragmatics*. Amsterdam: John Benjamins, 1–30.

Schleiermacher, F. (2004) On the different methods of translating, in Venuti, L. (ed.) *The Translation Reader*. London: Routledge, 43–63.

Scollon, R., Scollon S. and Jones, R. (2012) *Intercultural Communication: A Discourse Approach*. 3rd edition. Chichester, UK: Wiley Blackwell.

Searle, J. R. and Vanderveken, D. (1985) *Foundations of Illocutionary Logic*. Cambridge: Cambridge University Press.

Sechrest, L., Fay, T. L. and Zaidi, S. M. H. (1972) Problems of translation in cross-cultural research. *Journal of Cross-Cultural Psychology*, 3(1), 41– 56.

Séguinot, C. (1988) Pragmatics and explicitation hypothesis. *Traduction, terminologie, rédaction*, 1(2), 106–113.

Sengupta, S. (2005) Editorial. *Journal of English for Academic Purposes*, 4, 287–289.

Shamim, F. and Qureshi, R. (2010) Research North and South: introduction, in Shamim, F. and Qureshi, R. (eds) *Perils, Pitfalls and Reflexivity in Qualitative Research in Education*. Karachi: Oxford University Press, 2–9.

Shamin, F and Qureshi, R. (2013) Informed consent in educational research in the South: tensions and accommodations. *Compare: A Journal of Comparative and International Education*, 43(4), 464–482.

Siegal, M. (1995) Individual differences and study abroad: women learning Japanese in Japan, in Freed, B. (ed.) *Second Language Acquisition in a Study Abroad Context*. Amsterdam: John Benjamins Publishing, 225–244.

Sikes, P. (2006) Decolonizing research and methodologies: indigenous peoples and cross-cultural contexts. *Pedagogy, Culture and Society*, 13(3), 349–358.

Sikes, P. and Piper, H. (2010) Ethical research, academic freedom and the role of ethics committees and review procedures. *International Journal of Research and Method in Education*, 33(3), 205–213.

Skillen, J. and Purser, E. (2003) Teaching thesis writing: policy and practice at an Australian university. *Hong Kong Journal of Applied Linguistics*, 8(2), 17–33.

Skutnabb-Kangas, T. (2002) Linguistic human rights in education: Western hypocrisy in European and global language policy. Paper presented in the 5th International Congress of Hungarian Studies.

Smith, L. T. (1999) *Decolonizing Methodologies*. London: Zed Books.

Sperber, D. and Wilson, D. (1986) *Relevance: Communication and Cognition*. Oxford: Blackwell.

Steiner, G. (1998) *After Babel: Aspects of Language and Translation*. Oxford: Oxford University Press.

Street, B. V. (1984) *Literacy in Theory and Practice*. Cambridge: Cambridge University Press.

Street, B. V. (1993) *Cross-Cultural Approaches to Literacy*. Cambridge: Cambridge University Press.

Stroud, C. and Prinsloo, M. (2015) *Language, Literacy and Diversity: Moving Words*. New York and Abingdon, UK: Routledge.

150 Bibliography

Swadener, B. and Mutua, K. (2004) Afterword, in Mutua, K. and Swadener, B. (eds) *Decolonizing Research in Cross-Cultural Contexts: Critical Personal Narratives,* New York: State University of New York Press, 255–262.

Swales, J. M. (1998) *Other Floors, Other Voices: A Textography of a Small University Building.* Mahwah, NJ: Lawrence Erlbaum Associates.

Tajfel, H. (1981) *Human Groups and Social Categories: Studies in Social Psychology.* Cambridge: Cambridge University Press.

Temple, T. and Young, A. (2008) Qualitative research and translation dilemmas, in Atkinson, P. and Delamont, S. (eds) *Representing Ethnography* Vol. 3. London: Sage Publications, 90–107.

Tillich, P. (1963) *Morality and Beyond.* London: Routledge & Kegan Paul.

Trompenaars, F. and Hampden-Turner, C. (1997) *Riding the Waves of Culture: Understanding Cultural Diversity in Business.* London: Nicholas Brealy.

Turner, J. (2003) Writing a PhD in the contemporary humanities. *Hong Kong Journal of Applied Linguistics,* 8(2), 34–53.

Turner, J. (2011) *Language in the Academy: Cultural Reflexivity and Intercultural Dynamics.* Bristol, UK: Multilingual Matters.

Turner, J. C. (1982) Towards a cognitive redefinition of the social group, in Tajfel, H. (ed.) *Social Identity and Intergroup Relations.* Cambridge: Cambridge University Press, 15–40.

Van Maanen, J. (1988) *Tales of the Field: On Writing Ethnography.* Chicago: The Chicago Press.

Venuti, L. (1998) *The Scandals of Translation: Towards an Ethics of Difference.* London: Routledge.

Venuti, L. (2004) *The Translation Studies Reader.* London: Routledge.

Venuti, L. (2011) Film adaptation and translation theory: equivalence and ethics. *Translation: A Transdisciplinary Journal,* 1, 37–40.

Verschueren, J. (2008) Intercultural communication and the challenges of migration. *Language and Intercultural Communication* 8(1), 21–35.

Wadensjö, C. (1998) *Interpreting as Interaction.* London: Longman.

Ward, K. (1976) *The Divine Image.* London: SPCK.

Warwick, D. P. and Osherson, S. (1973) Comparative analysis in the social sciences, in Warwick, D. P. and Osherson, S. (eds) *Comparative Research Methods: An Overview.* Englewood Cliffs, NJ: Prentice-Hall.

Welland, T. (2002) Research and the 'fate of idealism': ethical tales and ethnography in a theological college, in Welland, T. and Pugsley L. (eds) *Ethical Dilemmas in Qualitative Research.* Aldershot: Ashgate Publishing, 135–139.

Wijsen, F. (2007) *Seeds of Conflict in a Haven of Peace: From Religious Studies to Interreligious Studies in Africa.* New York: Rodopi.

Wilson, S. (2008) *Research is Ceremony: Indigenous research methods.* Manitoba, Canada: Fernwood.

Wilson, D. and Sperber, D. (2004) Relevance Theory, in Horn, L. R. and Ward, G. (eds) *Handbook of Pragmatics.* Oxford: Blackwell, 607–632.

Wolf, A. (1999) Context and Relevance Theory in language teaching: an exploratory approach. *International Review of Applied Linguistics in Language Teaching,* 38(1), 95–108.

Wolf, A. (2005) *Subjectivity in a Second Language: Conveying the Expression of Self.* Oxford: Peter Lang.

Wolf, A. (2009) Mobilizing meaning?: religious symbolism in film adaptations of C.S. Lewis's The Lion, the Witch and the Wardrobe. *Journal of Adaptation in Film and Performance,* 2(3), 239–254.

Wolf, A. (2010) Inferential meaning in drama translation: the role of implicature in the staging process of Anouilh's 'Antigone', in Baines, R., Marinetti, C. and Perteghella, M. (eds) *Staging Translation: Text and Theatre Practice*. London: Palgrave MacMillan, 87–104.

Wolf, A. (2015) George Eliot's French: transcending the monocultural self in Daniel Deronda. *Language and Intercultural Communication*, 15(4), 494–512.

Wong, J. P. and Poon, M. K. L. (2010) Bringing translation out of the shadows: translation as an issue of methodological significance in cross-cultural qualitative research. *Journal of Transcultural Nursing*, 21(2) 151–158.

Yates, L. and Trang, N. T. Q. (2012) Beyond a discourse of deficit: the meaning of silence in the international classroom. *The International Education Journal: Comparative Perspectives*, 11(1), 22–34.

Ye Lan. (2005) *Social Science in Twentieth-Century China: On Education*. Shanghai: Shanghai People's Press. [叶澜.(2005).二十世纪中国社会科学 (教育学卷).上海:上海人民出版社.]

Ye Lei. (1995) Complimenting in Mandarin Chinese, in Kasper, G. (ed.) *Pragmatics of Chinese as Native and Target Language*. Manoa: University of Hawaii, 207–295.

Žegarac, V. (2009) A cognitive pragmatic perspective on communication and culture, in Kotthoff, H. and Spencer Oatey, H. (eds) *Handbook of Intercultural Communication*. Berlin: Mouton De Gruyter, 31–53.

INDEX

academic literacies 11–14, 15, 16, 58–9, 92–3; *see also* writing across cultures
academic publishing 129; in English 13–14, 120–1, 123–8; geopolitics of 13–14, 106, 107, 118
act sequence 28
action research 16, 91; *see also* Participatory Action Research
addressee 28
addressor 28
affective meaning 70
Andrews, J. 10
Anscombe, G. E. M. 68
Arundale, R. B. 49
Ashraf, D. 115
Atkinson, P. 115
audience 11, 92–3; relational dimension of writing 103–8; writing for multiple audiences 91, 118–23; *see also* academic publishing
audio recordings 95, 97–8
Austin, J. L. 54

Bach, K. 47
back translation 80–1
Bakhtin, M. 30
Bautista, M. L. S. 86
Becher, V. 114
Bhabha, H. K. 7, 46, 76
Birbili, M. 61, 69, 80, 81
Blakemore, D. 31, 32
Blum-Kulka, S. 45
Bradby, H. 58, 59, 74–5, 81, 91

Brooks, R. 15
Byram, M. 8

Camus, A. 68
Canagarajah, A. 12, 13, 14, 18n5, 22, 118, 123, 124, 129, 131
Castello, M. 14
centre/periphery 18n4–5, 22, 135n1
channels 29
Chesterman, A. 77
Chilisa, B. 5, 6, 13–14
Cicero 65, 66
Clifford, A. 78
Clifford, J. 90
code meshing 14, 124
code-switching 14, 59–60, 60*t*, 74–6, 126, 138
cognitive effects 32, 36
communication x, 29; ostensive-inferential communication 33–4; *see also* ethics of mediated communication; intercultural communication; miscommunication
communicative polyphony 51–2
communicative practices 5, 7
conceptual meaning 69–71
conduit model of interpreter training 78, 83n9
Conjoint Co-Constituting Model of Communication 49
connotative meaning 20, 61–2, 69–71
context 10; background knowledge context 103–4; co-textual context 103, 104, 105–6; definitions 24–6;

dynamic features 25, 31–8; ethics of 35–7, 38; and language x; local contexts 21; miscommunication 34–5, 49–51; prejudice and trust 40–3; Relevance Theory 31–4, 36, 37, 38; situational context 103, 104; stable features ('SPEAKING') 25, 26–30; truth 35; in writing across cultures 103–8, 109; concluding remarks 30–1, 37–8
contextualisation cues 34–5, 39n5
Convention of Lausanne (1923) 40
conversational inferences 34–5
conversational maxims 36–7, 39n6
Cook-Gumperz, J. 34, 35, 39n5
Cooperative Principle 36–7
cross-cultural educational research 19–23
cross-cultural pragmatics 8, 45–6
cultural difference 45–6
culture 92; centrality of in research 1–3; 'small culture' 92, 108
Curry, M. J. 13, 119, 139
Cutting, J. 103

Daily Mail 50
data collection x; as 'gift' to the researcher 51, 54
decolonising methodology 5–7, 118, 136, 138
Devereux, S. 4, 9
dialogical co-construction 49, 51–4
discourse 12, 14, 20–2, 30–1, 52, 54; *see also* publishing in English; writing across cultures
Dolet, E. 66
domestication 68–9, 76–7
Ducrot, O. 51–2

education in China: history of 22; local contexts 21–2; second language education 20, 21
emergence 4, 11, 30, 45, 46, 49, 51, 53–4
ends (of an event) 28
English language: as a global language 20, 87; and power 2, 7; *see also* discourse; publishing in English; textualisation; translation
Ercikan, K. 80
ethics of context 35–7, 38
ethics of mediated communication x, 76, 77, 115; alterity 77; communication 77, 78; faithfulness to people rather than utterances 78–9; faithfulness to source text 79–80; representation 77; sense for sense approach 66–7; service 77

ethics of research 6, 16, 30, 138
ethnography 12, 25, 26, 89, 90–1, 96, 99, 115
etic–emic construct 99, 111n1; *see also* 'insider–outsider'
explicature 32, 34, 88
explicitation 114–15; grammatical level 74; semantic/conceptual level xviii, 69–71

face 9–10
Fairclough, N. 20
feedback 84–7, 102, 132
fieldnotes 94; audio recordings 95, 97–8; and 'headnotes' 94; language 2, 13, 94–9
fieldwork practice: decolonising methodology 5–7, 118, 136, 138; intercultural communication 7–10; the research relationship 4, 5–7, 9–10, 11, 59, 90; *see also* writing relationships
Flowerdew, J. 132
foreignisation 68–9, 71, 74, 76–7
form–function pairings across languages 72–4
Forster, E. M. 30–1
free ('sense for sense') translation 65, 66–7, 68, 74
Frey, F. 62, 70

Geertz, C. 53
gender roles 7, 9, 76–7
genre 12, 29–30
Gilbert, S. 68
Gonzalez, E. 91, 129–30
Goodall, H. L., Jr 113
Goody, J. 11
grammar *see* form–function pairings across languages
Grice, H. P. 36–7, 46–7
Gumperz, J. 34, 35, 39n5
Günthner, S. 30
Gupta, Achala 58–62

Halliday, M. A. K. 38–9n3
Hammersley, M. 115
Hampden-Turner, C. 29
Harris, M. 111n1
Hasan, R. 38–9n3
Haugh, M. 48, 49, 50, 51
'headnotes' 94
al-Hilali, Sheik Taj Din 49
Hoffman, C. 59
Hofstede, G. 8, 45, 101
Holliday, A. 46, 53–4, 55, 90, 91, 92, 99, 108
Horace 66

154 Index

hospitality 54, 56
House, J. 45
Human Capital Theory 16–17, 18n6
human rights 18n6, 21
Hyland, K. 92–3, 100, 103, 128
Hymes, D. *see* SPEAKING

identity 15–16, 91; and code-switching
74–6, 138; crisis of identity 92; multiple
identities 92–3; researcher identity 7,
99; spoken and written terms of address
112–14; writer identity 11–13, 14, 88,
99, 101–2, 131
illocutionary acts 54, 73, 74
implicatures 37, 46, 47–9;
miscommunication of 49–51
inferences 47, 48, 49–50
'insider–outsider' 5–7, 18n3, 99, 111n1
instrumentalities 29
intention: ambiguity of 35–7, 71; failing
to recognise 33–5; miscommunication
of implicatures 49–51; in multilingual
research 46–9, 50–1
intercultural communication 1–5;
performativity 7–8, 54–5; and
research interviews 7–10; the research
relationship 4, 5–7, 9–10, 11
intercultural learning 128–9
interlingual translation (translation proper)
64, 65
international community of researchers
16–17, 117–18; alternatives 128–32;
career progression 13, 119–22,
124–5; collaborative writing 132, 139;
constructing knowledge for multiple
audiences 16, 118–23; cross-cultural to
intercultural 1–3; discursive dimension
129–30; disseminating research 13–14;
material constraints and strategies 131–2;
mobility 15; publishing in English
13–14, 120–1, 123–8; conclusion 133–5
interpreter/translator role 4, 9, 10, 63–4,
98; code-switching 59–60, 60t, 74–6,
138; conceptual meaning 69–71; conduit
model of interpreter training 78, 83n9;
domesticated *vs.* foreignised translations
in research 68–9, 71, 74, 76–7; ethical
judgements 66–7, 69, 76–7; explicitation
xviii, 69–70, 74, 114–15; form–function
pairings across languages 72–4; important
'tips' 80–2; myth of translation
63; pre-testing 81; in the research
context 69–77; researcher–interpreter
relationship 81; responsibilities 70–1,

74; 'sense for sense' approach 65, 66–7,
68, 74; terminology 64–6; transcription
conventions xviii, 84, 85f; 'word for
word' approach 65, 67–9, 83n4; of
words, meaning, culture? 3–4, 85–7; *see
also* ethics of mediated communication
intersemiotic translation (transmutation)
83n3
interviews 7–10, 30; *see also* fieldnotes;
fieldwork practice
intonation 34
intralingual translation 83n3
Iranian Journal of Language Teaching Research
131
Ivanic, R. 11, 12, 92, 93, 100, 103

Jakobson, R. 64, 83n2–3
Jankie, D. 5, 6
Jerome, St 65, 66, 83n8
Jones, C. *et al.* 11
journals, centre-based 13, 14, 18n4–5, 123,
130, 131–2, 135n1

Kamler, B. 9
key (of speech act) 28–9
Khamis, A. 16–17
King James Bible 66–7, 81
Klein, W. 72
knowledge 11; background knowledge
context 103–4; constructing knowledge
16, 118–23; hierarchies of knowledge 6,
16; mutual knowledge 31
Konidari, Eleni 38, 40–3
Kumari, R. *et al.* 28
Kvale, S. 30

language: centrality of in research x, 1–3,
7, 9–10; defined ix–x; for disseminating
research 13, 100–3; in fieldnotes 2, 13,
94–9; hierarchies of languages 14, 16;
learning 4; proficiency 72–3; theory and
power 19–23
Lapadat, J. C. 84
Lea, M. 11
Lefevere, A. 65
Levinson, S. C. 31
Lewin, K. 3
Liamputtong, P. 91, 99
Lillis, T. 11, 13, 119, 139
Lincoln, Y. 91, 129–30
Lindsay, A. C. 84
literacy ix; hierarchies of literacies 14
literal ('word for word') translation 65,
67–9, 83n4

Index **155**

localisation 64, 121
location 9, 21
Lontoc, Gina 82, 84–7
Luther, M. 66–7
Lutz, H. 58

McConnell-Ginet, S. 112, 113
Magyar, A. xvii, 105
manner (conversational maxim) 37, 39n6
Marcus, G. 90
Matsuda, A. 87
Matsuda, P. K. 87
meaning: affective meaning 70; conceptual
    meaning 69–71; connotative meaning
    20, 61–2, 69–71; definition 46; *see also*
    intention
mediators 28, 41–2
Mehrotra, R. R. 113
Mey, J. 48
Michael-Luna, S. 14, 124
migration and mobility 15, 58, 59
miscommunication 34–5, 49–51
Moses, I. 69
Munday, J. 65
Mutua, K. 6, 99, 123–4, 136

Nair, Joanna 110, 112–15
Nelson, N. 14
Nikander, P. 85
non-verbal features 28–9
Nord, C. 67, 77
norms of interaction 29

Ochs, E. *et al.* 84
Ohlstain, E. 45
Osherson, S. 80
ostensive-inferential communication 33–4
the Other 7, 23, 52, 54, 77, 78–9, 80

Panikkar, R. 52, 55
Pannwitz, Rudolf 76
Pardhan, A. 27–8
participants (in speech act) 28
Participatory Action Research and
    participatory approaches to research 16,
    91
Paul, St 66–7
Paxton, M. 92
peer review 106–7
Pennycook, A. 12, 123, 124, 125, 126, 129
performativity 7–8, 54–5
perlocutionary acts, 54
Pillay, H. D. 72–3
politeness 29, 41, 52, 73, 74

Pomerantz, A. 45
Poon, M. K. L. 61–2, 76
postcolonial theory 5, 6–7, 16, 18n4, 91
power relations: in the academy 10, 92, 93,
    101–3, 105, 107, 111n2; in the field 9,
    15, 20, 30, 42, 115; North–South/
    East–West 7, 9, 18n4–5, 21–3, 108
pragmatics 25, 38n1, 44; cross-
    cultural pragmatics 8, 45–6;
    dialogical co-construction 49, 51–4;
    miscommunication of implicatures
    49–51; performativity 7–8, 54–5; speaker
    meaning: intention 46–9, 50–1; trust and
    charity 52, 54, 55–6; *see also* translation
prejudice 40–3
Pring, R. 24, 25
Prinsloo, M. ix–x
Pu Shi 19–23
publishing in English 13–14, 120–1, 123–8
Purser, E. 117
Pym, A. 77

qualitative research 2, 53
quality (conversational maxim) 37, 39n6
quantity (conversational maxim) 39n6
Qureshi, R. 113

Ramsden, P. 69
Rancière, J. 48
reading across cultures 12–13, 81, 92, 93,
    105–6, 108–9, 125–7
referencing 12, 13, 14, 88–9, 104–5, 108,
    109
registers 29
relation (conversational maxim) 37, 39n6
Relevance Theory 31–4, 36, 37, 38
research dissemination 13–14, 17
research ethics 6, 16, 30, 138
research relationships 4, 5–7, 9–10, 11, 59,
    81, 90
researcher: as amateur linguist 3–5; identity
    7, 99; 'insider–outsider' 5–7, 18n3, 99,
    111n1; *see also* writer identity
responsibilities 70–1, 74
Ricoeur, P. 94
Risager, K. 8
Rizvi, F. 14
Robinson-Pant, A. xvii, 13, 69, 74, 105
Rogers, A. 8

Sadeghi, K. 121, 131
Sanjek, R. 95
Sarangi, S. 8
scene 26–7

156 Index

Schleiermacher, F. 67–8, 83n5
Scollon, R. *et al.* 9
Scott, M. 11
second language education 20, 21
Séguinot, C. 114, 115
sender 28
Sengupta, S. 10
'sense for sense' (free) translation 65, 66–7, 68, 74
setting (of speech act) 26–8
Sikes, P. 91
situation 26, 38–9n3, 103, 104
Skillen, J. 117
'small culture' 92, 108
Smith, L. T. 5–6
Socrates 66
Source Language (SL) 64
Source Text (ST) 64
speaker 28
SPEAKING 25; Setting 26–8; Participants 28; Ends 28; Act Sequence 28; Key 28–9; Instrumentalities 29; Norms of interaction 29; Genre 29–30
speech styles 29
Sperber, D. 31–2
story crafting 9
Street, B. V. 11, 13
Stroud, C. ix–x
Swadener, B. 6, 99, 123–4, 136

Target Language (TL) 64
Target Text (TT) 64
teknonymy 113–14
Temple, T. 91
terms of address 112–14
textualisation 10–14, 89, 94–9
Threadgold, T. 9
topoi 52
Trang, N. T. Q. 20
transcription 2, 61–2, 84; conventions xviii, 84, 85f; purpose of 95–7
translation x; back translation 80–1; cost and effectiveness 4; cultural connotations 58–62; myth 63; terminology 64–6; in written texts 130; *see also* interpreter/ translator role
translation proper (interlingual translation) 64, 65
Translation Studies 64–5, 77
The Translator 77
transmutation (intersemiotic translation) 83n3

Trompenaars, F. 29
trust 41–2, 52, 54, 55–6
truth 35
TT (Target Text) 64
Turner, J. 8, 12, 100, 101, 109, 118, 129

utterances 25, 31, 36–7, 38n2, 39n3

Van Maanen, J. 90, 94, 99
Venuti, L. 68–9, 79, 83n5
Verschueren, J. 35, 45
voice 4, 5, 6, 22, 51–2; of participants 91, 96; in research text 16–17, 99–100; and writer identity 11–13, 14, 88, 101–2, 131

Warwick, D. P. 80
Waters, J. 15
Wilson, D. 31–2
Wilson, S. 6
Wittgenstein, L. 68
Wolf, A. 37, 72
Wong, J. P. 61–2, 76
Woolfe, Sylvia 79–80
'word for word' (literal) translation 65, 67–9, 83n4
'World Englishes' 87
writer identity 11–13, 14, 88, 99, 101–2, 131
writing across cultures 88–9; in the academy 89, 92–3, 101–3, 105, 111n2; audience and readers 11, 93, 103–8; citations 12; collaborative writing 132, 139; and context 103–8, 109; disseminating research 13–14; genre and style 12; issues of identity and voice 11–12, 99–103; learning from ethnographers 90–1; multilingual perspective 10–14, 94–5; peer review 106–7; references 88–9; research outcome 17; textualising data 10–14, 89, 94–9; conclusion 108–11
writing relationships 112, 116f; lost or gained in translation? 114–15; spoken and written terms of address 112–14; *see also* ethics of mediated communication

Yates, L. 20
Ye Lan 22, 45
Young, A. 91

Žegarac, V. 25, 33–4